THE CONTINUITIES OF GERMAN HISTORY

In this controversial work of German history, Smith argues that German historians have become ever more focused on the twentieth century and on twentieth-century explanations for the catastrophe at the heart of it: the Holocaust. Against conventional wisdom, he considers long-term continuities – in the concept of nation and the ideology of nationalism, in religious exclusion and violence, and in race and racism. Exploring these topics in novel ways, he argues for deep continuities in German history, even as he insists that Germany was not on a special path to destruction. The result is a series of challenging reflections on nationalism, anti-Semitism, and race, as well as a novel interpretation of modern German history.

Helmut Walser Smith earned his PhD at Yale and is the Martha Rivers Ingram Professor of History at Vanderbilt University. He is the author of *German Nationalism and Religious Conflict* (1995) and *The Butcher's Tale: Murder and Anti-Semitism in a German Town* (2002), which won the Fraenkel Prize for the best work in contemporary history and was named an L.A. Times Non-Fiction Book of the Year.

THE CONTINUITIES OF GERMAN HISTORY

Nation, Religion, and Race across the Long Nineteenth Century

HELMUT WALSER SMITH
Vanderbilt University

CAMBRIDGE
UNIVERSITY PRESS

CAMBRIDGE UNIVERSITY PRESS
Cambridge, New York, Melbourne, Madrid, Cape Town, Singapore, São Paulo, Delhi

Cambridge University Press
32 Avenue of the Americas, New York, NY 10013-2473, USA

www.cambridge.org
Information on this title: www.cambridge.org/9780521720250

First published 2008

Printed in the United States of America

A catalog record for this publication is available from the British Library.

Library of Congress Cataloging in Publication Data

Smith, Helmut Walser, 1962–
The continuities of German history : nation, religion, and race across the long nineteenth
century / Helmut Walser Smith.
p. cm.
Includes bibliographical references and index.
ISBN 978-0-521-89588-0 (hardback) – ISBN 978-0-521-72025-0 (pbk.)
1. Germany – History – 1789–1900 – Historiography. 2. Nationalism – Germany –
History – 19th century. 3. Jews – Germany – History – 19th century
4. Germany – Ethnic relations – History – 19th century. 5. Europe – Ethnic relations –
History – 19th century. I. Title.
DD204.S56 2008
943'.07072 – dc22   2007037925

ISBN 978-0-521-89588-0 hardback
ISBN 978-0-521-72025-0 paperback

For Henry Turner and Peter Gay

CONTENTS

INTRODUCTION

On February 21, 1519, the citizens of Regensburg tore down the synagogue of the venerable Jewish community, whose documented existence in the city dated to circa 1000, making it at the time the oldest Jewish community in Germany. As in many German cities throughout the fifteenth and early sixteenth centuries, razing the synagogue signaled the onset of expulsion. As he sketched the synagogue interior, Albrecht Altdorfer knew the expulsion was imminent; he sat on the same city council that gave the Jews two days to clear the synagogue and five days to evacuate the city.[1] Edicts of expulsion did not mandate that citizens tear down synagogues, but this was the usual way, with Christian churches symbolizing victory atop the rubble of Jewish houses of worship. Yet in Altdorfer's etching, it is the overwhelming sense of architectural durability, supported by massive arches, that strikes us. To heighten the synagogue's solidity, Altdorfer illuminated its supporting walls, vaults, and the column on the left with fiercer light than realism demanded. In the etching, the actual light comes from a window, with the light of the protective Star of David casting a faint shadow beyond the man leaving the synagogue for the last time. The man looks at us as his shadow reaches toward us, as if to implicate us in his fate. But the pull of history is with the woman before him, and she exits the door into a space where there is no light. For the Jews of this community, this is "the hour," to cite W. G. Sebald, "when the shadow falls."[2]

---

[1] Christopher S. Wood, *Albrecht Altdorfer and the Origins of Landscape* (London, 1993), 251.

[2] W. G. Sebald, *After Nature*, tr. Michael Hamburger (New York, 2002), 36.

If Altdorfer rendered death-quiet interiors, it takes an act of imagination to conceive of the lively clamor outside the synagogue, as exultation accompanied its razing and the destruction of the wide aerial that constituted the Jewish quarter. Amidst this clamor, a stonemason fell from a beam in the synagogue, and the people assumed him dead until the next day when he returned. Astonished, the people proclaimed a miracle and promptly erected a wooden chapel and a stone pillar crowned by a statue of Maria holding the infant Jesus. The pope issued an indulgence for a pilgrimage to the site of the miracle, and swarms of the devout descended onto the square where once the synagogue had stood. They were in a state of religious ecstasy, and this circumstance drew the criticism of Martin Luther, who in his "Open Letter to the Christian Nobility" (1520) opined that people "run to these places in excited crowds, as though they had lost their reason, like herds of cattle."[3] But if Luther denounced the pilgrimage at Regensburg, he passed over in silence the expulsion of the Jews and the destruction of their community. His antipathies would soon be clear enough, however. In his infamous *The Jews and Their Lies*, written in 1543 after the great wave of expulsions had already occurred, he urged Christians "to set fire to [the Jews'] synagogues or schools and to cover over with dirt whatever will not burn, so that no man will ever again see a stone or cinder of them." "Their houses," he also advised, should "be razed or destroyed."[4] Often historians quote these words as presaging the calamity of the twentieth century; in fact, however, they merely described a ubiquitous practice of an earlier era. By the time Luther wrote these words, the numbers of synagogues to be razed had dwindled precipitously; left were not artifacts of Jewish life but markers of Christian triumph.

The years between the first Jewish settlement in Regensburg and its destruction in 1519 roughly correspond to the arc of time that separates us from that destruction. It will come as a surprise to many readers that historians rarely think in long time spans, electing instead to confine themselves to more manageable chronological units, measured at most

---

[3] Martin Luther, "An den christlichen Adel," in *Martin Luther: Studienausgabe*, vol. 2, ed. Hans-Ulrich Delius (Berlin, 1982), 143.

[4] Martin Luther, "On the Jews and Their Lies," in *Luther's Works*, vol. 47, ed. Franklin Sherman (Philadelphia, 1971), 268–9. On Luther and anti-Semitism generally, see the brief but incisive remarks in Heiko A. Oberman, *Wurzeln des Antisemitismus: Christenangst und Judenplage im Zeitalter von Humanismus und Reformation* (Berlin, 1981).

in decades, rarely in centuries. The closer one gets to the present, the more chronologically myopic historians become, confining questions of continuity and rupture to the recent past. In German history, a subject in which twentieth century cataclysms understandably dominate historical concerns, this problem is especially pronounced and is becoming more acute. If historians once severed the nineteenth century from the early modern period, now they truncate the twentieth century from the rest. The result, in my view, is a sense of German history that shies from considering chronological depth and the historical connections across long spans of time.

I first began to think about these questions in Regensburg, where in 2003 we lived a few houses away from the *Neupfarrplatz*, a large, empty square, save for the awkwardly placed parish church in the middle. The new parish church was built upon the ruins of the synagogue whose interior Altdorfer had so carefully etched. At first, there was just a wooden pilgrimage church; then, in 1542, when Regensburg for a time embraced Protestantism, the wooden structure was rebuilt in stone and became the first Protestant church in the city. But nearly 500 years later, there was no gainsaying the spatial alienation of the church or the purpose-lessness of the square's graceless dimensions. For 300 years, the square was hardly used, save by the French occupiers, who in 1796 practiced troop formation there. By the mid-nineteenth century, merchants occupied the place on market days, and in the twentieth century, the Nazis disgraced it again by burning books there.

But the shadow first fell at the time of the initial destruction – not that 1519 prefigured 1933, or that Germany was already on a special path, but I did feel that there was a connection, etched in stone and evident in the architecture, that my training as a historian hardly equipped me to talk about. It is perhaps indicative that historians have come to think of these matters not because historical argument necessitated revision but because the precise poetic eye of W. G. Sebald forced us to look at the landscape of the past, its hidden traces and enduring shadows, with new intensity.[5]

This is the theme of this book. I am interested in how the centuries connect in German history, and in particular how it is possible to think

---

[5] But see also the immense success of Etienne François and Hagen Schulze, eds., *Deutsche Erinnerungsorte*, 3 vols. (Munich, 2002).

about historical change over long periods of time. The attempt, of course, is not entirely novel. Scores of books once saw German history as a kind of "hearse in reverse," backing into the past with the knowledge of the corpses it has piled up. This way of envisioning history, the opposite of a lachrymose conception, led historians to pattern the whole of the German past as if it portended its violent present. "The history of the Germans is a history of extremes," proclaimed A. J. P. Taylor in the first sentence of *The Course of German History*, written in 1944.[6] Nowadays, historians emphasize instead the shattered quality of the past. Frank Tipton, for example, begins his *History of Germany* with the figure of *Germania* – not the angry, confident woman guarding the Rhine, but the marble, jack-hammered fragments of floor that Hans Haacke intended visitors of the Venice Biennale in 1993 to walk over, disoriented and mournful.[7]

In German history, images of shattering and fragmentation have increasingly served as a "root metaphor," which, following the philosopher Max Black, may be defined as "a systematic repertoire of ideas by means of which a given thinker describes, by analogical extension, some domain to which those ideas do not immediately and literally apply."[8] The root metaphor of a shattered history profoundly influences how German historians connect the present to the past, and the past of contemporary history to earlier periods. According to some, it has even become "a new orthodoxy."[9]

The metaphor derives in part from a general postmodern stance, informed by "incredulity towards master narratives," as Jean François Lyotard has famously put it.[10] On a deeper level, however, shattered images also haunt testimonies of the Holocaust, strongly implying the collapse of transparency and the impossibility of insight, as if the sheen of civilization were as thin and impenetrable as the single row of barbed

---

[6] A. J. P. Taylor, *The Course of German History: A Survey of the Development since 1815* (New York, 1962), 13.

[7] Frank B. Tipton, *A History of Modern Germany since 1815* (Berkeley, 2003), 1.

[8] Max Black cited in Victor Turner, *Dramas, Fields, and Metaphors: Symbolic Action in Human Society* (Ithaca, 1974), 26.

[9] Interview with Geoff Eley and David Blackbourn, in *German History*, 22.2 (2004), 243, 245.

[10] Jean François Lyotard, *The Postmodern Condition: A Report on Knowledge*, tr. Geoff Bennington and Brian Massumi (Minneapolis, 1984), xxiv.

wire around Auschwitz-Birkenau. Something like this image informed Primo Levi's description of Dr. Pannwitz, who gazed upon Levi with a look that "was not one as between two men," and more resembled the view "across the glass window of an aquarium between two beings who live in different worlds."[11] As in much Holocaust testimony, glass separates, paradoxically blocking the possibility of human understanding.[12] Shattered glass renders this impossibility permanent and irreparable. As an image, it is also more implacably final than reference to ruins, which can serve as new foundations, and which, as its romantic lineage suggests, enables longing and the imaginative reconstruction of home.

The "shattered past" implies, then, that the catastrophe of the twentieth century precludes traditional historical narrative as a vehicle for understanding what occurred. Historians can tell stories, but the attempt to bind them together into a coherent whole necessarily rings false. In their influential consideration of major themes in modern German history, Konrad Jarausch and Michael Geyer emphasize that German history is a "permanently fractured history," best told not with Walter Scott's confident cadences but with Uwe Johnson's "fragmented multi-local and cross-temporal narrations."[13] Perhaps, but metaphors of fracture and shatter draw their power from experience, and experience – lived, remembered, recounted – is not quite the same as history, which seeks to understand, to put things together and connect them, offering limited generalizations that allow for more insightful, if still imperfect, statements about the past. One can represent experience as shattered, but history tells differently (as does the chronologically ambitious, analytical narrative of *Shattered Past*).[14] The difference is significant. In his analysis of the Holocaust testimonies collected at the Fortunoff Archive at Yale University, Lawrence L. Langer relates the story of how a daughter struggles to understand the experience of her parents,

---

[11] Primo Levi, *Survival in Auschwitz*, tr. Stuart Woolf (New York, 1993), 105.

[12] Lawrence L. Langer, *Holocaust Testimonies: The Ruins of Memory* (New Haven, 1991), 56–57.

[13] Konrad H. Jarausch and Michael Geyer, *Shattered Past: Reconstructing German Histories* (Princeton, 2003), 15, 358.

[14] See the highly analytic, close-to-the-current-state-of-historiography account offered in ibid.

Mr. and Mrs. B., who between them survived the Lodz Ghetto, Auschwitz, Dora-Nordhausen, and Bergen Belsen. "She draws on a vocabulary of chronology and conjunction," Langer writes, "while they use a lexicon of disruption, absence, and irreversible loss."[15] Are we not, in fact, closer to the position of the daughter, with history our "system of ladders . . . out and over the abyss"?[16]

This must imply a history less confident than Scott's narration suggests, but with an emphasis on human connections, not only the proximate causes but also the longer lineages, without assuming that continuities run in only one direction or that past events determine future disasters. This attempt at historical understanding, which in Inga Clendinnen's words is both "cumulative and never complete," governs the form of what follows, namely the essay, a series of attempts to construct bridges across chronological chasms.[17]

The essays – literally, attempts – address a series of questions that derive from what I call the altered "vanishing point of German history." The first essay, Chapter 1, suggests that a central reference point of German history, a vanishing point in the painterly sense of the term, has shifted from 1933, when Hitler seized power, to 1941, when the genocidal killing of the Holocaust commenced, and that this shift has considerable implications for the writing of German history. I try to understand how this shift came about and explore its potential impact. In painting, a vanishing point focuses the viewer's attention and determines the relative size of detail throughout the canvas. By analogy, the vanishing point in history determines the central focus of a disciplinary community, establishing central questions and deciding the scope of what counts. It does this not only for events chronologically close to the vanishing point, but also for those at considerable distance. In this sense, vanishing points pattern the writing of history, whether or not we wish them to. When Hitler's seizure of power in 1933 constituted the vanishing point, historians worked out interpretations of the nineteenth century that centered Germany's authoritarian traditions and illiberal politics. The new vanishing point of 1941 again challenges German historians to think in the long term, against what I see as an emerging

[15] Langer, *Holocaust Testimonies*, xi.
[16] The quote, and the line of argument, is from Inga Clendinnen, *Reading the Holocaust* (Cambridge, 2002), 4.
[17] Ibid.

historiographical consensus that confines questions concerning the continuities of German history to the short, violent twentieth century. The new vanishing point also suggests different kinds of continuities, as the thing to be explained is not the political failure of elites but the collapse of fellow feeling among ordinary men.

In Chapter 2, I ask about the origins of modern nationalism and try to understand this problem against the background of an early-modern conception of the German nation. I do not agree with Ernest Gellner, who argued that as far as nationalism was concerned, any old scrap of nation sufficed, and that nationalists made nations, not the reverse. On the contrary, in Germany, as in France and England, the Netherlands and Spain, nations predated nationalism. Nationalists did not invent nations; they made sense of them in radically new terms. This new understanding involved the shift from an exterior sense of nation to an interior sense, from the nation as emblem to the nation as identity. It is, I contend, the invention of national identity, predicated upon a modern understanding of personhood that made the (German) nation of the (German) nationalists into a powerful, revolutionary, and portentous idea.[18]

In Chapter 3, I take up the legacy of catastrophic religious violence and follow Ernest Renan's famous suggestion that nations must also learn to forget. I compare the inter-Christian violence of the Thirty Years War with the Christian-Jewish violence of massacres and expulsions and ask whether, in the early modern period and into the nineteenth century, forgetting occurred in the sense that Renan implied. I have come to believe that after the Thirty Years War, which for the German population exceeded World War II in destructive fury, a blanket of forgetfulness covered over the experience, and that this covering lasted not decades but more than a century. When Germans rediscovered the Thirty Years War at the end of the eighteenth century, and with more engagement at the beginning of the nineteenth, it was a rediscovery of an

---

[18] For this line of thinking, a number of works have been formative. On the novelty of collective identity, see Lutz Niethammer, *Kollektive Identität: Heimliche Quellen einer unheimlichen Konjunktur* (Reinbek bei Hamburg, 2000); on modern subjectivity, Jerrold Seigel, *The Idea of the Self: Thought and Experience in Western Europe since the Seventeenth Century* (Cambridge, 2005); Dror Wahrman, *The Making of the Modern Self: Identity and Culture in Eighteenth-Century England* (New Haven, 2004); Heinz D. Kittsteiner, *Die Entstehung des modernen Gewissens* (Leipzig, 1991); Charles Taylor, *Sources of the Self: The Making of Modern Identity* (Cambridge, Mass., 1989).

experience forgotten. Conversely, memory of the expulsion had a vital place in German culture, especially in local communities, the German hometowns. When debate about Jewish inclusion began, the reaction against it drew on this memory, which had become codified in ritual and in exclusionary practices. Continuity with the deep past proved strong; the history of Jewish inclusion vexed, with lasting results.

One lasting result was the continuing salience of anti-Semitic violence. Throughout the nineteenth century, this violence, which is the subject of Chapter 4, involved anti-Semitic theater: Rioters threatened and beat Jews, but rarely murdered them. I ask how anti-Semitic violence became murderous and approach the problem by collecting and analyzing all the incidences of anti-Semitic violence that required the intervention of military forces. Moreover, I collect these incidences of violence not just for Germany but for non-Ottoman Europe and suggest their novelty against the backdrop of a quieter eighteenth century and a seventeenth century in which the killing of Jews occurred amidst murderous clashes that involved other antagonisms. This approach enables us to discern the transition from community-based violence to violence defined in national terms; it allows us to see when and where the dam inhibiting murder broke; and it makes us appreciate the role of the state in halting, encouraging, and furthering anti-Semitic violence.

In Chapter 5, I explore the interconnection of modern anti-Semitism with racism, racism with the idea of the elimination of peoples, and anti-Semitism with the kind of racism that posited elimination. The long nineteenth century witnessed the transition from thinking about the annihilation of peoples in a cultural sense to conceiving of it in physical terms. Racism, as a theory and as a reflection of the practice of colonial rule, proved a powerful motor driving this dismaying transition. Yet elimination in the strong sense of the term, as genocide, remained inconceivable, whether in the mainstream or on the margin, except when it legitimated mass murder that had already occurred in colonial wars. The same does not hold for eliminationist experiments short of genocide, such as expulsion, ethnic cleansing, incarceration in concentration camps, and the creation of human reservations. Political publicists of liberal and conservative provenance entertained these possibilities, if reluctantly. In the nineteenth century, it was not yet possible to think, as Hannah Arendt wrote of the twentieth-century concentration camp universe, that anything is possible.[19]

This is a book about the continuities of German history – about how ideas and political forms are traceable across what historians have taken to be the sharp breaks of history. In common parlance, continuity implies that something is uninterrupted, and in history that suggests that forms of ideas and politics remain homologous, of similar magnitude and like ratio, across significant political ruptures. In this spirit, Fritz Fischer famously argued for the continuities of German history, seeing the annexationist program of the German leadership prior to and during World War I as a direct precursor to Hitler's visions of world domination.[20] Differences in detail between the two sets of annexation plans seemed to Fischer insignificant when compared to their overall similarity in form. This continuity was, moreover, undergirded by an alliance of elites, which meant that at two different points of time leaders from the same social station brought into being Germany's aggressive politics. There are other arguments for fundamental continuity, notably those advanced with greatest cogency by Hans Rosenberg and Hans-Ulrich Wehler, emphasizing the political preponderance over the long term of conservative-reactionary elites in a period of rapid economic and social change.[21] This understanding of continuity posits a high degree of identity between the initial and terminal point of the continuum, and it suggests not merely structuring force but causal explanation. Advanced with élan, these continuity theses have been highly influential in German history. But they were always vulnerable to criticism that derived from arguments of contingency: that history is open and multivalent and that events can dramatically change structure.[22] These

---

[19] Hannah Arendt, *The Origins of Totalitarianism*, rev. ed. (New York, 1973), 437.

[20] For a penetrating recent discussion, see Klaus Große Kracht, *Die zankende Zunft: Historische Kontroversen in Deutschland nach 1945* (Göttingen, 2005), 47–68.

[21] Hans Rosenberg, *Bureaucracy, Aristocracy and Autocracy: The Prussian Experience 1660–1815* (Boston, 1958); Hans-Ulrich Wehler, *Deutsche Gesellschaftsgeschichte*, 4 vols. (Munich, 1987–2003) – with a fifth volume forthcoming.

[22] See Thomas Nipperdey, *Gesellschaft, Kultur, Theorie* (Göttingen, 1976), 360–389. But see also the historicist moments in David Blackbourn and Geoff Eley, *The Peculiarities of German History: Bourgeois Society and Politics in Nineteenth Century Germany* (Oxford, 1984), where the authors, in their words, attempt "to redirect(s) primary attention away from the deeper historical continuities" (50). In his review of Blackbourn and Eley, Nipperdey points out this historicist affinity, grounded in the necessity of preserving

criticisms chiseled away at the explanatory force of the continuity theses and opened important questions about the degree to which profound ruptures cut through the continuities of German history. We will return to these debates. Suffice here to say that I think of them as being largely over, but with fallout that cannot be satisfying from the standpoint of German history in the long term. Such a history must still think about connections across time, and connections require us to think across what are undeniably caesuras in the German past.

I take as my starting point connections within symbolic forms of German history, and in particular those forms – nation and nationalism, religion and religious exclusion, racism and violence – that have long histories, that are at the center of the German past, and that did not emerge, "*per saltum*," in the modern world. Within this context, continuity means something quite specific.[23] It does not mean that events from a given point tend to a certain outcome, or that the later point merely reiterates a starting point. The first position is teleological, the second theological, at least in the sense that circular understandings of history derive from Christian precedents.[24] Nor is it my claim that, from a certain point, change is mainly endogenous (i.e., unaffected by events external to the system) and thus determined by factors specific to Germany – as Fritz Fischer, for example, argued. Instead, I make two kinds of assertions about continuity. The first is that adequate explanations of twentieth-century events ought to have historical reach, and this reach ought to encompass periods longer than the lifetime of an individual. This kind of long-term explanation requires us to consider ideas, institution, and politics over significant periods of time, both within German history and across it. The "across" is important. Continuity need not imply particularity, and precisely the most important continuities – seen

---

a sense of contingency. See Nipperdey's review in *Historische Zeitschrift*, 249 (1989), 434–437.

23 For the following discussion, I am indebted to Alexander Gerschenkron, "On the Concept of Continuity in History," *Proceedings of the American Philosophical Society*, 106.3 (June 1962), 195–209. Gerschenkron describes five kinds of continuity: constancy of direction, periodicity of events, endogenous change, length of causal regress, and stability of the rate of change (200). When I refer to "the continuities of German history," I intend the term continuity mainly in the fourth sense, length of causal regress, but sometimes in the fifth, which, even in Gerschenkron, is mainly a method for seeing not continuity but break.

24 M. H. Abrams, *Natural Supernaturalism: Tradition and Revelation in Romantic Literature* (New York, 1971), 197–252.

from the standpoint of twentieth-century catastrophes – are not peculiar to Germany. The second claim is related to the first: It is that only by considering continuity of form – the nation, for example, or anti-Jewish violence, or the discourse and practice of annihilation – is it possible to see with acuity the specific kink, the significant shift, that structures later developments.

I cannot claim specific originality in looking at things this way. Historians are generally familiar with insights that emphasize the persistence of form – the continuing hold of late medieval piety in the figurative imagination of Martin Luther, for example – or how the religious imagination gripped radical Jacobins as they attempted to invent novel conceptions of God and time.[25] Yet the emphasis on the long term, on a *histoire croisée* across chronological rupture, no longer represents conventional wisdom in the narrower field of modern German history.[26]

---

[25] The first famously by Ernst Troeltsch in 1913 in "Renaissance and Reformation," in Ernst Troeltsch, *Schriften zur Bedeutung des Protestantismus für die moderne Welt*, ed. Trutz Rendtorff (Berlin, 2001), vol. 8 of Ernst Troeltsch, *Kritische Gesamtausgabe*, 329–374; Mona Ozuf, *Festivals and the French Revolution*, tr. Alan Sheridan (Cambridge, Mass., 1988).

[26] There are, however, a number of historians who have recently written books that address the long term of German history, mainly in the early modern period. They include William H. Hagen, *Ordinary Prussians: Brandenburg Junkers and Villages, 1500–1840* (Cambridge, 2002); Isabel V. Hull, *Sexuality, State and Civil Society in Germany, 1700–1815* (Ithaca, 1996); David Sabean, *Property, Production and Family in Neckarhausen, 1700–1870* (Cambridge, 1990); David Sabean, *Kinship in Neckarhausen 1700–1870* (Cambridge, 1998) – to list only a few of the recent English language works. See also, and including the more recent periods, David Blackbourn, *The Conquest of Nature: Water, Landscape, and the Making of Modern Germany* (New York, 2006); Philippe Burrin, *Warum die Deutschen?: Antisemitismus, Nationalsozialismus, Genozid*, tr. from the French by Michael Bischoff (Berlin, 2004); Ute Frevert, *Die Kasernierte Nation: Militärdienst und Zivilgesellschaft in Deutschland* (Munich, 2001); Dieter Gosewinkel, *Einbürgern und Ausschließen: Die Nationalisierung der Staatsangehörigkeit vom Deutschen Bund bis zur Bundesrepublik* (Göttingen, 2001); Suzanne L. Marchand, *Down from Olympus: Archaeology and Philhellenism in Germany, 1750–1970* (Princeton, 1996); and the challenges put forth in Thomas A. Brady Jr., *The Protestant Reformation in German History, GHI in Washington D.C. Occasional Paper, No. 22* (Washington, D.C., 1998). Finally, it is true that modern German history has been blessed with synthetic works of remarkable quality and force. They include, most notably, David Blackbourn, *The Long Nineteenth Century: A History of Germany, 1780–1918* (New York, 1998); Christopher Clark, *The Iron Kingdom: The Rise and Fall of Prussia, 1600–1947* (Cambridge, Mass., 2006); Thomas Nipperdey, *Deutsche Geschichte 1800–1866: Bürgerwelt und starker Staat* (Munich, 1983); *Deutsche Geschichte 1866–1918*, 2 vols. (Munich, 1990); James J. Sheehan, *German History, 1770–1866* (Oxford, 1989); Hans-Ulrich Wehler, as cited in note 21; and Heinrich August Winkler, *Der lange Weg nach Westen: Deutsche Geschichte*, 2 vols. (Munich, 2000).

Instead, assumptions that have become common in the aftermath of the *Sonderweg* debate (whether Germany was on a peculiar historical path) have contributed to a reluctance to consider continuities over the long term. The *Sonderweg* debate and its aftermath hardly constitute the only reason why historians of modern Germany now bid the nineteenth century *adieu*, as Paul Nolte has recently asserted.[27] But as that debate turned on the question of what made Germany peculiar, it led historians to concentrate on ever slimmer strands of continuity, with continuity defined as what was unique in German history and how that uniqueness carried over and contributed to mid-twentieth century catastrophes. I take up this issue in the conclusion, entitled "Continuities of German History," and try to discern significant continuities over long spans of time, with the Holocaust being the event that shapes my questions. In this conclusion, I also address the conventional wisdom concerning the "modernity" of the Holocaust and suggest that it has constricted our vision for the many ways in which what transpired in Nazi Germany had historically profound roots.

In what follows, I instead emphasize broader continuities, centered on violent ideologies that have accompanied transformations in nation, religion, and race across the long nineteenth century. These transformations have specifically German histories but remain enmeshed in Europe. They represent the thick strands of continuity, rather than the thin. And they cannot be set aside simply because European history dyed into them, coloring over their German specificities. On the contrary, the wider continuities command our attention precisely because they are part of what Alain Finkielkraut called the history of a lost humanity.[28]

---

[27] Paul Nolte, "Abschied vom 19. Jahrhundert oder Auf der Suche nach einer anderen Moderne," in *Wege der Gesellschaftsgeschichte*, eds. Jürgen Osterhammel, Dieter Langewiesche, and Paul Nolte (Göttingen, 2006), 103–132. See also the now nearly classic exposé of the problem, Suzanne L. Marchand, "Embarrassed by the Nineteenth Century," in *Consortium on Revolutionary Europe: Selected Papers* (Tallahassee, 2002), 1–16; and the important arguments for connecting the nineteenth and the twentieth centuries contained in James Retallack, *The German Right, 1860–1920: Political Limits of the Authoritarian Imagination* (Toronto, 2006).

[28] Alain Finkielkraut, *Verlust der Menschlichkeit: Versuch über das 20. Jahrhundert*, trans. Susanne Schaper (Stuttgart, 1998).

THE VANISHING POINT
OF GERMAN HISTORY

"The purpose of a historian depends on his point of view."
> Leopold von Ranke, *Histories of the Latin and Germanic Nations from 1494–1514*

When it comes to history, every student seems to understand that at the end of the day, the person with the Gatling gun determines who tells the subsequent story and how. There is, nevertheless, a richer way of looking at historical perspective; it derives from perspective in painting, and more precisely from the intersection between modern historical thinking and the discovery of linear projection.

In his dedication of *The Prince* to Lorenzo de Medici, Niccolò Machiavelli hinted at this intersection. "Just as men who are sketching the landscape put themselves down in the plain to study the nature of the mountains and the highlands, and to study the low-lying land they put themselves high on the mountains, so," Machiavelli wrote in 1513, "to comprehend fully the nature of the people one must be a prince, and to comprehend fully the nature of princes one must be an ordinary citizen."[1] The perspective of an observer outside the thing being observed, Machiavelli implies, is the precondition for comprehension. For Machiavelli, perspective had a particular, painterly resonance. Roughly a century earlier, Filippo Brunelleschi had conducted

---

[1] Niccolò Machiavelli, *The Prince*, tr. George Bull (New York, 1961), 30, "Letter from Niccolò Machiavelli to the Magnificent Lorenzo de Medici." The relation of this passage to the general problem of perspective is pointed out in Gisela Bock, "Machiavelli als Geschichtsschreiber," in *Quellen und Forschungen aus Italienischen Archiven und Bibliotheken*, 66 (1986), 175. See also Carlo Ginzburg, *Wooden Eyes: Nine Reflections on Distance*, tr. Martin Ryle and Kate Soper (New York, 2001), 153.

his famous experiments leading to the discovery of linear perspective, which Leon Battista Alberti then systematized for the use of his fellow artists in his famous treatise, *On Painting*, published in 1436. The essential discovery is that from the perspective of a viewing eye, the lines of a three-dimensional image on a flat plane converge in what Alberti called the "centric point."[2] In English, in the course of the eighteenth century, this "sign," as Alberti also called it, became known as a "vanishing point."[3] In mathematically precise fashion, it determined the relative size of all other objects on the canvas.

The vanishing point suggests that perspective generates as well as limits knowledge, and raises questions about how the canvas is structured.[4] Linear perspective is of course a metaphor, the use of one kind of thing to better understand another. As love is not a red, red rose, so history is not a Renaissance canvas with a vanishing point. But for the writing of history, the painterly metaphor is an old one, and if not merely a cliché, it tells us something. When Voltaire, for example, compared his chapters of the *Age of Louis XIV* to "frescoes of the great events of the time," he added, revealingly: "the principal figures are in the foreground; the crowd is in the background. Woe to details!"[5] Conversely, when the social historians of the 1960s and 1970s talked about widening the canvas, foregrounding the crowd, and empathetically rendering the details of the everyday, old-school critics wondered where the center was now to be. They were not wrong to ask. When taken seriously, the painterly metaphor helps us consider the place of significant facts in a larger image; it allows us to see what is in the foreground and what is placed out of view. It also enjoins us to consider these things from an analytical position that does not necessarily privilege our present perspective or reduce perspective to a putative political ideology. Instead, the metaphor suggests that while we now see certain historical forces with greater clarity, the price of this clarity is a necessary blindness in other spheres.

The above may seem self-evident, yet it bears recalling that the current ruling metaphor in the historical profession for how we structure

[2] Leon Battista Alberti, *On Painting*, tr. Cecil Grayson (London, 1972), 54.
[3] *The Oxford Companion to Art*, ed. Harold Osborne (Oxford, 1970), 849.
[4] John Berger, *Ways of Seeing* (London, 1972), 16.
[5] Voltaire to Jean Baptiste Dubos, October 30, 1738, excerpted in *The Varieties of History: From Voltaire to the Present*, ed. Fritz Stern (New York, 1973), 39.

things is poetic not painterly, a trope not a canvas. The figurative difference has consequences for our sense of what we do. Alberti believed
that the laws of painting arise "from roots within nature herself," and
that painting involved getting the proportions that are given in nature
right from the standpoint of the viewer.[6] For Alberti and for painters
in the mimetic tradition generally, painting involved a "three way negotiation" – between the subject, the painter's perception of the subject,
and the social conventions and artistic techniques that condition and
enable the painter's rendering of the subject.[7] As in painting, so in history, the stress falls on negotiation. Constructivist accounts, by contrast,
privilege the narrative imagination of the historian over the recalcitrant
material he orders.

Hayden White's *Metahistory* still constitutes the *locus classicus* of
the narrative argument. White considers historians of "distinctly classic
achievement" – men such as Ranke, Michelet, de Tocqueville, and Burckhardt – and argues that "their status as models of historical narration
and conceptualization depends, ultimately, on the perceptual and specifically poetic nature of their perspective on history and its processes."[8]
He then maps this poetic nature on a grid, with different "modes of
emplotment" suggesting affinities to "modes of argument" and "modes
of ideological implication."[9] As these emplotments are fictional tropes,
tied to political ideologies, history tendentiously places fiction before
fact.

If White's analysis helps us understand the likes of Michelet and de
Tocqueville, towering solitary figures before the age of professional communities, it strikes me as misleading with respect to ordinary historians
who spend their days, as J. H. Hexter famously wrote, reading "things
written between 1450 and 1650 or books written by historians on the
basis of things written between 1450 and 1650."[10] Hexter implied that

[6] Alberti, *On Painting*, 35.
[7] Simon Schama, *Rembrandt's Eyes* (New York, 1999), 329.
[8] Hayden White, *Metahistory: The Historical Imagination in Nineteenth-Century Europe*
(Baltimore, 1973), 4.
[9] Ibid., 29. On White, and whether his formalism takes sufficient account of the destabilizing moments of richly textured works, see especially Dominick LaCapra, "The Poetics of
Historiography: Hayden White's Tropics of Discourse," in LaCapra, *Rethinking Intellectual History: Texts, Contexts, Language* (Ithaca, 1983), 72–83.
[10] J. H. Hexter, *Reappraisals in History: New Views on History and Society in Early Modern
Europe*, 2nd ed. (Chicago, 1979), 6.

the central events of the past, perhaps even more than the issues of our day, determine how we carve away the hours of our historical work. Sometimes these events become the focal point, explicit and implicit, of whole disciplinary communities. In histories marked by trauma, these events powerfully structure fields, overshadowing the narrative tropes historians might otherwise employ.

These events we call vanishing points. They should not be confused with turning points of history, though they may be that as well. A vanishing point is a focus of research that structures the whole image, while a turning point is where history bends in one direction and not another. For A. J. P. Taylor, for example, September 1939 constituted the vanishing point, as the problems created by German aggression in Europe structured his work. By contrast, the Revolution of 1848 was, at least for Taylor's Germany, the turning point where German history famously "failed to turn." Subsequent German history, starting with Bismarck, and passing through 1914, then converged on the vanishing point of 1939.

Rich in cataclysmic events, modern Germany illustrates how vanishing points structure fields. Whether located in 1914, 1918, 1933, 1939, 1945, or 1989, the vanishing points of modern German history belong to the twentieth century, dictating the questions we ask and the issues we debate. Their structuring powers are not just issues of metahistorical discourse or grand narrative. Vanishing points often evince intense debate about the veracity, even the authenticity, of documentary evidence at points close to the center. Sometimes these debates derive their force from generational conflict. "Every generation writes its own history," George Herbert Mead memorably wrote, often with a new vanishing point.[11] Now, after a very long period, roughly the half-century from 1949 to 1989, the utter centrality of January 1933 is ceding way to another vanishing point: the summer of 1941, when Operation Barbarossa began and the mass killing of the Holocaust commenced.

In what follows, I examine how the vanishing point of 1933 structured the historical field; I then trace the historical debates that spurred the shift from 1933 to 1941 and suggest that problems and possibilities that

---

[11] George H. Mead, "The Nature of the Past," in *Essays in Honor of John Dewey*, ed. John Coss (New York, 1929), 240.

inhered in the first vanishing point may yet be instructive for the second, especially as it pertains to the Holocaust.

I

For the Germans who remained in the country after defeat in World War II, the experience of the Third Reich necessitated a reconsideration of the entire sweep of German history. It was not obvious, however, that 1933 should constitute the vanishing point of their work. Consider Friedrich Meinecke's *The German Catastrophe*. Written in 1946, when Meinecke was eighty-four and nearly blind, it is easily the most famous historical reflection written in the immediate postwar years. For Meinecke, the year 1933 represented the point when German history irrevocably turned; the catastrophe, "the abyss," was however the war – Hitler's "unscrupulous and ruinous exploitation of the people's last drop of strength."[12] By placing the vanishing point in the lost war, Meinecke necessarily foregrounded not politics but the failed "synthesis of power and culture."[13] It is for this reason that King Frederick William's dismissal of Wilhelm von Humboldt and Hermann von Boyen in 1819 constituted an important turning point in German history. This dismissal may be regarded, Meinecke wrote, "as a victory in the Prussian State of the soul that was hostile to culture over the soul that was capable of culture."[14] The balance between culture and power was also at the center of Meinecke's critique of Bismarck, who nevertheless still maintained a sense of the balance characteristic of statesmen before the age of demagogues, and it informed Meinecke's image of the irrational in modern politics – mass Machiavellianism, he revealingly called it. Finally, this lost sense of balance inspired Meinecke's deeply felt, if easily ridiculed, prescription for German renewal: the building of local Goethe communities throughout the land.

In the context of defeat, it seems indicative that a censured document counts among the first reassessments by a German historian that truly placed 1933 at the vanishing point. Written by Ludwig Dehio in 1949

[12] Friedrich Meinecke, *The German Catastrophe*, tr. Sidney Fay (Cambridge, Mass., 1950), 50–51.
[13] Ibid., 14.
[14] Ibid., 11.

upon his assumption of the editorship of the *Historische Zeitschrift*, the document was to be a foreword to the first number of the journal, scheduled to resume publication after a hiatus of five years. But the publisher, *Oldenburg Verlag*, considered the "confession of guilt" unnecessary and refused to publish it. The document is nevertheless instructive. For Dehio, 1933 represented the year "in which something hitherto unimaginable became reality." That something, foreshadowed in 1918, was a fact of cultural, not political history, and Burckhardt, not Ranke, offered the conceptual tools to understand what Dehio called "the fragility of the Christian-humanistic cultural personality in the age of total civilization."[15] If Dehio's language remained tinctured with the polemics of the First World War, he nevertheless placed the vanishing point square in the middle of a civilizational canvas. "Our catastrophe is only a section (*Auschnitt*) of the crisis of the west, of the world," he wrote.[16] Yet he penned the foreword from a national perspective, from "the sorrows of a people half liberated, half destroyed" – referring, of course, to the Germans.[17]

By contrast, German historians in exile unequivocally placed the vanishing point in 1933, and had a different sense of the larger context. If Meinecke and Dehio located the German catastrophe as part of a western cataclysm, the German historians in exile argued that Germany had veered away from the values of the west. About this, they could not have been clearer. In the *Mind of Germany*, published in 1960, Hans Kohn offered, as he wrote, "a tentative reply to the one question upon which much of the fascination of German history rests: how the alienation of Germany from the west came about."[18] According to Kohn, the divergence began with the progenitor of radical nationalism, Johann Gottlieb Fichte, and it was best understood by the philosopher of power, Friedrich Nietzsche. In his influential essay, "German Idealism in the Light of Social History," Hajo Holborn followed a similar line of reasoning. "The only question that is of concern here," he wrote, "is the

---

[15] The foreword is reprinted in Winfried Schulze, *Deutsche Geschichtswissenschaft nach 1945* (Munich, 1989), 101–104.

[16] Ibid.

[17] Ibid.

[18] Cited by Kenneth D. Barkin, "German Émigré Historians in America: The Fifties, Sixties, and Seventies," in *An Interrupted Past: German-Speaking Refugee Historians in the United States after 1933*, eds. Hartmut Lehmann and James J. Sheehan (New York, 1991), 158.

origin of the separation of Germany from Western Europe and America."[19] Like Kohn, Holborn located the divergence "during the age of German idealism, by which is meant the great intellectual movement in Germany during the years 1770–1840."[20] The end of German idealism, in turn, represented the decisive chronological marker between volumes two and three of his monumental *A History of Modern Germany*.[21]

What impresses about the exiled historians, many of them students of Meinecke, is their abiding sense that the magnitude of the German catastrophe required an understanding of history with depth of field. The major figures all wrote important books on earlier periods: Hans Kohn on the origins of the idea of nationalism, Holborn on Ulrich von Hutten, and Hans Rosenberg on the origins of Prussian feudalism, which he located in the seventeenth century. Strongly determined by liberal-democratic positions, their angle of vision foregrounded the epic struggle of left and right, carried out in the twin realms of ideas and politics, and ending in disaster. Hans Rosenberg put the point with characteristic force. In a postscript to *Bureaucracy, Aristocracy and Autocracy, The Prussian Experience 1660–1815*, he referred to "the long protracted counterrevolution in Germany [that] was brilliantly executed by the old ruling groups."[22] This counterrevolution, which cemented social and political power, spelled the demise of Weimar, a victim of the conservative "alliance with the captains of big industry which went back to the 1870s."[23]

This unholy alliance is also the linchpin of a German work that commenced the radical recasting of German history writing in the Federal Republic: Fritz Fischer's *Germany's Aims in the First World War* (*Griff nach der Weltmacht*), published in 1961. It is difficult to overestimate the sensation Fischer's work elicited; in our own day, only Daniel Goldhagen's *Hitler's Willing Executioners* generated a similar atmosphere of historical passion.[24] Yet it was not the audacity of Fischer's archival work, his discovery of Bethmann-Hollweg's annexationist

---

[19] Hajo Holborn, *Germany and Europe: Historical Essays* (New York, 1971), 2.

[20] Ibid.

[21] Hajo Holborn, *A History of Modern Germany*, 3 vols. (New York, 1959–1969).

[22] Cited in Barkin, "German Émigré Historians in America," 161.

[23] Ibid.

[24] Fritz Fischer, *Griff nach der Weltmacht: Die Kriegszielpolitik des kaiserlichen Deutschland, 1914–1918* (Düsseldorf, 1961).

September program notwithstanding, that impressed and enraged. Rather, Fischer quickened Clio's pulse by drawing bold lines of continuity from the Third Reich back to the Second. He argued that in 1914, as in 1939, the civilian leadership of Germany willed war; that the war, in 1914 as in 1939, was fought for a hitherto unrecognized degree of continental hegemony and world power; and that a powerful alliance of civilian elites, agrarian and industrial, furthered these goals in order to shore up a repressive status quo. Continuity, collusion of elites, internal strategy, and foreign expansion, these became the clarion calls for an assault against the national tradition of German historical writing. As the debate wore on, Fischer's positions became more radical. In *War of Illusions*, which Fischer published in 1969, he argued that Germany does not bear the main responsibility for the war, but the sole responsibility.[25]

For Fischer, the experience of the Third Reich gave renewed salience to 1914, imparting to the earlier date the quality of a displaced vanishing point. This displacement was partly a generational phenomenon. Born in 1908, Fritz Fischer belonged to those too young to fight in World War I but old enough, in Fischer's case barely, to recall the loss and sorrow it brought. His career as a historian, preceded by his work in theology, did not begin until the Third Reich, where it manifested an all-too-commonplace mix of conformity and racist expression. A member of Hitler's SA in 1933, theologically close to the "German Christians," Fischer received his doctorate in history in 1936 and became a member of the Nazi Party in 1937.[26] Two years later, he received a scholarship from the *Reichsinstitut für Geschichte des neuen Deutschlands*, then under Walter Frank, the most powerful and important exponent of National Socialist historiography. In 1941, Fischer looked forward to holding lectures on such topics as "the infiltration of Judaism in the culture and politics of Germany in the last two centuries" and "the infiltration of Jewish Blood in the English upper class."[27] Instead, and with a recommendation from Frank, he was appointed "*Ausserordentlicher*" professor of history at the University of Hamburg in 1942. Clearly,

---

[25] Fritz Fischer, *War of Illusions: German Policies from 1911 to 1914*, tr. Marian Jackson (London, 1975).

[26] Klaus Große Kracht, "Fritz Fischer und der deutsche Protestantismus," *Zeitschrift für neuere Theologiegeschichte*, 10.2 (2003), 224–252.

[27] Ibid., 239–40.

Fischer's was not a career that suffered. When called to arms, Fischer fell into American captivity, from which he was released in February 1947 and reinstated at the University of Hamburg in May of the same year.[28]

Fischer's experiences of active obedience in the Third Reich, then captivity by the Americans, must have been profound, for something caused him to perform a *volte face* of his previously held views. In 1949, at the first *Historikertag* in postwar Germany, he dripped vitriol on Protestant doctrines of obedience to the state. Working from a strong *Sonderweg* thesis, Fischer believed that in Germany the conservative forces of throne and altar had in the course of the nineteenth century co-opted Protestant religiosity, rendering disobedience of the state sinful whereas in the west it was the abuse of power that attracted moral opprobrium. "The history of the relation between politics and religion in Protestant Germany in the nineteenth century," Fischer bluntly concluded, "represents a singular mistaken path."[29]

Fischer's argument about German culpability for World War I appeared a decade later.[30] The dates are important mainly because of the generational division that drove the subsequent Fischer debate. With few exceptions, Fischer's major critics belonged to a generation for whom World War I lingered as a real-life experience. Whether Gerhard Ritter, born 1888, Hans Rothfels, born 1891, or Egmont Zechlin, born 1896, they had all served in World War I, an ordeal central to their outlook as historians. Of his prominent critics, only Karl Dietrich Erdmann, born 1910, could count among Fischer's generation.[31] Conversely, Fischer's supporters were a generation younger. Whether his prominent students, like Helmut Böhme (b. 1936) and Dirk Stegmann (b. 1941), or historians such as Hans-Ulrich Wehler (b. 1931) or Volker Berghahn (b. 1938), they were too young to have played a role in World War II, and they came of scholarly age at a time of a significant expansion of the German university system. Against the German nationalist tradition of historical

---

[28] Schulze, *Deutsche Geschichtswissenschaft nach 1945*, 27.

[29] Fritz Fischer, "Der deutsche Protestantismus und die Politik im 19. Jahrhundert," *Historische Zeitschrift*, 171 (1950), 473.

[30] Fritz Fischer, "Kontinuität des Irrtums. Zum Problem der deutschen Kriegszielpolitik 1914–1918," *Historische Zeitschrift*, 191 (1959), 249–310.

[31] For a revealing account of Erdmann's writings and activities during the Third Reich, see Martin Kröger and Roland Thimme, *Die Geschichtsbilder des Historikers Karl Dietrich Erdmann: Vom Dritten Reich zur Bundesrepublik* (Munich, 1996).

writing, they instinctively sided with Fischer's political and diplomatic conclusions, even as they were more interested in the structural walls that supported it.

A characteristic of the vanishing point is that it powerfully structures the visual field, even to the point of distortion. In the ensuing debate, the distortions came from those who agreed with Fischer and those who did not; they were reflected in interpretive syntheses and in specialized studies, indeed even in the presentation of the documents themselves. The fate of the Riezler diaries, a central document from the pen of Bethmann-Hollweg's personal secretary in the *Reichskanzlei*, may illustrate the point. Immediately after World War II, Hans Rothfels – Jewish but German national to the core – advised Riezler's brother against publication, as the diaries might damage the German national image. Twenty-five years later, Karl Dietrich Erdmann published the diaries in Germany, though it soon became apparent that Riezler's entries for the July crisis consisted of summaries. More problematic, the entries for the period July 7 to August 14 were written on a different kind of paper than the rest of the diary, and this paper, one chemical analyst maintained, was produced after, not before, World War I.[32] Distortions in Fischer's camp were never as spectacular, and it is perhaps one important reason why scholarly opinion largely considers Fischer to have carried the day, with one of his enthusiastic supporters comparing Fischer's *"explicandum"* to "Thucydides' work on the Great Peloponnesian War of antiquity."[33] Nevertheless, among the supporters of the Fischer thesis there were also problems of proof, though they typically involved sins of omission, arguing from a lack of documentation rather than from specious evidence.

A case in point involved Volker Berghahn's elaborate elucidation of Tirpitz's *Sammlungspolitik*, the crux of a conscious strategy to solve the social problem by dint of an aggressive naval build-up calculated to exacerbate tensions between Germany and England. The interpretation's brilliance depended on its interlacing of domestic and foreign policy, which undermined a historiographically conservative insistence on the primacy of the latter. Berghahn attempted to show how the alliance

[32] Bernd Sösemann, "Die Tagebücher Kurt Riezlers: Untersuchungen zu ihrer Echtheit und Edition," *Historische Zeitschrift*, 236 (1983), 327–69.

[33] Roger Fletcher, introduction to Fritz Fischer, *From Kaiserreich to Third Reich: Elements of Continuity in German History, 1871–1945*, tr. Roger Fletcher (London, 1986), 23.

of iron and rye, battleship building for the first, protective tariffs for the second, supported a grand strategy to buy off (while actually rendering poorer) the working class and thus loosen the grip that socialism had on Germany's laboring poor. This was an elite social strategy – conscious, niggardly, and mean. Yet, as Geoff Eley suggested, its necessary evidence – Johannes Miquel, the domestic minister, or Alfred Tirpitz, the naval minister, explicating the common strategy – was wanting.[34]

We have come to think of the critique leveled by Geoff Eley, David Blackbourn, and Richard J. Evans against the "Bielefeld School" as largely concerning the alleged predominance of the old regime in an age of rapid industrialization and bourgeois ascendancy. Yet it may also be read, especially in the early work of Geoff Eley, against the grain: as a Rankean salvo at the perspectival distortions engendered by the Fischer thesis. Where Fischer saw an "alliance of elites," Eley posited the importance of the new men of the right, people like August Keim, director of the Pan-German League, organizer of the Navy and Defense Leagues, and "a man of violence."[35] Sharply critical of a functionalist approach that perceived ideology as a mere reflection of interest, Eley nevertheless insisted upon another kind of continuity, exchanging one set of elites (agrarian, conservative) for another (capitalist, bourgeois). He thus maintained the integrity of the left–right understanding of politics that undergird the interpretive edifice. And even if Eley overstated the influence of the new politicians (especially in the Navy League and at the local level), his analysis proved finely attuned to the explosive potential of mass politics; it made sense not from the displaced vanishing point of 1914 but from a different way of seeing 1933.[36]

II

That elites should be in the center of the picture seems obvious for 1914; it would also seem apposite for 1933. Yet the most important early work

[34] Geoff Eley, "*Sammlungspolitik*, Social Imperialism and the Navy Law of 1898," in Eley, *From Unification to Nazism: Reinterpreting the German Past* (Boston, 1986), 119–120.

[35] Geoff Eley, *Reshaping the German Right: Radical Nationalism and Political Change after Bismarck*, 2nd ed. (Ann Arbor, 1991).

[36] On the evidentiary distortions of Eley's important book, see Roger Chickering's critical review of *Reshaping the German Right* in *The American Historical Review*, 86.1 (February, 1981), 159–160. On the transition from *Honoratiorenpolitik* to populist politics in a new key, see especially James Retallack, *The German Right, 1860–1920: Political Limits of the Authoritarian Imagination* (Toronto, 2006), 76–107.

of history detailing the demise of Germany's first democracy depicted the fatal last months of the Weimar Republic not as an unholy collusion of power elites but rather in terms of a "power vacuum." This was Karl Dietrich Bracher's *The Dissolution of the Weimar Republic (Die Auflösung der Weimarer Republik)*, published in 1955. A political scientist, Bracher described the Brüning chancellorship, which since spring 1930 operated as a presidential cabinet, as the first step toward the collapse of the republic; it was a step, moreover, not yet justified by the pressure of the Great Depression or by narrowing political options. Elites were clearly implicated in this step, particularly the agrarian and military elites close to President Paul von Hindenburg. As the situation deteriorated, the ability of these elites to control events eroded, and the pillars of democracy, having been weakened, could no longer hold.[37] The German government then became an open stage for the struggle of one group against the next, with the National Socialists ending victorious. Bracher's monumental study was followed in 1960 by *The National Socialist Seizure of Power (Die nationalsozialistische Machtergreifung)*, and in 1969 by *The German Dictatorship (Die deutsche Diktatur)*, the first serious German synthesis of research on the Third Reich.[38] The emphasis of the third book, as its title suggests, was not on elites but on the wider public. Not Hitler's dictatorship or the dictatorship of the Nazi Party, but rather a dictatorship by the people over the people most accurately described as the Third Reich. Moreover, Bracher identified the central doctrine of Hitler and the regime not as a will to power, or as a diabolical drive to destruction, but as anti-Semitism. "The core," Bracher wrote of Hitler's master key to history and politics, had always been "anti-Semitism and race mania."[39]

German historians proved slow to warm to Bracher's perspective. Werner Conze, who we now know to have been implicated in the murderous population policies of the Third Reich, countered Bracher by arguing that Hindenburg's appointment of Heinrich Brüning as a presidential chancellor was the only way to save democracy. When, moreover,

---

[37] Karl Dietrich Bracher, *Die Auflösung der Weimarer Republik* (Düsseldorf, 1955), 377.

[38] Karl Dietrich Bracher, *Die Stufen der Machtergreifung*, Part I of Bracher, Gerhard Schulz and Wolfgang Sauer, *Die nationalsozialistische Machtergreifung* (Cologne and Opladen, 1960); Bracher, *Die deutsche Diktatur: Entstehung, Struktur, Folgen des Nationalsozialismus* (Cologne, 1969).

[39] Bracher, *The German Dictatorship*, tr. Jean Steinberg (New York, 1970), 67.

Hindenburg forced Brüning to resign in May 1932, the chancellor was "within a hundred yards of the goal."[40] Reopened after the publication of the Brüning memoirs in 1970, this debate elicited increasingly technical arguments concerning the state of the economy in the early years of the Depression; it nevertheless remained a central issue of contemporary history throughout the seventies and into the early eighties.[41]

Bracher's second argument, that a power vacuum existed at the vanishing point, was still more crucial and difficult to accept; it implied that at the decisive moment no "structural" alliance of elites existed, save for the baleful influence of agrarian and military leaders close to President Paul von Hindenburg. In his short book, *From Kaiserreich to Third Reich (Bündnis der Eliten)*, Fritz Fischer attempted to demonstrate nevertheless that leading agrarian and industrial circles played a central role in Hitler's seizure of power in January 1933.[42] Characteristically, Fischer typically referred to "industry" and "agriculture" as such – structures, not individual people, brought Hitler to power. A habit of mind, this way of writing also masked a paucity of genuine proof. The dearth of evidence became apparent in David Abraham's attempt to show empirically how Bracher's power vacuum was an illusion; real, Abraham believed, was the alliance of industrial and agrarian elites who stabbed the republic in the back and helped Hitler to power. After initial positive reviews, questions about Abraham's sources surfaced.[43] The ensuing debate, often erroneously depicted as a methodological struggle between conservative and Marxist historians, or "positivists and conceptualists," turned on Abraham's jumbled statistical evidence and incorrectly transcribed documents.[44] As it happened, leaders of big business did not support the National Socialist German Workers Party (NSDAP) in the decisive months in a decisive way; there was no critical

---

[40] Cited in Eberhard Kolb, *The Weimar Republic*, tr. P. S. Falla (London, 1988), 180.

[41] For a short review of this literature, see ibid., 180–184.

[42] Fischer, *From Kaiserreich to Third Reich*, 81–82. "Both sides," Fischer argued, "...agreed that the NSDAP was a political force which must be won over; that a mere return to the 'Papen system' was out of the question; that Nazi participation in government was, in any case, the lesser evil vis-à-vis Schleicher's attempt to draw the trade unions into the presidial state...."

[43] See Henry A. Turner in *The American Historical Review*, 88 (1983), 1143. For a full airing of the evidentiary problems, see Ulrich Nocken, "Weimarer Geschichte(n)," *Vierteljahresschrift für Sozial– und Wirtschaftsgeschichte* 71 (1984), 505–27.

[44] Peter Novick, *That Noble Dream: The "Objectivity Question" and the Historical Profession* (New York, 1988), 613–621.

collusion across the camps of iron and rye; and the Nazis, far from depending on the financial support of big business, largely raised their funds through grassroots activity.[45]

The alliance of elites proved the real illusion. It was, at some level, an illusion of the left, but it is perhaps more interesting to inquire what perspectives were, as a result, obscured. And here the force of independent populist politics suggests itself, as does the destabilizing influence of nationalist ideology, and the brutalizing consequences of colonialism and war.

The problems bequeathed by an overly schematic left-right understanding of elite politics were dyed deep into the fabric of modern German historiography. In one form, it already inhered in the émigré synthesis, as the émigrés focused on high politics and great ideas and insisted on rooting the German catastrophe in the long lines of battle between the political left and right. Following Eckart Kehr, Hans Rosenberg, for example, foregrounded the founding decade of the German Empire because the 1870s decided the struggle between the two great protagonists of the nineteenth century: conservative reaction and liberal progress. The decision, Rosenberg believed, fell to the detriment of the latter, and it is in this context that the Puttkamer purge assumed importance. The Prussian Minister of the Interior allegedly rid the bureaucracy of liberal officials, marking the beginning of what would become the second foundation of the German Empire based on illiberal protectionist tariffs, anti-Semitism, and anti-Socialism.

But in 1981, Margaret Lavinia Anderson and Kenneth Barkin convincingly showed that a full-scale purge had never taken place and that, if a purge had happened, it was directed mainly against Catholic, not liberal, officials.[46] Rosenberg reacted with an extremely piqued letter, uncharacteristically aggravated in tone, to Kenneth Barkin, in which Rosenberg warned the young scholar that publishing the article would seriously damage his good reputation.[47] Perhaps Rosenberg was overly

---

[45] Henry Ashby Turner, *German Big Business and the Rise of Hitler* (New York, 1985), 340–359.

[46] Margaret L. Anderson and Kenneth D. Barkin, "The Myth of the Puttkamer Purge and the Reality of the Kulturkampf," *Journal of Modern History*, 54.4 (1982), 647–86. For critical, but by no means conclusive, objections, see Thomas Kühne, *Dreiklassenwahlrecht und Wahlkultur in Preußen* (Düsseldorf, 1994), 61–63.

[47] The article was turned down by *The American Historical Review*, accepted by *The Journal of Modern History*, and, in the meanwhile, Hans-Ulrich Wehler, whose commitment

protective of Eckart Kehr, who had been a friend and who died tragically in 1930; if we follow the memoirs of Felix Gilbert, Kehr had been "the born leader" of a cohort of critical Meinecke students, of which Rosenberg later emerged as the most prominent member.[48] Yet the issue also concerned the meaning and centrality of the *Kulturkampf* to the founding of the Empire. Rosenberg, and many in the émigré generation, perceived the *Kulturkampf* as a manifestation of intolerance; as such, it represented a betrayal, not an expression, of liberal principles. The émigrés measured German liberalism with an idealist yardstick and, for this reason, often perceived personal failure when structural constraints were more apposite, or a political lapse when, in fact, a given position reflected German liberalism *wie es eigentlich gewesen*.[49]

The émigré historians similarly failed to appreciate the degree to which radical nationalism arose more from the liberal than the conservative camp, among modern pundits rather than pre-modern elites. And this blindness, in turn, led to an underestimation of the racist, indeed eliminationist ideas that inhered in liberal imperialism. German historians now associate this line of criticism with Geoff Eley and David Blackbourn, and with the rise of post-colonial criticism. Yet in a different form, the argument had long been on the table. When Hannah Arendt published *The Origins of Totalitarianism* in 1951, she focused on anti-Semitism and imperialism as significant antecedents of modern totality. Applauded for its brilliance, admonished for its eclecticism, the book received mixed reviews in professional journals, and appreciative, if guarded, evaluations in more popular venues.[50] Save for Hans

---

to the public airing of ideas contrary to his own has always been exemplary, had offered to publish it in *Geschichte and Gesellschaft*. Communication of Margaret Lavinia Anderson.

[48] Gilbert quoted in *Historiker Lexikon: Von der Antike bis zur Gegenwart*, eds. Rüdiger vom Bruch and Rainer A. Müller, 2nd ed. (Munich, 2002), 176.

[49] See James J. Sheehan, *German Liberalism in the Nineteenth Century* (Chicago, 1978), 2, for a criticism of the tendency of "a great deal of recent scholarship on German liberalism – especially work done by American historians since 1945 ... to explain the liberals' failure in terms of their moral deficiencies."

[50] For examples of reviews in professional journals, see Aileen Dunham in *The Journal of Modern History*, 24.2 (June, 1952), 184–186. C. H. Van Duzer, *The American Historical Review*, 57.4 (July, 1952), 933–935; in more popular venues: H. Stuart Hughes, *Nation* 172 (March 24, 1951), 280–81; Hans Kohn, "Where Terror is the Essence," *Saturday Review of Literature*, 34 (March 24, 1951), 10; E. H. Carr, "The Ultimate Denial," *New York Times*, March 25, 1951, 169.

Kohn and H. Stuart Hughes in the United States, and Golo Mann in Germany, a major German historian did not review it.[51] Partly, this disinterest derived from Arendt's different vanishing point – the universe of the concentration camps. Partly, we may speculate, *Origins* met silence because Arendt could not see the Third Reich as the result of the conservative crippling of German liberalism. Instead, the National Socialist regime had to be seen as the apotheosis of mass society, and the failure of the middle classes, indeed the obliteration of classes, in the face of it. Arendt's *Origins* therefore fit ill with the émigré synthesis centered on liberal-conservative political struggle. Totalitarian domination "invalidated all obsolete political differentiations from right to left," she argued: "The most important yardstick for judging events in our time" was instead "whether they serve totalitarian domination or not."[52]

Arendt's work, quickly appropriated by Cold War conservatives, also fell on unreceptive ears in Germany, especially among the historians born around 1930. These included Hans-Ulrich Wehler, Hans and Wolfgang J. Mommsen, Heinrich August Winkler, Gerhard A. Ritter, and Helmut Berding. They spent their youth in the Third Reich, though their formative political experience was postwar Germany and the Atlantic partnership. Hans-Ulrich Wehler has called this generation, his own, the generation of 1945, the implication being that not the Third Reich but the possibilities inherent in "Hour Zero" defined their intellectual horizons. Many of them had spent time in the United States and had developed close contacts with the émigré historians, especially Hans Rosenberg, but also Hajo Holborn, Dietrich Gerhard, and Felix Gilbert. Thereafter, they maintained close relations with a generation of American-born German historians who succeeded the émigrés, as well as those German-born, American-educated historians, such as Klaus Epstein, Hans Gatzke, Peter Gay, and Fritz Stern, who also powerfully shaped the field. Finally, and far more than their predecessors, the historians of the generation of 1945 cooperated in a common intellectual project with leading figures in auxiliary fields, most notably in sociology, and especially with those figures, like Jürgen Habermas, M. Rainer Lepsius, and Ralf Dahrendorf, who shared their understanding of the

---

[51] Important exceptions include Golo Mann's review in the *Die Neue Zeitung*, cited in *Hannah Arendt-Karl Jaspers Correspondence 1926–1969*, eds. Lotte Kohler and Hans Saner, tr. Robert and Rita Kimber (New York, 1992), 724.

[52] Hannah Arendt, *The Origins of Totalitarianism* (New York, 1951), 442.

"German Question" as being, in Dahrendorf's formulation: "Why is it that so few in Germany embraced the principle of liberal democracy?"[53]

As all German historians will know, it is the leading figures of the German generation of 1945 who developed history as a critical discipline that shifted the ground from Meinecke's intellectual history to a wider and deeper history of society. As for the émigrés, so too for the generation of 1945, 1933 was their unequivocal vanishing point – "the year," as Paul Nolte in his fine article on them points out, that "almost always remained the reference point of the history and histories of this generation."[54] They also developed a very particular canvas of the prehistory of 1933. Like Ludwig Dehio, they saw 1933 as a "civilizational break," but unlike the older generation, they did not see the civilizational break in European terms. Rather, like the émigrés, they located it squarely in Germany, as a German problem.

Their Atlantic ties, paradoxically, worked in the service of an increasingly national explanation of 1933. But the explanation depended on Germany representing the mirror image of successful liberal-democratic development in the United States and Great Britain. To look too close – at American racism, at the civilizational calamity of the slave trade, or at the limited suffrage of both the United States in the era of Jim Crow and England before and even after the Second Reform Bill – rendered the mirror image less sharp. For this reason too, Hannah Arendt's *The Origins of Totalitarianism* made little sense to them. She posited European (and particularly English) imperialism as the turning point of a history centrally marked by the "administrative massacre" of "superfluous peoples." At once the apotheosis of the nation-state and its death knell, imperialism is what linked the nineteenth century to the twentieth. Arendt also devoted considerable attention, one-third of the book, to an analysis of how Jews had become powerless in European society and, as such, a target of nationalist persecution. Why Jews should be the principal victims of totalitarianism in its German form is, then, the starting question of *Origins*. Arendt's answer, her analysis of Stalinism notwithstanding, is a west European one, with the stress falling heavily on the Dreyfus Affair, a dress rehearsal for subsequent destruction.

53 Ralf Dahrendorf, *Society and Democracy in Germany* (New York, 1967), 14.
54 Paul Nolte, "Die Historiker der Bundesrepublik. Rückblick auf eine 'lange Generation,'" *Merkur*, 53.5 (1999), 421.

Finally, for Arendt, totalitarianism represented a novel political form, not the politics of a place, like Germany, but the political expression of an experience: loneliness, uprootedness, superfluousness.

III

That until recently German historians did not place the Holocaust at the center of scholarly attention is not news. As readers of the great textbooks of earlier generations, whether by Hajo Holborn or Gordon Craig, will readily appreciate, the Holocaust, as such, barely makes a cameo appearance: in Holborn's three volumes, it occupies a page; in Craig's *Germany, 1866–1945*, the Holocaust is not mentioned once. For the postwar German historians who had remained in Germany, the silence was as conspicuous. "No one reading [Meinecke's] *The German Catastrophe* would ever know about slave labor, concentration camps, mass shootings, death factories, the murder of 6 million Jews," Lucy Dawidowicz pointed out more than two decades ago.[55] Popular works that did render the Holocaust more central, like Sebastian Haffner's *The Meaning of Hitler (Anmerkungen zu Hitler)*, implied that the greater tragedy "by far" involved the Germans, the people whom Hitler betrayed and who lost "more than seven million, more than the Jews and Poles."[56] Yet the reluctance to descend more deeply into the labyrinth of how the killings actually happened was not confined to non-Jews. When in 1959 Raul Hilberg submitted the manuscript of *The Destruction of European Jewry* to Princeton University Press, he received a rejection. The anonymous outside reader supposedly opined that Gerald Reitlinger, H. G. Adler, and Leon Poliakov had already written what there was to say about the subject. The reader, Hilberg discovered many decades later, was Hannah Arendt.[57]

Thanks to Nicolas Berg's *The Holocaust and West German Historians*, we now possess a detailed story of the tortured relation of the historians of the Federal Republic to the catastrophe. The story includes seeing the Third Reich as mainly a German, not a Jewish tragedy; refusing

---

[55] Lucy Dawidowicz, *The Holocaust and the Historians* (Cambridge, Mass., 1981), 58–59.

[56] Sebastian Haffner, *Anmerkungen zu Hitler* (Frankfurt, 1981), 142.

[57] Raul Hilberg, *The Politics of Memory: The Journey of a Holocaust Historian* (Chicago, 1996), 156–157.

to consider the historical work of Holocaust survivors as "objective"; writing about the destruction process as if individual Germans, ordinary or otherwise, were not part of it; beclouding the Holocaust with *Faschismustheorie*; and nearly extinguishing the subject in the "critical" 1970s.[58] It was not until the 1980s that a set of events came together in such a way as to affect a significant shift. In a narrow sense, these events included the January 1979 airing of the miniseries "The Holocaust" on German television, the debate surrounding Ronald Reagan's visit to the cemetery of German soldiers (including members of the Watten SS) at Bitburg, the founding of the U.S. Holocaust Museum in the United States, and the fallout of the *Historikerstreit* in Germany. In a wider sense, the postmodern focus on identity, on culture and experience, agency and victimization, also played an important role in bringing the Holocaust to the fore of historical research. This large-scale shift encouraged paying closer attention to the actual details of the Holocaust – with less assurance that a single narrative, such as modernization or Germany's turn away from the values of the west, could explain the enormity of the crime at hand.

As we should expect, the Holocaust as vanishing point elicited intense historiographical debate focusing on the legitimacy and veracity of documents. We now know that Martin Broszat, the director of the Institute for Contemporary History in Munich from 1972 until his death in 1989, turned away and derided as "merely journalistic" the documentary editions of Joseph Wulf. A survivor of Auschwitz, Wulf put together some of the earliest and most comprehensive collections of documents on the Holocaust, in particular on the ghettos of Warsaw and Lodz. While Broszat insisted on the necessity of exploring structures of persecution, Wulf pleaded in vain for admitting Jewish testimony as well. The case, moreover, was not an isolated one, as Jewish historians including Leon Poliakov and H. G. Adler were similarly marginalized. Berg suggests that Broszat's reluctance to consider this evidence, and indeed his proclivity for "processes" and "structures," resulted from his own complicity in the Third Reich. In 1944, Broszat had applied for membership to the Nazi Party, a fact that he subsequently hid his life long.

Yet Broszat's proclivity for "processes" and "structures" reflected not an individual but a generational predisposition, and many of the

---

[58] Nicolas Berg, *Der Holocaust und die westdeutschen Historiker* (Göttingen, 2003).

historians who shared it, like Hans Mommsen (b.1930), were simply too young to have been active participants in the Third Reich. Born in 1926, and therefore a bit older, Broszat nevertheless belonged to the generation of West German historians for whom 1933 remained the vanishing point: The problem was not to explain the motives of individual perpetrators but the collapse of German civilization in that decisive year, and the seductive power of the regime to ordinary citizens.[59]

It is this interest that underwrote Broszat's directorship of a major project in *Alltagsgeschichte*: "*Bayern in der NS-Zeit*." It was history from below, and between 1977 and 1983 the "Bavaria Project," as it came to be called, produced six thick volumes comprising thirty separate monographs. By international standards, the research proved ground-breaking, for it rendered concrete a great deal of abstract theory about the limits of totalitarianism. It was also accessible, a genuine *histoire humaine*, and in this sense represented an important break with a social history of elite politics.[60] Finally, the Bavaria Project signaled a shift of the vanishing point from 1933 to the first six years of the regime. Obviously, other researchers had tread the ground before, but for the first time there existed a concentrated, well-funded effort to understand the social history of ordinary Germans in the Third Reich.

Yet there were problems with the Bavaria Project in particular and the new *Alltagsgeschichte* more generally. "Where did all the Nazis go?" Peter Fritzsche acidly, tellingly, asked of the new research, which tended to concentrate on "*Resistenz*."[61] Broszat had defined "*Resistenz*" as "any effective defense, limiting, or damming in of dominance" regardless of motivation or origin.[62] If this had the salutary effect of taking into its analytical purview mundane acts against the regime, it had the unfortunate consequence of downplaying the role of Germans who supported Nazi rule. Broszat himself perceived the problem as one of perspective.

[59] See Ian Kershaw's review of Berg, "Beware the Moral High Ground," in *Times Literary Supplement*, 10 (October 2003). See also the interview with Hans Mommsen in Rüdiger Hols and Konrad H. Jarausch, *Versäumte Fragen: Deutsche Historiker im Schatten des Nationalsozialismus* (Stuttgart, 2000), 180.

[60] See Broszat, "Plädoyer für Alltagsgeschichte. Eine Replik auf Jürgen Kocka," in Broszat, *Nach Hitler* (Munich, 1988), 194–200.

[61] Peter Fritzsche, "Where Did All the Nazis Go? Reflections on Collaboration and Resistance," *Tel Aviver Jahrbuch für deutsche Geschichte* 23 (1994), 191–214.

[62] Martin Broszat, "Resistenz und Widerstand," in Broszat, *Nach Hitler*, 144.

In his "Plea for the Historicization of National Socialism," he argued as follows:

It is difficult to historicize the Nazi regime because of the need to view its two sides both together and separately: the proximity and the interdependence of its capacity for success and its criminal energy, of its mobilization for achievement and for destruction, of people's participation and dictatorship.[63]

In Broszat's "Plea," success, achievement, and people's participation ranged on one side, criminal energy, destruction, and dictatorship on the other. Yet historicization, rendering the Third Reich less strange, meant focusing on aspects of its history that made it comprehensible to those people who participated in it and those born after. But this led to a more fundamental problem, which Saul Friedländer raised in his exchange with Martin Broszat in 1987.[64] Broszat's historicization, Friedländer rightly claimed, lost sight of the criminal nature of the regime, and while already problematic for the period between 1933 and 1939, this obtuseness was indefensible in the face of the Holocaust. Over the possibility of innocent historical knowledge, Friedländer implied, the vanishing point of 1941 cast a pall.

Perspective was the crux of the matter. Much as he had in his debate with Wulf in the early 1960s, Broszat insisted that history "from the perspective of the victims of National Socialist persecution," was "understandable," but "formulated in absolute terms . . . it would serve to block important avenues of access to historical knowledge, and would also hardly satisfy the demands of historical justice."[65] Against the "mythical memory" of the victims and their descendents, "which acts to coarsen historical recollection," Broszat urged a rational understanding of the Third Reich. In this way of seeing the problem, there were two irreconcilable perspectives: one German, complex, insistent on nuance; the other Jewish, putatively moralistic, black and white. The figure of the bystander illustrates the problem. From one perspective, he is a man or woman consumed with the quotidian; from another, he is a passive accomplice to murder.

---

[63] Martin Broszat, "A Plea for the Historicization of National Socialism," in *Reworking the Past: Hitler, the Holocaust, and the Historians' Debate*, ed. Peter Baldwin (Boston, 1990), 82.

[64] Martin Broszat and Saul Friedländer, "A Controversy about the Historicization of National Socialism," in *Reworking the Past*, 102–132.

[65] Broszat, published letter to Saul Friedländer, 10/26/1987, in *Reworking the Past*, 113.

The problem, once posed, can hardly be rendered if historians start with the vanishing points that have structured German history in the postwar era. We are here far from the collusion of elites that provided the Fischer thesis with its argumentative élan. We are also far from the problems of liberal democracy that preoccupied the émigrés and exercised the critical imagination of the generation of 1945. Nor does the problem of the bystander admit of easy dispensation through the vessel of systemic criticism. "Unhappy the land that needs heroes," Bertolt Brecht has Galileo say. Yet the literary context discloses why the analogy with bystanders deceives. Galileo wants to think and act differently. Whether this is true of the bystander is not clear. And yet the bystander is also the object of historical forces, and historical understanding demands that his or her experience of totalitarianism be explicated as well. At this moment, the single vanishing point begins to break down, for as Broszat intimated, and Friedländer understood, there are two histories here. They can never have the same center, and they cannot be understood in isolation, as if cocooned realities.

The writing on perpetrators reveals the problem in still sharper contours. Since the "phase of the second repression," as Ulrich Herbert calls German history writing in the 1970s, there has been a stream of new work on the perpetrators of the Holocaust, which in the wake of Daniel Goldhagen's *Hitler's Willing Executioners* became a torrent.[66] But even without "the Goldhagen phenomenon," the volume of new work would have been remarkable. A generation of German historians (my own, born around 1960) has meanwhile published a series of detailed local and regional studies showing how the killing actually happened. Some, like Christian Gerlach and Mark Roseman, have also investigated the timing of the order and the modalities of planning in Berlin.[67] Taken together, these works offer a detailed image of a killing apparatus with a wide array of perpetrators with varying motivations for their participation in genocide.[68] When combined with the studies of

---

[66] Ulrich Herbert, *Nationalsozialistische Vernichtungspolitik, 1939–1945* (Frankfurt, 1998), 19.

[67] Christian Gerlach, *Krieg, Ernährung, Völkermord* (Hamburg, 1998), 85–166; Mark Roseman, *The Villa, the Lake, the Meeting: Wannsee and the Final Solution* (London, 2002).

[68] For a good introduction, see Herbert, *Nationalsozialistische Vernichtungspolitik*; see also Dieter Pohl, *Holocaust: Die Ursachen – das Geschehen – die Folgen* (Freiburg, 2000).

Christopher Browning, Omer Bartov, Peter Longerich and others, this collective scholarly enterprise has established a new vanishing point. Like previous vanishing points, this one has an effect on the whole canvas.

A comparison of two synthetic accounts of Hitler's rule – Karl Dietrich Bracher's *The German Dictatorship* and Michael Burleigh's *The Third Reich: A New History* – may illustrate the change. In Bracher, the war takes up one chapter in nine, the murder of the Jews, eleven of 502 pages. In Burleigh, the divisions are not so neat, but the war consumes roughly four of ten chapters; there is a separate chapter on "German Jews and their neighbors from 1933 to 1939," consisting of more than sixty pages, and another chapter on "the racial war against Jews," which comprises more than ninety pages (of 812). Where Bracher rendered topics such as state and party and the role of the churches as central, Burleigh devotes attention to eugenics and euthanasia. The result is a very different image of National Socialism, with one emphasizing politics, the other violence. The two books also differ with respect to chronological sweep. As Bracher's vanishing point is 1933, he devotes nearly half of the book to events leading up to the *Machtergreifung* and includes a trenchant analysis of nineteenth-century strands in German and European history (including anti-Semitism), which contributed to the German dictatorship. Burleigh, whose vanishing point is 1941, starts his book in August 1914. A cataclysm without deep roots, the Third Reich is for him a twentieth-century phenomenon, and more a mark of its time than an expression of its place. Put simply, Burleigh's "new history" has severed its ties to the deep structures of the German and European past.

Burleigh is not alone in rendering the Third Reich as a twentieth-century phenomenon. A conspicuous result of the shifted vanishing point has been to foreground World War I – for its brutalization of men, for the quality of its extreme nationalism, and for the more virulent strain of anti-Semitism it brought forth. Ian Kershaw, for example, sees anti-Semitism as taking on decisive new form in the years 1916 to 1923.[69] World War I also assumes a prominent place in the work of

[69] Ian Kershaw, "Antisemitismus in der NS-Bewegung vor 1933," in *Vorurteil und Rassenhaß: Antisemitismus in den faschistischen Bewegungen Europas*, eds. Hermann Graml, Angelika Königseder, and Juliane Wetzel (Berlin, 2001), 29–32.

Omer Bartov, who begins his essay, "The European Imagination in the Age of Total War," with an arresting sentence: "One of the most striking aspects of battlefield descriptions in Great War literature is the extent to which they resemble accounts of the Holocaust."[70] Even Richard J. Evans, whose most important publications concern the nineteenth century, is already in 1914 by page forty-one of his remarkable *The Coming of the Third Reich* – and this after posing the rhetorical question: "Is it wrong to begin with Bismarck?"[71] The Revolutions of 1989 have arguably accelerated this tendency, bringing forth new periodizations centered on the "short twentieth century" (Hobsbawm) in which the "new Thirty Years War" assumes an especially prominent place. Yet as Charles Maier has convincingly argued, if the "short twentieth century" has come to serve as a "moral narrative," highlighting the spectacular atrocities at its center, its utility as an explanatory paradigm remains less evident.[72]

In this context, few historians have reached back into the nineteenth century for genuine explanation, with Daniel Goldhagen constituting an exception. Yet Goldhagen's historical reach exceeded his grasp, and the earlier chapters of his book are replete with oversimplifications, errors, and distortions. Generalizing from the thinnest sliver of evidence, he tarred the mental predisposition of nineteenth-century Germans with a wide, thick brush of eliminationist anti-Semitism, which he saw as being peculiar to Germany. Both the national frame and the muscular sense of causality conspire to prevent Goldhagen from offering a plausible interpretation for what is genuinely original, indeed groundbreaking, in his book: namely his investigation of the cruelty of ordinary men. Not the sadism of the psychologically disturbed, but the utter collapse of a sense for the humanity of others is at issue, and this collapse can be understood in historical terms.[73] That from the scholarly standpoint Goldhagen's historical preface constituted the most objectionable part of his work certainly says something about the quality of Goldhagen's historical

---

[70] Omer Bartov, *Murder in our Midst* (New York, 1996), 33.

[71] Richard J. Evans, *The Coming of the Third Reich* (New York, 2004), 2.

[72] Charles S. Maier, "Consigning the Twentieth Century to History: Alternative Narratives for the Modern Era," *The American Historical Review*, 105.3 (2000), 807–831. See also Manfred Hettling, "Der Mythos des kurzen 20. Jahrhunderts," *Saeculum*, 49.2 (1998), 327–345.

[73] See the brilliant sketch, which has strongly influenced my own position, by Alain Finkielkraut, *L'Humanité perdue* (Paris, 1996).

imagination. It also may suggest something about what, given the structuring force of this vanishing point, historians cannot easily see. Here the comparison with Christopher Browning's *Ordinary Men* is telling. In a work rendered with a finer historical hand, and justly celebrated, Browning desists from tracing the cruelty of men historically. Instead, he appeals to timeless social–psychological explanations, centered on the pressures for group cohesion among the men of a killing battalion, thus rendering the vanishing point as a twentieth-century event without historical depth of field.[74]

What should this depth of field look like? This, I would submit, is an important question. For if my metaphor of the vanishing point convinces, it means that we cannot write nineteenth-century German history without cognizance of the problem. Some themes, such as anti-Semitism, will be foregrounded.[75] But the picture that emerges cannot just be about anti-Semitism, as Goldhagen believed, or even about the specifically German prehistory of the twentieth-century calamity, as the émigrés, the generation of 1945, and Goldhagen all assumed. Rather, the new vanishing point suggests wider themes to foreground: how humanity came to think of itself as divided, and some parts less human than others; how the institution of slavery and the prejudice of race gave these human predispositions a long pedigree; how race and nation came in the course of the eighteenth and nineteenth centuries to be seen as permanent markers, emblems of unalterable difference; and how these markers justified the enslavement and the cultural and physical extermination of peoples.

These are events of the nineteenth and preceding centuries. They are German events but not just German events. And they speak to the larger history of the value of life. As such, they address not so much the destruction of reason as the collapse of fellow feeling.[76] This is a history

---

[74] Christopher R. Browning, *Ordinary Men: Reserve Police Battalion 101 and the Final Solution in Poland* (New York, 1992). It is perhaps indicative that in his new and magisterial work, *The Origins of the Final Solution: The Evolution of Nazi Jewish Policy, September 1939–March 1942* (Lincoln, Neb., 2004), Browning pays a great deal of attention to the historical roots of anti-Semitic policy.

[75] See now the penetrating essay of Philippe Burrin, *Warum die Deutschen? Antisemitismus, Nationalsozialismus, Genozid*, trans. Michael Bischoff (Berlin, 2004).

[76] A central text for this way of seeing the problem is Michael Geyer, "Resistance as Ongoing Project: Visions of Order, Obligations to Strangers, and Struggles for Civil Society, 1933–1990," in *Resistance against the Third Reich, 1933–1990*, eds. Michael Geyer and John W. Boyer (Chicago, 1994), 325–350. See also Enzo Traverso, *Moderne und Gewalt: Eine*

of sentiment, and ties, how they worked, and how they came asunder. It is history beyond identity. And it is a history that evinces concern for how, as Wordsworth put it in the year 1800, modern life came to "blunt the discriminatory powers of the mind," reducing it to "a state of almost savage torpor." Finally, it is a history of seeing, of regarding the pain of others.[77]

Not to insist on depth of field, on the necessity of integrating the history of the nineteenth century into the history of the twentieth, and the longer life of the past into the shorter moment of cataclysm, is, as previous generations of German historians understood, a failure of imagination.

It would mean our loss of mastery.

europäische Genealogie des Nazi-Terrors (Cologne, 2003), which maps out many of these connections, if perhaps too schematically.
[77] Susan Sontag, *Regarding the Pain of Others* (New York, 2003).

2

THE MIRROR TURN LAMP

Senses of the Nation before Nationalism

"It must go further still, that soul must become its own betrayer; its own deliverer, the one activity, the mirror turn lamp."

W. B. Yeats

In a little-known pamphlet entitled "Explanation of the New Instruments of the Sun," published in 1528, the mapmaker and cosmographer Sebastian Münster attempted to enlist his fellow countrymen in a collaborative effort that would reveal the "hidden beauties" of "our common German fatherland" and create a work "in which one will see all of Germany...as if in a mirror." The mirror would reflect "Germany's territories, cities, towns, villages, distinguished castles and monasteries, its mountains, forests, rivers, lakes, and its products, as well as the characteristics and customs of the people, the noteworthy events that have happened, and the antiquities which are still found in many places."[1] But as one man alone could not "describe Germany properly,"

---

[1] Arthur Dürst, *Sebastian Münsters Sonneninstrument und die Deutschlandkarte von 1525: Begleittext zur Faksimileausgabe von Sebastian Münster, Erklärung des neuen Sonnen-Instruments* (Oppenheim, 1528). This passage also cited and translated in Gerald Strauss's *Germany: Its Topography and Topographers* (Madison, Wisc., 1959), 26, which remains the standard work in any language on the subject of the humanist discovery of Germany. Steeped in the classical heritage that the humanists shared, Strauss adeptly showed how a sense of nation, and consummate skill in describing its features, grew out of an injured pride deriving from the slights that classical authors and contemporary Italians leveled against Germany and its cities. A work of great erudition, it remains a book to which scholars turn. There is, however, good reason to revisit the terrain Strauss so expertly mapped out. For one, since the 1960s, there has been an explosion in scholarly work on nations and nationalism, and this allows us to rethink the achievements of the topographers Strauss described. In particular, Benedict Anderson's *Imagined Communities* (London, 1983), 15, itself nearly a quarter-century old, continues to offer possibilities for understanding how

it would be necessary to collaborate.[2] For Münster, "properly" meant by observation and measurement, and to aid his collaborators, the leading humanists of the day, Münster sketched a regional map of the area around Heidelberg, where he then taught. Modest in appearance, the map was the first to use sighting lines to form triangles, from which Münster could measure angles to the towns he depicted and then estimate the distances to them. A primitive form of triangulation, Münster's method represented a small but significant step forward in geographical accuracy.

Münster thereafter spent eighteen years gathering evidence, taking measurements, collecting manuscripts, and entreating his fellow humanists to contribute histories, topographies, and maps from their regions and cities. The work soon grew beyond the boundaries of the nation and was first published as the *Cosmographia* in 1544, then substantially revised in 1550; thereafter, it went through nineteen more editions by 1628 and sold roughly 50,000 copies in German and another 10,000 in Latin. It was also translated into French, Italian, Czech, and English.[3] If the new wide angle has led modern historians to overlook the national import of the *Cosmographia*, the more perceptive contemporary, Jean Bodin, was not so easily fooled; he called it a "*Germanographia*," as more than half of its 1,000 plus pages described Germany.[4]

The *Cosmographia* was also fitted with a prodigious number of land maps, a relatively new phenomenon: the first map of Germany having been made in 1500 by a Nuremberg clockmaker named Erhard Etzlaub in order to aid pilgrims on their way to Rome; the second in 1515 by Martin Waldseemüller, the Lorraine mapmaker better known for his world map of 1507 in which "the new islands" appear for the first time as the fourth part of the earth and are named America. The sixteenth century was the first great age of German mapmaking, with *Germania*

---

nationalism emerged "not from self-consciously held political ideologies" but out of "the large cultural systems that preceded it."

[2] Cited in Peter H. Meurer, *Corpus der älteren Germania-Karten* (Alphen aan den Rijn, Holland, 2001), 186 – the standard work on the subject of the early *Germania* maps.

[3] Karl Heinz Burmeister, *Sebastian Münster: Versuch eines biographischen Gesamtbildes* (Basel, 1963), 181–2.

[4] Consider Hans Kohn, who treated "incipient German nationalism" in his *Idea of Nationalism: A Study in its Origins and Background* (New York, 1944), 120, 139, but then set its claims aside as "largely confined to historians and poets." Bodin cited in Anthony Grafton, *New Worlds, Ancient Texts: The Power of Tradition and the Shock of Discovery* (Cambridge, Mass., 1992), 107.

maps a part of a general cultural efflorescence. By 1650, according to the most meticulous attempt to estimate the scope of early *Germania* maps, there were 130 such maps, 270 if one counts variations, if almost all of them are based on seven foundational maps.[5]

I

Before there was a German nation conceived as an extension of the interiorized self, there was a nation of the exterior senses, primarily sight, secondarily sound. The nation of the self, the very meaning of the term national identity, was the product of the late eighteenth and early nineteenth century; it is the nation of Herder and Fichte, and in the latter's *Identitätsphilosophie* one can already discern the broad band of dangers that inhere in the political doctrine of modern nationalism. The nation of the senses is also a nation, but it is exterior to the self, and this exteriority must be taken literally: sight being "vision brought about by a picture of the thing seen," as Johannes Kepler wrote in 1604, "on the concave surface of the retina."[6] Similarly, the sound of language, the cadences of the "mother tongue" (as Luther called the vernacular) was not the road to the soul of the people, but a receptacle for communication. Luther translated the Bible, after all, not to found a national language but to allow the common people to communicate more easily with God.

This division into two categories of nations, one external, one internal, locates the first discovery of the German nation firmly in the sixteenth century and suggests that there were two discoveries: one primarily associated with Renaissance ways of seeing, the other with the late enlightenment search for the nation's center of gravity in its poetry and its language.

One can strain dichotomies: between sight and sound, painting and poetry, exterior and interior. Yet the dichotomies also reveal the degree

---

[5] Meurer, *Corpus*, ix.

[6] Cited in Svetlana Alpers, *The Art of Describing: Dutch Art in the Seventeenth Century* (Chicago, 1983), 34. Her book has been very influential for my way of thinking about early modern nations, especially her opposition of the surface in Dutch painting to the narrative of the Italian art of the Renaissance. For a work that takes up some of these themes, see Richard Helgerson, *Forms of Nationhood: The Elizabethan Writing of England* (Chicago, 1992).

to which our understanding of nation remains tied to what J. H. Parry called the second age of discovery (referring to the systematic exploration of the Pacific, but let us use his felicitous phrase to refer to the scientific reconnaissance of the eighteenth century more generally).[7] In Germany, that reconnaissance begins with Herder. Every national culture has its own notion of the good, the true, and the beautiful, Herder argued, and this wonderful plurality, far from denting the progress of mankind, was its essential precondition. Not along the "deceiving and dreary path of political and military history" could one arrive at the soul of a people, but only through its poetry and, therefore, through its language. "Through language," Herder asserted, "nations are raised and cultivated (*erzogen* und *gebildet*)."[8] Here the vocabulary of construction, a better translation for *gebildet*, seems more apt than discovery, though it must be remembered that the Romantic project of gathering the tales, myths, legends, and sayings of the "people," and the philological work of rendering the German language historically, had just begun. And while it is possible to see in this work a feat of sheer imagination, it was also a scholarly reconstruction of monumental proportions, as well as a journey into an exotic, strange, and foreign home – the past as a different country, if at the same time one's own.[9]

What if we emphasized the searching aspect of the national imagination and suggested that nations were as much discovered as imagined? We would underscore the work that went into finding the nation, seeing it, mapping it, rendering its cities and its nature, describing it, and understanding its "center of gravity," as Herder called it. These are no small matters, but as historians know, to allow the stress to fall in this way is not the conventional wisdom. That wisdom holds that nationalists make, imagine, or invent nations, and it places the nationalist invention of the nation in the relatively recent past. If "nationalism is a doctrine invented in Europe at the beginning of the nineteenth century," as Elie Kedourie maintained, and if "it is nationalism which engenders nations, not the other way around," as Ernest Gellner famously asserted, then

---

[7] J. H. Parry, *Trade and Dominion: The European Overseas Empires in the Eighteenth Century* (London, 1971), 244.

[8] Johann Gottfried Herder, *Sämtliche Werke* (Berlin, 1883), vol. 5, 57.

[9] John Toews, *Becoming Historical: Cultural Reformation and Public Memory in Early Nineteenth-Century Berlin* (Cambridge, 2004), 322–3.

nations must arise in the eighteenth or nineteenth centuries – for nations cannot antedate the nationalists who invented them.[10]

I would suggest that this line of argument remains enmeshed in the categories of the second discovery, privileging the word over the image, sound and language over sight and space, interiority over exteriority, and the nation as an extension of the self as against what the art historian Svetlana Alpers calls an "additive way of piecing together the world."[11] Herder is again the hinge. He began his famous *Ideas on the Philosophy of the History of Mankind* with the arresting sentence, "Our earth is a star among stars."[12] His remains an additive way of piecing together the world – nations exist, as they do in maps, next to other nations, *jedes Volk an Stelle und Ort*, each in its own position and place, or "like plants in a garden," as he wrote in his "Letters for the Furthering of Humanity."[13] The echo is not to the cosmopolitanism of his day but to an older way of thinking about nation – as nations in coexistence.

That older way derives from the sixteenth century, when nations, as they were on maps, could only be thought in the context of other nations. Sebastian Münster was not alone in this way of seeing nations. We find the first description of Germany, penned by Johannes Cochlaeus in 1512, as an appendage to a classical treatise of world geography. That description, the *Brevis Germanie Descriptio*, was itself a commentary on the Rome Way Map of 1500, where the nation, far from being imagined as above all things, is the starting point for a pilgrimage to Rome.[14] This imperative – to place the description of the nation among descriptions of other nations – is central to the sixteenth-century discovery, whether in cosmographical works, of which Münster's was only the

---

[10] Elie Kedourie, *Nationalism*, rev. ed. (New York, 1961), 9; Ernest Gellner, *Nations and Nationalism* (Oxford, 1983), 55. For the argument that nationalism and nation ought to be separate, as nation is an older category, see David A. Bell, *The Cult of Nation in France: Inventing Nationalism, 1680–1800* (Cambridge, Mass., 2001), 5–15.

[11] Alpers, *The Art of Describing*, 163.

[12] Herder, *Sämtliche Werke*, vol. 13, 13.

[13] Herder, *Sämtliche Werke*, vol. 18, 284, 249.

[14] Johannes Cochlaeus, *Brevis Germanie Descriptio*, ed. and tr. Karl Langosch (Darmstadt, 1976). On Etzlaub, see Meurer, *Corpus*, 133–43; and Herbert Krüger, "Des Nürnberger Meisters Erhard Etzlaub älteste Straßenkarte von Deutschland," *Jahrbuch für fränkische Landesforschung* 18 (1958), 17.

most spectacular, or in the tradition of mapmaking from Waldseemüller to Gerhard Mercator, whose conformal projection continues to shape the way we see the world.

The early maps set the contours of Germany as humanists across Europe set them – from Maas to Vistula, and from the Alps to the *Mare Germanicum*. But Germany was a cultural not a political nation, as evidenced by the silence of any serious discussion about the location of its borders. Even among the most precise mapmakers of the sixteenth century, Germany's borders remain indistinct, rendered, if at all, by colors (often painted by assistants in the mapmaker's workshops, and sometimes according to the whims of patrons). Not until Matthias Quad's atlas of 1604 will dotted lines begin to mark country borders on European maps.[15] And even with Matthias Quad, the dotted lines suggest less the fixity than the porous nature of borders.

The requirement of fixity is the product of a later age – when the nation wedded the absolutist state and became concerned with the precise demarcation of sovereignty. The nation of the sixteenth century knew no such precision. Armed with a battery of surveying instruments and complex calculations for projections and triangulations, geographers measured the distance between cities and towns, the course of rivers, and the shape of coastlines. By contrast, borders are discussed as if the precise line hardly mattered. In the *Brevis Germanie Descriptio*, for example, Cochlaeus adduces of the Silesians that "their language is to a large extent German, but that beyond the Oder, Polish is also spoken." "For this reason," he asserts, "the border of Germany to the east is there."[16] Conversely, Trier is a German city, older than Rome, but "most ascribe Trier more to France than to Germany, although German is the local language."[17]

A half-century later, with a revolution in cartography in between, this general situation had not radically changed, even as mapmakers attained greater mastery in national description. Tilemann Stella's memorandum for "a national and historical description of the entire Germany" composed in Latin in 1566 illustrates this new mastery. A

---

[15] John Hale, *The Civilization of Europe in the Renaissance* (New York, 1993), 35.
[16] Cochlaeus, *Brevis Germanie Descriptio*, 119.
[17] Ibid., 49.

student of the Reformer Philipp Melanchthon, Stella envisioned his portrayal of Germany in two parts: a map of Germany that precisely situated its towns and cities and that detailed routes; and an explanation "in which Germany as a whole and details worth knowing are exhaustively explained." The map was to have a large format, and it was to display accurately towns and regions, mountains, rivers, forests, spas, and mines. And, as we learn from an independent source, the whole was to be underpinned by nearly a hundred separate regional maps of different sizes and formats.[18] Taken together, then, this was the most ambitious cartographical project focusing on Germany in the entire sixteenth century.

Stella also considered borders. "The borders, which Germany will have on four sides," are, he writes, as follows: "in the east Königsberg in Prussia and Vienna in Austria, in the south Venice and Trent, in the west Calais, in the north Kolding in Jütland and the Danish capital Copenhagen." Modern historians, attuned to Germany's unstable mix of national aspiration and power, may find these borders alarming – yet chauvinism plays scarcely a role in the defense of the map. Unfortunately, we can only infer motivation indirectly – from Herzog Johann Albrecht of Mecklenburg's letter to Maximilian II in 1569 requesting renewal of regal privilege for Stella. The map, Albrecht writes, "was begun and intended to praise and honor God, the beneficent creator of all things, whose creation's reflection is painted before us for our observation and consideration."[19] Albrecht then describes the map as "painting" the "German Nation of the current time, the supreme shelter of dear Christianity" and as praising its authorities, heroes, and artisans.[20] The map, in essence, portrays Germany's cities and towns, the sites of civilization and culture, and these sites are also markers on the borders of his map. They are not, strictly speaking, linguistic borders, but instead represent the outer limits of a circle drawn, as with a compass, around a center. Put differently, they frame the picture.

Even though he worked at it for at least eighteen years, Stella's project was never completed. But circa 1560, he rendered an early version of

---

[18] Meurer, *Corpus*, 306.
[19] Das Priveleg von 1569, reproduced in Meurer, *Corpus*, 331.
[20] Ibid.

the *Germania* map, which Abraham Ortelius considered but did not use in his famous *Theatrum Orbis Terrarum* of 1570, the first printed atlas. Tellingly, Ortelius felt compelled to clarify the question of boundaries. "We will border contemporary Germany as it is in reality," the great Dutch mapmaker wrote, "according to its language, which is German."[21]

Seeing the nation in the context of the world, which an atlas allows one to do, evolved into a powerful tradition, and enjoyed considerable public appeal well into the seventeenth century. Its *Meisterwerk* was, however, also its death knell. This was Matthäus Merian's *Topographia Germaniae*, a sixteen-volume compendium published between 1642 and 1655 describing Germany's cities and towns, most of which were rendered by an elegant copper engraving.[22] Carefully etched by Merian's deft stylus, the engravings communicated idyllic harmony just as the destruction of the Thirty Years War descended. The text accompanying the engravings is by Martin Zeiller, the great seventeenth-century perambulator and author of travel books who believed one had to see the country in order to describe it. With 1,568 descriptions, and over 1,000 copper engravings, the *Topographia Germaniae* became a vast pointillist rendering of "the whole wide Germany," as Merian called it. Embraced by Protestants and Catholics alike, the project received the support of city and townsmen throughout the Empire. There was, in fact, something deeply irenic about the *Topographia Germaniae*. As Wolfgang Behringer has recently pointed out, most of the topographical works of the early modern era stem from religious dissidents who attempted to find a religious space between religious camps. Against religious dogmatism, and the cataclysmic violence it engendered, topographical descriptions, with Merian's work paramount among them, rendered an enduring image of a nation in repose.[23]

Historians have largely disregarded these monuments to the nation – a testament to how our discipline slights the visual faculties and to

[21] Ibid., 303.
[22] Ulrike Valeria Fuss, *Matthaeus Merian der Aeltere: Von der lieblichen Landschaft zum Kriegsschauplatz – Landschaft als Kulisse des 30 jährigen Krieges* (Frankfurt am Main, 2000).
[23] Wolfgang Behringer, "Die großen Städtebücher und ihre Voraussetzungen," in *Das Bild der Stadt in der Neuzeit, 1400–1800*, eds. Wolfgang Behringer and Bernd Roeck (Munich, 1999), 91.

what Richard J. Evans has called the "historian's strange aversion to maps."[24] This aversion is especially remarkable with respect to the study of nations. Whether penned by Carleton Hayes, Hans Kohn, Karl Deutsch, Ernest Gellner, Elie Kedourie, or Eric Hobsbawm, the great classics of the field are completely or largely bereft of maps or a discussion of them. In his groundbreaking *Imagined Communities* (1983), Benedict Anderson considered maps in the second edition, but only to emphasize how cartography became a tool for the imperialist domination of space. The specialized literature focusing on Germany has hardly been more attentive.[25] A recent, learned study of the rise of German national identity stretches out for more than 500 pages; but on not one of its many pages will the reader find a map or a discussion of the making of maps. In the index, there are no mapmakers.[26]

II

The omission is telling – indicative of how historians continue to project eighteenth-century understandings of language as interiorized back to the fifteenth and sixteenth century. In the earlier period, language was important, but as something exterior to the self, emblematic not constitutive of the nation. Although we commonly associate language with sound and thus with our sense of hearing, it is the analogy of sight that helps us understand the place of language in the nations of early modern Europe.

The key is the revolution in printing. The printing press, Walter J. Ong has argued, inaugurated the sweeping shift from a culture of primary orality, marked in literature by the "set phrase, the formula, the expected qualifier" that served as mnemonic aid, to script-based language communities, in which words were things to be arranged on a page, and writing analytic and abstract rather than aggregative and close to life. The shift implies, according to Ong, a sensory world dominated

---

[24] A notable exception is Peter Sahlins, *Boundaries: The Making of France and Spain in the Pyrenees* (Berkeley, 1991).

[25] For recent introductions, see Hans-Ulrich Wehler, *Nationalismus: Geschichte – Formen – Folgen* (Munich, 2001); Dieter Langewiesche, *Nation, Nationalismus, Nationalstaat in Deutschland und Europa* (Munich, 2000).

[26] Jörg Echternkamp, *Aufstieg der deutschen Nation, 1770–1848* (Frankfurt, 1998), may count as indicative.

by sight, even with respect to the word.[27] Partly, this is a point about the way in which the printing press stabilized language.[28] More profoundly, Ong points to the cognitive possibilities that the written word affords the reader, including the ability to backward scan, edit, and focus on particular passages and precise points, with an eye to style as well as accuracy. With the printed page, words become divorced from authors and take on a life of their own; they can be analyzed and dissected, refuted and improved, and placed together with images – as was indeed the case in a wide array of sixteenth-century genres, from the chapbook to the broadside, the illustrated Bible to the great cosmographical works of the age.

The shift did not start with printing. Writing in German was, of course, older, and in the century before Gutenberg the wider availability of paper allowed many more scholars to be their own scribes.[29] Yet printing brought a new permanence to language, arresting linguistic drift and slowing the decay and dissipation of new insights. It also brought ideas to a wider audience, not only in the cities but also in the villages, where the literate man reading books aloud slowly replaced storytellers who worked from memory.[30] This wide social shift, from primary orality that had to be kept in one's head to the word on the page that could be seen and read, allowed for new kinds of "cognitive styles" and new kinds of links across space and time, even if oral habits of thought persisted well into the era of the eye. The predilection for counting ranks among these new cognitive styles, as well as an increasingly precise and measured understanding of time and place. So too does the new sense of nation, conceived of as a two-dimensional space and situated within a continent. Within this exteriorized nation, vernacular language assumed an important place, as a marker of similarity, as a communicative medium, as something that evinced pride, and as emblematic of the nation.

---

[27] Walter J. Ong, *Orality and Literacy: The Technologizing of the Word* (London, 1982).

[28] Even if as late as 1593, Sebastian Helber, the author of a *Teutsches Syllabierbüchlein*, could still complain of seven different printing languages. Cited in Werner Besch, *Die Rolle Luthers in der deutschen Sprachgeschichte* (Heidelberg, 1999), 8.

[29] Elizabeth L. Eisenstein, *The Printing Revolution in Early Modern Europe* (Cambridge, 1983), 8.

[30] Ibid., 93.

Yet throughout the early modern period, the reification of the vernacular as the essence of the nation remained all but unthinkable. There were partial exceptions: the unknown "Upper Rhenish Revolutionary," who believed in 1495 that "Adam was a German man" and his ancient German the *Ursprache*; and the ever imaginative Conrad Celtis, who remained convinced that the Druids had taught Greek to the Germanic tribes in the caves of the Hercynian wood, thus imparting to modern German a classical heritage. But Luther eschewed such speculation, as he well understood that God had revealed himself to man in Hebrew and Greek, and that Latin was the language in which Christianity had been spread to the pagan peoples of Europe.[31] Luther nevertheless lauded German as a truth-telling language. "I thank God that I hear and find my God in the German tongue," he wrote in his preface to the *Theologia Deutsch*.[32] The mother tongue brought people closer to God, not to the nation as such.[33] The first work to explicitly emphasize Luther's contribution to the formation of an emerging German language was Johann Clajus's grammatical treatise of 1578, composed, tellingly, in Latin.[34]

The sixteenth and seventeenth century constituted a great grammatical age, with grammars written for no fewer than sixty-three languages, according to one estimate.[35] Few of these grammars were written in the vernacular they intended to codify, and their overriding motivation

---

[31] On these questions, see Arno Borst's panoramic, *Der Turmbau von Babel: Geschichte der Meinungen über Ursprung und Vielfalt der Völker*, 5 vols., (Stuttgart, 1957–1963), here vol. 3, part 1, 1048–1090.

[32] *Luther's Works*, vol. 31, ed. Harold J. Grimm (Philadelphia, 1957), 76.

[33] Besch, *Die Rolle Luthers*, 30. Luthers's Bible is the key, his translation of the New Testament both spurring linguistic convergence, especially in middle and upper Germany, and serving as its most felicitous measure. When Luther's *New Testament* first appeared in Wittenberg in 1522, its publication in Upper Germany in the following year required a word glossary and some orthographic changes; twenty years later, the glossary fell by the wayside; and 100 years later, the lower German, or *Plattdeutsch*, edition fell away as well.

[34] John T. Waterman, *A History of the German Language* (Seattle, 1966), 134–5. John Rowe, "Sixteenth and Seventeenth Century Grammars," in *Studies in the History of Linguistics: Traditions and Paradigms*, ed. Dell Hymes (Bloomington, 1974), 364. Clajus hoped to reach readers beyond the boundaries of Germany. Like many grammars of the period, Clajus's *Grammatica Germanicae Linguae* aimed not to knit disparate dialects into a coherent language but to teach German, however inconsistent a language it may have seemed, to those who spoke another language.

[35] Rowe, "Sixteenth and Seventeenth Century Grammars," 361.

was understanding not one's own, but other languages. Latin remained the first language of most grammar books, followed by Spanish and Portuguese. The discovery of new worlds proved, in fact, to be the principal impetus for the explosion in the production of grammatical works, with the first grammatical accounts of Asian and American languages following closely the composition of the first European grammars. It is instructive to keep in mind this wider dimension, analogous to the cartographic explosion that set in after 1492. Discoveries, in this sense, fueled the "first sociolinguistic revolution" – the term given by the late French linguist, Daniel Baggioni, to the linguistic stabilization of major national languages in western Europe in the course of the sixteenth and seventeenth centuries. While this "stabilization" was built upon the first literary products of the vernacular, the early grammatical works, rhetorical manuals, orthographies, lexica, and dictionaries drove it forward. A long road then marked the distance from the first attempt to stabilize to actual stabilization, and a still longer stretch from stabilization to successful standardization – which in Germany did not occur until the late eighteenth century. As Eric Blackall has elegantly shown, the stabilization of the German language also endured setbacks, especially in the half-century between the end of the Thirty Years War and the age of Leibniz, circa 1700.

Torn by religious strife, ravaged by war, beset by economic misfortune, Germany in the seventeenth century also witnessed the creation of the first language programs that were motivated more by nation-thinking than by religious impulse. The Fruitbearing Society (*Fruchtbringende Gesellschaft*), founded in Weimar in 1617 to purify German language and support German literature, remains the most famous. Its circle of scholars made genuine strides in the stabilization of the language. From the assiduous collecting and transcribing of Georg Henisch, for example, comes the first major monolingual dictionary. Detailed, voluminous, attentive to the precisions of rhetoric and to the variations of lexical connotation, Henisch's *German Language and Wisdom* (*Teutsche Sprach und Weißheit*), published in Augsburg in 1616, was a remarkable feat, cut short only by Henisch's death two years after the first volume, which only extended to the letter "F." In the Latin-language dedication, Henisch praises the German language for its manly and onomatopoetic qualities, and for its antiquity. "Ours is without doubt one of the original languages and one of the first to emerge from the futile attempt to build the Tower of Babel," he writes.[36] Henisch was also a humanist. Words, he believed, were adequate to describe the world; one must only use them precisely.

Precision meant precisely mirroring, even in the domain of sound. German, the language reformers argued, relied on one-syllable tonality, and as single syllables were rooted in nature, they became vehicles of near-perfect mimesis. "It was the greatest miracle of nature," wrote Justus Georg Schottelius, the author of the very influential *The Art of the German Language* (*Teutsche Sprachkunst*, 1641), "that our mouth curtly forms diverse tones and expressions and can bring forth precise and differentiated sound."[37] Like Henisch and the poets of the so-called *Pegnitz-Schäfer*, Schottelius was especially interested in German's onomatopoetic qualities, creating effects "as if the thing were actually there."[38] Or, as Georg Philipp Harsdörffer put it, German "talks with the tongue of nature ... it thunders with the heavens, strikes lightening with fast words, streams with hail, whistles with the wind," and so on.[39] This insight was mixed with a cultural patriotism; and this patriotism soon shaded into efforts at language purification, which in the course of the Thirty Years War became more pugnacious. By 1644, Georg Philipp Harsdörffer, in his *Defense of German Language Work* (*Schutzschrift für die deutsche Spracharbeit*), developed a program to preserve "the high German language in its actual essence and condition, without the admixture of strange and foreign words."[40]

Hearing is a sense like sight, and what strikes one as remarkable is the degree to which nation-thinking and the sound of language have in fact converged, if only in the thought of a small coterie of Baroque scholars and poets, many of them of aristocratic background. For them, the sound of the language had become a positive attribute of Germany,

---

[36] A translation into German by Claudia Barthold and Peter Barthold in Heidrun Kämpfer, "Einführung und Bibliographie zu Georg Henisch, Teutsche Sprach und Weisheit (1616)," in Henne, *Deutsche Wörterbucher des 17. und 18. Jahrhunderts*, 67–70. On such dictionaries in an international context, see *Wörterbücher: Ein internationales Handbuch zur Lexikographie*, eds. Franz Josef Haussmann et al. (Berlin, 1989–1991).

[37] Cited in the standard work of Irmgard Weithase, *Zur Geschichte der gesprochenen deutschen Sprache* (Tübingen, 1961), 117.

[38] Ibid., 117.

[39] Ibid.

[40] Cited by Helmut Henne, *Deutsche Wörterbucher des 17. und 18. Jahrhunderts* (Hildesheim, 2001), 16.

akin to the visual delight in Germany's mountains and rivers. Hans Just Winkelmann, for example, listed more than fifty adjectives describing the superiority of the German language, among them "pleasant," "expansive," "rich," "powerful," "regal," and "bejeweled."[41] There is no talk here about essences, no supposing that the nation, in some elemental way, is based on language. In his dedication to the Archduke of Austria, Henisch praised the German language alongside his encomium to other German contributions to civilization, like the cannon and the printing press, two inventions literally emblematic of Germany. Emblem, something on the outside, something that stands for Germany – this, in fact, is precisely how they came to view the relationship between language and nation. And this language, like the course of rivers and the heights of mountains, had still to be reconnoitered, explored for its variety, and structured according to rules that allowed for more precise description and greater conformity with the world of things.

III

"It must go further still," William Butler Yeats wrote, "that soul must become its own betrayer; its own deliverer, the one activity, the mirror turn lamp."[42] In his brilliant elucidation of Yeats's description of this epistemic shift in western culture, M. H. Abrams describes the change as one from art reflecting nature "out there" to art emanating from the poet himself. "The change," he writes, is "from imitation to expression, and from the mirror to the fountain, the lamp, and related analogues."[43] To grasp the abiding and fundamental nature of the shift, according to

---

[41] Cited in Thorsten Roelcke, "Der Patriotismus der barocken Sprachgesellschaften," in *Nation und Sprache. Die Diskussion ihres Verhältnisses in Geschichte und Gegenwart*, ed. Andreas Gardt (New York, 2000), 153. On the larger question of language patriotism, see also Andreas Gardt, "Sprachpatriotismus und Sprachnationalismus: Versuch einer historisch-systematischen Bestimmung am Beispiel des Deutschen," in *Sprachgeschichte als Kulturgeschichte*, eds. Andreas Gardt, Ulrike Haß-Zumkehr, and Thorsten Roelcke (Berlin, 1999), 89–114, where, however, the early modern connection between language and identity is overly emphasized. For the wider European context, and its complexity, see G. A. Padley, *Grammatical Theory in Western Europe, 1500–1700* (Cambridge, 1985), 325–348.

[42] Quoted in M. H. Abrams, *The Mirror and the Lamp: Romantic Theory and the Critical Condition* (Oxford, 1953), frontispiece.

[43] Ibid., 57.

Abrams, one must imagine the transition from Leon Battista Alberti ("What should painting be called except the holding of a mirror up to the original") to John Locke (for whom the mind, a "*tabula rasa*," was likened to a *camera obscura* in which "the pictures coming into such a dark room [would] but stay there") to Gotthold Ephraim Lessing (who saw painting and poetry as representing different mimetic domains, the former depicting what in nature is next to each other, the latter what follows in time) to William Wordsworth (for whom poetry was "the spontaneous overflow of feeling") and John Stuart Mill (for whom "all poetry is of the nature of soliloquy").[44] From an exterior to an interior understanding of culture, from painting as a foundational metaphor to poetry and language as its constitutive analogue, the shift structured possibilities in a deep sense. One is here tempted to speak, as Michel Foucault did in *The Order of Things*, of an epistemological rupture that rendered the past unintelligible to the present. Less ambitiously, but perhaps more precisely, we might follow Abrams in seeing the mirror and the lamp as expository analogues not merely illustrative but constitutive of knowledge. Such analogues, Abrams argues, "yield the ground plan and essential structural elements of a literary theory, or any theory."[45]

The transition occurred in the European context of the late Enlightenment, but its beginnings in Germany might be fixed more precisely in the late 1760s, between the publications of Lessing's *Laokoon* in 1766 and Herder's critique in the first *Critical Forests* (*Kritische Wälder*) in 1769. Lessing had argued against a conventional notion, according to which poetry was likened to painting, as in Horace's formula, *ut pictura poesis* (as in painting so in poetry), and which every eighteenth-century schoolboy knew in the adage that painting is mute poetry and poetry a painting that speaks.[46] Lessing aimed to demarcate poetry and painting, not in their common purpose of imitation but in the means they have available to achieve imitative effects. "Poetry and painting, both are imitative arts," Lessing wrote in an early unpublished sketch, "the purpose of both is to awaken in us the liveliest, most sensate representations

---

[44] Ibid., 57, 25.
[45] Ibid., 31.
[46] Gotthold Ephraim Lessing, *Werke und Briefe* (Deutsche Klassiker Ausgabe), vol.5, 2; *Gotthold Ephraim Lessing Werke, 1766–1769*, ed. Wilfried Barner (Frankfurt am Main, 1990), 632.

of their objects.... Painting uses figures and colors in space. Poetry articulates tones in time. The signs of the former are natural. Those of the latter are arbitrary."[47] In the insistence that not the ends but the means of painting and poetry diverge, Lessing liberated poetry, as Goethe would later claim in *Poetry and Truth* (*Dichtung und Wahrheit*), from the tyranny of an impoverished way of seeing.[48] But by maintaining that the signs of painting are natural, while those of poetry arbitrary, Lessing also betrayed the enduring weight of the mimetic tradition. He did not, in short, go far enough, and this hesitation was the target of Herder's critique. Poetry, Herder explained, effects not through its physical presence but by the power it has to convey meaning, and this power (*Kraft*) inheres in the words themselves. "Poetry effects through power," Herder writes, "through power that inheres at once in words, through power, that although it goes through the ear, affects the soul directly."[49] The essence of poetry, then, lies not in its mimetic abilities, whether in terms of spatial coexistence or temporal succession, but in its ability to move us. As this thought is now commonplace, it is easy to forget its novelty in the 1760s, and the conceptual rupture that the turn away from the mimetic tradition entailed. For understanding the impact of this turn for nation-thinking, it is also necessary to point out that for Herder the essence of poetry still lies in its ability to convey something between people, and it is not yet, as it will be for the later Romantics, a vehicle of expression for the feeling "I." Put differently, the nature of poetry is not yet in soliloquy. Instead, there is a crucial connection between the expression of a poet and the soul of his readers, and this connection would become the source of a fascination with the bardic tradition in which a poet, or a body of poetry, expresses the soul of a nation.[50]

---

[47] Cited in David Wellbery, *Lessing's Laocoon: Semiotics and Aesthetics in the Age of Reason* (Cambridge, 1984), 103.

[48] Johann Wolfgang von Goethe, *Aus meinem Leben, Dichtung und Wahrheit*, in Goethe, *Werke*. Hamburger Ausgabe, vol. 9, *Autobiographische Schriften* I, (Munich, 1981), 316.

[49] Herder, *Die kritischen Wälder zur Aesthetik*, in Herder, *Werke*, vol. 2, *Schriften zur Aesthetik und Literatur*, ed. Gunter E. Grimm (Frankfurt am Main, 1993), 194. On Herder's aesthetics, see especially Robert E. Norton, *Herder's Aesthetics and the European Enlightenment* (Ithaca, 1991).

[50] Katie Trumpener, *Bardic Nationalism: The Romantic Novel and the British Empire* (Princeton, 1997).

This tradition only made sense in the context of the crystallization of the modern self, a self not defined by exterior social relations and the role that a particular person qua character was expected to play, but by interior depth, and by the notion, as Charles Taylor has put it in his remarkable study of the problem, that this interior depth represents the voice of personal truth.[51] The transition from an exterior to an interior understanding of the self is perhaps the most dramatic story of eighteenth-century thought, and historians are only now exploring its ramifications across a wide spectrum of social life, with some, like Dror Wahrman, placing the dawn of a new identity regime at the dusk of the century.[52] Here the point is more modest: that the bardic tradition introduced a notion of authenticity – poetry expressing the genuine values and sentiments of a people – that only cohered when the nation, like the self, possessed interior depth.

It is, of course, commonplace in German historical writing to place Herder at the beginning of a new kind of thinking about the nation. To generations of historians steeped in the history of ideas, Herder was the founder of a cultural nationalism conceived in a humanistic context. Hans Kohn, in his magisterial *The Idea of Nationalism*, apportions Herder an extended discussion, subtly aware that Herder's thought embodied the full measure of paradox that inhered in the modern idea of nation.[53] The emphasis of Kohn and earlier generations was not misplaced, even if a second wave of studies of nationalism, beginning in the 1980s, has tended to downplay the influence of specific nationalist intellectuals. "What Herder thought about the *Volk*," Eric Hobsbawm blithely asserted, "cannot be used as evidence for the thoughts of the Westphalian peasantry."[54] Yet it can be used to take measure of the beginnings of an epistemological shift that had profound influence on the way nations were conceived in the modern era. This shift, I have argued, is a shift from exteriority to interiority and, in terms of senses,

---

[51] Charles Taylor, *Sources of the Self: The Making of Modern Identity* (Cambridge, Mass., 1989).

[52] Dror Wahrman, *The Making of the Modern Self: Identity and Culture in Eighteenth-Century England* (New Haven, 2004), 176, who charts the transition from a "non-essential notion of identity" to an identity "anchored in a deeply seated self."

[53] Kohn, *The Idea of Nationalism*, 427–451.

[54] E. J. Hobsbawm, *Nations and Nationalism since 1780*, rev. ed (London, 1992), 48.

from sight to sound. Herder, more than any other thinker, theorized the change and made language its linchpin.

In his "Treatise on the Origins of Language," published in 1772, Herder argued that language was essential to what it means to be human. Animals, he reasoned, live in a specific environment, where instinct suffices and understanding is not essential to survival; but humans, being free, live in the world, where mere instinct is insufficient. Language, according to Herder, is the reflective activity that allows us to understand and make our way in the world. He emphasizes the cumulative nature of this reflective activity and its social dimension, as a tool to implant knowledge in others and to touch the soul.

From the start, Herder associated language with the operations of the soul – a turn from the tradition of perceiving language as an exterior communicative medium, or at best a mimetic reflection of our reason, as it still was for Lessing. Historians have traditionally traced this shift to Herder's pietism, a Protestant religiosity that emphasized the subjective experience of Christ – "Christ within us" rather than "Christ for us," as the seventeenth-century theologian and historian of religion, Gottfried Arnold, put it.[55] But the shift also has to do with a new understanding of the senses. In his essay, "On the Knowing and Feeling of the Human Soul," published in 1778, Herder posited an "enmity" between "the clarity of the eye" and the "deep interiority of the ear" but nevertheless insisted that the senses can only "feel from the inside" (*in sich empfinden*). Crucially, Herder's image of how this works is drawn from biology – from Albrecht Haller's notion that organisms respond to external stimuli by self-contraction and expansion, a quality Haller defined as their *Reizbarkeit*, which might in this context be translated as sensitivity. Herder then generalizes this image to develop a notion of an inner self responding actively to the environment around it. The inner response is crucial.[56] Herder calls it an inner sense; language is its medium, and as language can be cultivated, so too can the senses.

---

55 Cited in a still-classic work by Koppel Pinson, *Pietism as a Factor in the Rise of German Nationalism* (Columbia, 1934), 41.

56 M. H. Abrams, *The Mirror and the Lamp*, 204. Herder, *Die kritischen Wälder zur Aesthetik*, 194. For extremely suggestive reflections on the relationship of touch to feeling and "Innerlichkeit," see Ulrike Zeuch, *Umkehr der Sinneshierarchie: Herder und die Aufwertung des Tastsinns seit der frühen Neuzeit* (Tübingen, 2000), esp. 144–152.

This cultivation is at the heart of what Herder thought of as humanity: "The more one strengthens, directs, enriches, and cultivates the inner language of a person, the more one shapes his reason and makes the divine come alive."[57]

For Herder, the inner language is the mother tongue, and for the first time, at least in German history, it is not defended because of its laudable characteristics or because of its ancientness or even because it allows one to understand the word of God, but only because it is the most natural language, the language of parents and children. The difference is of immense importance and thinkable only in the context of ideas of childhood accepted after the publication of Jean Jacques Rousseau's epochal work, *Emile ou de l'éducation*, which insisted on the "natural education" of children based on precise observation of their first impressions, sounds, and attempts to interact with their environment. Herder, like Rousseau, wanted to perfect natural sensibilities and to this end repeatedly returned to the image of the hearth.[58]

The sound of the hearth was not prose but poetry. Nowadays, poetry seems almost antithetical to everyday speech, yet Herder thought genuine poetry "a gift to mankind and to all people, not the private inheritance of a few refined and educated persons."[59] Against Lessing's rules, Herder extolled the language of "the streets and alleys and fish markets."[60] As poems disclosed the bard's inner voice, he argued, the untutored melodies of ordinary people expressed the nation. Herder asked not whether the songs were accurate but whether they were genuine, not whether they reflected the preoccupations of the people but whether they expressed its soul. This was "the mirror turn[ed] lamp," nationally inflected.

There was, from the start, a tension in Herder's writing – between his enthusiasm for the primitive and his insistence on cultivation, *Bildung*. But *Bildung* could not be something imposed from the outside; it had to be aligned with the inner sense of a people. This was true for all nations. Unlike the Renaissance grammarians, or the scholars of the

---

[57] Herder, "*Vom Erkennen und Empfinden der menschlichen Seele*," in Herder, *Werke*, vol. 4, *Schriften zu Philosophie, Literatur, Kunst und Altertum 1774–1787* (Frankfurt am Main, 1994), 358.

[58] Herder, *Auch eine Philosophie der Geschichte zur Bildung der Menschheit*, in ibid., 93.

[59] Herder cited in Kohn, *The Idea of Nationalism*, 442.

[60] Herder, *Von deutscher Art und Kunst*, in Herder, *Werke*, vol. 2, 480.

"*Fruitbearing society*," Herder possessed no reasonable basis to suppose that German was a language superior to another. German was only better for the Germans, just as Polish was better for the Poles. It was the imposition of foreign languages on subject peoples that Herder decried, and the obsequious propensity, most pronounced in the upper classes, to speak in the language of the powerful rather than the powerless. Herder's anti-French diatribes have often been cited to document a long-standing Germanic Francophobia – their real context, however, was Herder's abhorrence for the cultural impact of imperial rule.

Herder twined language and nation, language and humanity, in a way that made language not merely emblematic of either nationhood or humanity, but constitutive of it: "Only through language are nations made, only though common language do people achieve humanity."[61] Speech, hearing, the ear rather than the eye, sound rather than sight in this way became the locus of the nation's sense; it bound its members together, not merely as a society defined by eased communication, but as a community marked by sympathy: "Whoever has learned sorrow and joy, whoever has been brought up in the same language in which he empties his heart and learns to express his soul, belongs to the people of this language."[62]

Herder's strong sense of nation as constituted by language quickly became commonplace. "Wherever we encounter a distinct language," Fichte would write, "there is also a distinct nation." "The true homeland," Wilhelm von Humboldt declared, "is actually one's language." And as Friedrich Schleiermacher intoned: "To one language alone does the individual belong entirely."[63] Nations existed prior to the eighteenth century, and language was one of a number of markers of them; but prior to the epistemic shift, from mirror to lamp, mimesis to expression, outer to inner, language could not, in the way that the German nationalists imagined, constitute nations as such. Nationalists did not make nations, as Ernest Gellner thought, but they could, and did, put nations on an

---

[61] Cited in Haase, *Zur Geschichte der gesprochenen deutschen Sprache*, 374, from Herder's short essay, "Über die Fähigkeit zu sprechen und zu hören."

[62] Herder, *Briefe zur Beförderung der Humanität*, in Herder, *Werke*, vol. 7 (Frankfurt am Main, 1991), 304.

[63] Fichte, Humboldt, and Schleiermacher cited by R. J. W. Evans, *The Language of History and the History of Language* (Oxford, 1988), 25–27.

altogether different epistemological ground. They made sense of them anew.

IV

I have argued that the central distinction is between a nation conceived as exterior and a nation conceived as interior. The first involved the revolution in printing and the primacy of sight; the second emphasized sound as the avenue to the nation's inner soul and center of gravity. The first kind of nation was seen for the first time and surveyed, pictured, measured, mapped, and described in "the century of intense wonder," as Stephen Greenblatt calls the hundred years following Columbus's landfall.[64] Writing two centuries later, Herder remains remarkable because he exudes this wonder, but the turn inward would soon be politicized, and the "additive way of understanding the world," still extent in Herder's writing and in his relentless collecting, will soon give way to an altogether more radical and constructivist epistemology that assumes that both our categories and our sensations are products of the human mind.

Fichte is the starting point of the new nationalism, not because of the famous *Addresses to the German Nation*, oft quoted, seldom read, and at the time hardly heard by anyone, but because he put the nation onto an altogether new philosophical ground – beyond the senses. He was the first German intellectual whose substantial work was composed after the French Revolution, and the new world of possibilities promised by the events in France continued even after the Terror of 1794 to backlight Fichte's thought. But for Fichte there was another context, critical to the German generation of the 1790s: the philosophy of Immanuel Kant. For Fichte, who rose to prominence with an anonymous essay that the literary public mistook to be from the master's hand, there were two determining Kantian insights, one concerning epistemology, the other concerning freedom.

The insight concerning what we can know stems from Kant's *Critique of Pure Reason*, published in 1781. Put simply, Kant argued that the

---

[64] Stephen Greenblatt, *Marvelous Possessions: The Wonder of the New World* (Chicago, 1991), 14.

mind cannot fully know the phenomenal world without the aid of pre-existing categories – with the consequence that the world could never be comprehended by sense perceptions, even if there existed an independent realm outside the mind of "things-for-themselves." Yet for Fichte, to cite Yeats, "it must go further still," as Kant's necessary distinction, between things as they appear and things as they are, proved untenable. Extreme skepticism, asserting the impossibility of knowing, was one possible response, but Fichte pushed in the opposite direction, asserting that in the realm of practical reason there are no "things-for-themselves" but only an "I" that constructs them. This is the starting point of his *Wissenschaftslehre*, or *Science of Knowledge*, first published in 1794, but revised many times over the next two decades.

Fichte's *Wissenschaftslehre* contrasts starkly with a view that sees the senses as mirroring nature, and even with Herder's understanding of the soul as a repository of depth and a site of empathy, reacting from within to the real material and intersubjectivity of the outside world. Fichte starts from the opposite end. "I ought to begin thinking with the thought of the pure 'I'," he wrote, "and I ought to think of this pure 'I' as absolutely self-active – not as determined by things, but as determining them."[65] This is the constructive moment of identity.[66] The "I" posits its opposite, the "not I," and these two spheres, the "I" and the "not I," remain restrictive, with the "I," not the world, acting. Empowering what he called the "productive imagination," Fichte saw his breakthrough as a great moment of freedom. The parallel with events across the Rhine was more than merely fortuitous. Fichte claimed that it was the French struggle for freedom that inspired his epistemology. "Just as France has freed man from external shackles," he wrote at the height of the terror in 1794, "so my system frees him from the fetters of things in themselves, which is to say from those external influences with which all previous systems – including the Kantian – have more or less chained man."[67]

It is tempting to directly link the ego in Fichte's philosophy to the nation of modern nationalism. Yet in the mid-1790s, this link was not yet apparent, and Fichte remained a philosopher who thought about

---

[65] Quoted in Jerrold Seigel, *The Idea of the Self: Thought and Experience in Western Europe since the Seventeenth Century* (New York, 2005), 365.

[66] George Armstrong Kelly, *Idealism, Politics and History: Sources of Hegelian Thought* (London, 1969), 207.

[67] Quoted in Seigel, *The Idea of the Self*, 362.

humanity as such before he thought about nation in particular.[68] This fix on humanity was grounded in Fichte's ethics, and this too turned on Kant's understanding of absolute freedom, which entailed the convergence of the free ethical choices of the individual with the requirements of the wider community. This sense of freedom, as Leonard Krieger famously argued, was not based on an invisible hand bringing together the actions of men pursuing their own interests; rather, it was based on self-reflection – on the notion, Pietist in origin, that when men look into themselves they discover not self-love but the moral law, and that this moral law is a fact of reason and a condition of freedom.[69] Kant's categorical imperative – act in such a way that your action may at the same time be willed as a universal law – harmonizes, in theoretical terms, the individual ethical insight with the collective moral law and defines full freedom in terms of their convergence. For Fichte, who first read Kant's *Critique of Practical Reason* in 1790, the imperative and its philosophical proof engendered a conversion experience, lifting Fichte, as he wrote to a friend, into "a new world," "above all earthly things."[70] Throughout the 1790s, Fichte worked to bring together these two spheres, individual and collective morality. Yet the frame of his thinking as regards this project was not the nation but the state, and not a specific state, such as Prussia, but an abstract state.

He worked on this problem in his *Science of Ethics* of 1798 and in his *Closed Commercial Society* of 1800, the latter work a radical utopia. But it was a utopia with humanity not nationality in view. According to Herder, humanity could only be achieved in the first instance through a limited community, and this limited community, which allowed only a minimum of international trade and travel (except for scholars and creative artists), required a state – a state, moreover, that could impose morality by force.[71] Fichte bridged the apparent disjuncture – between his philosophy of individual freedom and the necessity of state

---

[68] On the importance of universal thinking to the genesis of modern patriotism, see Reinhart Koselleck, *Begriffsgeschichten* (Frankfurt am Main, 2006), 227–8.

[69] Leonard Krieger, *The German Idea of Freedom. History of a Political Tradition* (Boston, 1957).

[70] Cited in Anthony J. LaVopa, *Fichte: The Self and the Calling of Philosophy, 1762–1799* (Cambridge, 2001), 75.

[71] Fichte, "Der geschlossene Handelsstaat," in Fichte, *Werke 1800–1801*, eds. Reinhar Lauth and Hans Gliwitzky, in *J. G. Fichte – Gesamtausgabe*, Series I, vol. 7 (Stuttgart, 1988), 37–141.

coercion – by emphasizing the role of the intellectual, who can discern moral freedom and apply the universal law to others in the community. As the closed commercial society became more virtuous, the necessity of coercion declined, and the state withered away.[72]

It is within the context of these three intellectual moments – Fichte's radical epistemological deduction of the constructive "I" as against "things-in-themselves," his Kantian insistence that full freedom only occurs with the fusion of the individual moral law and the collective will, and his willingness to ascribe to the state (until it withers away) the power to shape and enforce morality – that one must place Fichte's discovery and unequivocal embrace of the nation.

At the turn of the century, few had embraced a political position that gave priority to the political nation over the cultural nation, or to German people over German states.[73] It is true that the prominent early Romantics, especially Friedrich Schlegel and Friedrich Hölderlin, had composed poems to the nation, but their verses remained exhortations to dawn a mantle of cultural leadership. In 1805, Ernst Moritz Arndt had written the first installment of his *Spirit of the Time* (*Geist der Zeit*), a fulminous diatribe against Napoleon, cowardly German princes, and the infirmities of the age. But this book, and the ferocity of its rhetoric, stood alone. For many German intellectuals, not the new century but the collapse of 1806 proved decisive. In this year, Father Jahn drafted his *German Peoplehood* (*Deutsches Volkstum*), and Arndt, the second installment of his *Geist der Zeit*. We find Kleist on the verge of collapse at the news of Jena and Auerstadt, but he will soon put his energy into his play, *Hermann's Battle*, whose visions of transformative violence and captured land denuded of foreign people presaged nationalism's darkest sides.[74] This is the context, too, of Fichte's nationalist writings, a corpus of work important not so much for its immediate influence as for its philosophical grounding of nationalism.

---

[72] On this topic, see Kelly, *Idealism, Politics, and History*, 283.

[73] For a judicious, brief discussion, James J. Sheehan, *German History, 1770–1866* (Oxford, 1989), 371–398.

[74] Wolf Kittler, *Die Geburt des Partisanen aus dem Geist der Poesie: Heinrich von Kleist und die Strategie der Befreiungskriege* (Freiburg in Br., 1987). See, in a broader context, David A. Bell, *The First Total War: Napoleon's Europe and the Birth of Warfare as We Know It* (New York, 2007), esp. 294–301.

From existing sources, it seems that Fichte first articulated his condemnation of Napoleon in the winter of 1805, soon after Napoleon's victory over the Austrians in Austerlitz.[75] By the summer of the following year, he wondered when he should intervene in events.[76] In a letter to Karl August von Hardenberg, dated August/September 1806, he referred to the widespread but deleterious opinion that "all men of talent tend to a certain harmful party" – which we may take as the party supporting Napoleon.[77] By now, Fichte had already committed himself to engaging the wider public; in June, he had composed one of his *Patriotic dialogues*, in which he, for the first time, etched with a sharp philosophical stylus the distinction between the state and the nation, Prussia and Germany. Fichte has his first speaker, "A," talk about patriotism in the old way, and the second speaker, "B," correct him about the new ways of thinking and feeling.

A: I don't want to be a German. I am a Prussian, and a patriotic Prussian at that.

B: Now, understand me correctly. The division of Prussia from the rest of Germany is artificial, based on half hazard and fortuitously erected institutions; the division of Germany from the other European nations is founded upon nature.[78]

For Fichte, the natural division involves language and character, and it is indicative that "A" understands the former but not the latter. Fichte also demarcates nationalism, which he calls patriotism (the word

---

[75] In a letter to Karl August von Hardenberg, dated August/September 1806, he writes that in the previous winter he had "loudly spoken according to his (Hardenberg's) principles." According to Eduard Fichte, *Johann Gottlieb Fichte: Lichtstrahlen aus seinen Werken und Briefen* (Leipzig, 1863), 290, Fichte rose up in the presence of company and stated, against the governing consensus, "that not a year will pass, before you mourn this defeat in the highest measure." See now also Johann Gottlieb Fichte, *Briefwechsel, 1801–1806,* eds. Reinhard Lauth and Hans Gliwitzky, *J. G. Fichte – Gesamtausgabe,* III, vol. 5 (Stuttgart, 1982), 365.

[76] Marie Johanne Fichte to Johannes Müller, 27.8.1806, in Fichte, *Briefwechsel, 1801–1806,* III, 5, 363.

[77] Fichte to Hardenberg, August/September, in ibid., 364–5.

[78] Fichte, "Der Patriotismus, und sein Gegentheil," in *J. G. Fichte – Gesamtausgabe,* II, vol. 9, *Nachgelassene Schriften,* eds. Reinhard Lauth and Hans Gliwitzky (Stuttgart, 1993), 403. On Prussian patriotism, see especially Christopher Clark, *Iron Kingdom: The Rise and Downfall of Prussia, 1600–1947* (Cambridge, Mass., 2006), 350–358, 378–385, and, especially for the use of "nation" to mean either Germany or Prussia or both, 386–387.

nationalism would not be coined in German until 1844) from cosmopolitanism. Cosmopolitanism wishes to approach the goal of humanity through humanity while patriotism is the "will that this goal be reached first in that nation of which we are members, and from there the success will be spread across the whole of mankind."[79]

The tone remained measured – but the defeat at Jena in the coming fall changed Fichte's conception. "What I have held for the true task of my life, a completely clear description of the *Wissenschaftslehre*, was not completed," he wrote in a letter to Hardenberg on October 18, just a few days after the Prussian defeat. But Fichte now resolved to address "the great questions of our day in writing and if possible in public speech in order to reach the hearts of the Germans and to fire their patriotic participation."[80] The letter signals Fichte's national turn. In the course of the next year, Fichte composed a series of short essays that deepened his national sentiment and connected his previous philosophical positions to it. Of these essays, the most remarkable is a fragment entitled *The Republic of the Germans at the Beginning of the Twenty-Second Century*. At the time of its composition between the fall of 1806 and the spring of 1807, it had had no kin in the history of German nation-thinking.

Consisting of isolated pages, paragraphs, and sometimes only scribbled sentences, *The Republic of the Germans* outlines Fichte's national utopia and places it 300 years into his future. By the twenty-second century, and as a result of the treason of the princes, the German nation had for a long time disappeared from the map, only to be resurrected again with a new generation, less selfish than the current one, more eager to learn, braver, and manlier. The state is, as the title suggests, a republic, but a republic with a strong "protector" elected by a Senate and supported by a self-selected inner council of advisors and an elected council of notables. In matters of war and peace, colonies and foreign policy, the "protector" makes decisions. In matters of education, culture, justice, military preparedness, and finances, a state administrator (*Statthalter*) governs affairs. The state's central goal was to create the most educated citizenry in the world.

---

[79] Ibid., 399.
[80] Fichte to Karl August von Hardenberg, 18.10.1806, in Fichte, *Briefwechsel 1801–1806*, III, 5, 371.

The state is a German state, and its borders expansive, if indistinct. They stretch from the north and the Baltic Sea to the Memel, the Vistula, and the Warthe, and south to include Bohemia, Moravia, and Austria, reaching all the way to Venice and Triest (in order to ensure German access to the Adriatic). The Island of Gibraltar must also become German.[81] Helvetia belongs to Germany, as does the Upper Rhine, though whether this includes Strasbourg, since 1681 in French hands, remains unclear.[82] Internally, the German Republic is organized according to historical regions, not dynastic states, with the telling exception of Brandenburg-Prussia. The republic is also a German state in terms of its citizens. "It is a basic principle," Fichte writes, "that only Germans can be citizens." He emphasizes this in the context of a remark concerning Poles who, three centuries hence, "have become to a large extent German, and those left over were allowed to emigrate to Russia."[83] The same fate has befallen the Jews, who have "either melted away or emigrated," many to "a very interesting state in Palestine," with the remaining Jews having "become members of the new church."[84]

The new church is a national church, the spiritual home of all free, educated men and women. The other Christian denominations, Catholic, Calvinist, and Lutheran, still exist, but they are slowly withering away, as more and more people freely join a church of "general Christianity." The Bible is the book of "general Christianity," and Christ is its greatest teacher, but his authority is based purely on the free, ethical insight of the individual members of the church. The church holds services every Sunday, and the services are revealing.

After gathering in the churchyard, the assembled enter into the hall, where the priest, a Justice of the Peace, awaits them. The walls are covered with weapons, "the symbol of citizenship," and every man carries one (since all men over twenty until death are soldiers). Service begins by commemorating the recently deceased. Cremated and buried in urns, the dead are arranged according to service to the nation, with the urns of

[81] Fichte, "Die Republik der Deutschen," in *Nachgelassene Schriften 1806–1807*, eds. Reinhard Lauth and Hans Gliwitzky, in *J. G. Fichte – Gesamtausgabe* (Stuttgart, 1994), II, 389.

[82] Ibid., 388–9.

[83] Ibid., 387.

[84] Ibid.

those who died in war receiving pride of place, followed by those who counseled the nation, and by those "good housefathers and housemothers who have lived peaceably and born and raised well-behaved children for the fatherland and have shown love and goodness to their fellow citizens."[85] There is also a fourth category, presumably for those who have neither served the nation nor born children; their ashes will be put into unmarked urns. Then newborns are consecrated. The "eldest and most worthy" women approach the altar with the newborns in their arms. When the child is blessed, the woman with the child in her arms (not the mother) steps forward and the child is named, and the name is placed in the citizen's book. Then the preacher places his hand on the child's head and says the words, which are to be repeated by the community: "We name you . . . as a sign that we, and through us the whole Fatherland of the German Nation, recognize you as a *being capable of reason*, as *participating in the rights of our citizenship*, and as *an inheritor of everlasting life, for which we also hope*."[86]

The hold of the French example is evident, with the imitation of Christian practices, Fichte's atheism notwithstanding, especially striking.[87] Much as Fichte had attempted in his epistemology to transfer the freedom of the French Revolution to the realm of mind, now he would "transfer sacrality" in order to infuse the nation with meaning and ritual.[88] It was a nation divorced from history. Reason, Fichte believed, could transcend Germany's problem of religious division, now nearly three centuries old. He had no interest in the history-heavy, earth-rooted peasants that Herder had extolled. Instead, Fichte placed the constructive moment of a new German national identity at the center, divorced, or nearly divorced, from the exigencies of time or the weight of prior cultural formation. In this too, Fichte's affinity to the later phase of the French Revolution is evident, especially in the revolution's

---

[85] Ibid., 417–8.

[86] Ibid., 423.

[87] Mona Ozuf, *Festivals and the French Revolution*. tr. Alan Sheridan (Cambridge, Mass., 1988), 262–283.

[88] There is a vast literature on the transfer of sacrality to the nation. To my mind, the most illuminating insights are to be found in the chapter provocatively entitled "Die Nation – von Gott erfunden?" in Friedrich Wilhelm Graf, *Die Wiederkehr der Götter: Religion in der modernen Kultur* (Munich, 2004), 102–133, and George S. Williamson, *The Longing for Myth in Germany: Religion and Aesthetic Culture from Romanticism to Nietzsche* (Chicago, 2004).

self-enclosed moments, which allowed the revolutionaries, in the historian David Bell's words, "to imagine forms of harmonious human coexistence whose ordering principles did not derive from any entity or authority external to the human community itself."[89]

This self-enclosed moment, akin to the initial identity of I = I that Fichte posited in the *Wissenschaftslehre*, allowed Fichte to conceive of the nation as a projected space of identity. The space was not empty; it contained a grid of divisions. Birth and education ensured equality, but gender and sacrifice divide the space again, foreshadowing two themes central to the subsequent history of nations and nationality and pairing, quite literally, male with death and female with birth.[90] To men who sacrifice for the republic as intellectuals or soldier the highest place of honor is given, and in this way Fichte twines male reason and male violence. This twining was not about foreign aggression; for the weapons of men, Fichte argues, ought only to protect the community. This point bears emphasis. For Fichte, unlike Arndt, not hatred of the foreigner counts, but only the community as a product of putatively free individuals. That the community is walled off from outsiders, as in the *Closed Commercial State*, results not from the ethnic inferiority of others, but instead because the Germans are, as the revolutionaries in France imagined themselves to have been in the 1790s, the vehicle of reason for humanity as a whole. Still, the national community, which presupposes an unmediated relationship between the individual and the nation, exercised the kind of control over the individual that foreshadowed later horrors. Fichte's suggestions for penal law, for example, hold out the harshest punishments for cowardice and desertion, and this harshness consists not only in judicial murder but in the eradication of the person's traces and the return of his land to the earth.[91] In Fichte's nation, there is equality, not just before the law but also in educational opportunity, but there is also sacrifice, which governs the terms of inclusion in the nation and the possibilities of expulsion from it.

---

[89] Bell, *The Cult of the Nation in France*, 199.

[90] On Fichte as a theorist of gender, see especially Isabel V. Hull, *Sexuality, State, and Civil Society in Germany, 1700–1815* (Ithaca, 1996), 314–323. On the convergence of masculinity and national ideas, see also the brief but incisive comments in Clark, *Iron Kingdom*, 377–378; and, in more detail, Ute Frevert, *Die kasernierte Nation: Militärdienst und Zivilgesellschaft in Deutschland* (Munich, 2001), 18–62.

[91] Fichte, "Die Republik der Deutschen," 393–4.

Fichte's *Addresses to the German Nation*, delivered in fourteen lectures at the rotunda of the Academy of Sciences in Berlin from December 1807 to March 1808, bring together the epistemological radicalism of Fichte's early years with the national turn of 1806 and represent a major departure from earlier traditions of nation-thinking. As the *Addresses* have been the object of considerable scholarly scrutiny, often unduly overshadowing Fichte's other writings, suffice here to underscore central themes: the critique of the corruption of the preceding age, the insistence that "the means of salvation" involves "the fashioning of an entirely new self," the centrality of education to that fashioning, and the emphasis that the new person thereby created will pursue the love of good rather than the love of self. Fichte further argued that a bond of brotherhood defines a nation, "an organic unity in which no member regards the fate of another as the fate of a stranger"; that the nobility of a man consists not in being well-born but in a willingness to sacrifice himself for his people; and that the only true aim of the people is freedom in the sense of following his inner moral law (and the convergence of that law with the law of the community). The appropriate state for the Germans is a republic, and the state now has a higher calling: to protect, educate, and serve the nation, to which the state is subordinate.[92]

Fichte has left the empirical ground of earlier concepts of nationhood, and his epistemology stamps every facet of the new nation. First and foremost is the denial of exterior senses. This will start with the earliest education. In the ninth address, he draws the distinction explicitly.

As a rule, the world of the senses was formerly accepted as the correct, authentic, true and really existing world; it was the first brought before the pupil in education. From it (the world of the senses) alone he was led to thinking, and mostly to thinking about it and in its service. The new education exactly

[92] Quoted citations from Johann Gottlieb Fichte, *Reden an die deutsche Nation*, in Fichte, *Werke 1808–1812*, eds. Reinhard Lauth et al., in *J. G. Fichte – Gesamtausgabe* (Stuttgart, 2005), 106, 112. For particularly insightful analyses of this work, see Ulrich Bielefeld, *Nation und Gesellschaft: Selbstthematisierungen in Deutschland und Frankreich* (Hamburg, 2003), 121–137. Kelly, *Idealism, Politics and History*, 260–268; Eli Kedourie, *Nationalism* (New York, 1961), 32–50, is brilliant but quirky. For the broader context of the *Addresses*, see Jörg Echternkamp, *Der Aufstieg des deutschen Nationalismus, 1740– 1840* (Frankfurt am Main, 1998), 216–275; Matthew Levinger, *Enlightened Nationalism: The Transformation of Prussian Political Culture, 1806–1848* (Oxford, 2000), 97–126; and, still classic, Aira Kemiläinen, *Auffassungen über die Sendung des deutschen Volkes um die Wende des 18. und 19. Jahrhunderts* (Helsinki, 1956).

reverses this order, making the world that is comprehended by thought the true and really existing world, to which it wishes to introduce the pupil from the very beginning.[93]

Fichte never tires of emphasizing that this will be a national education in love of fatherland, but the empirical world is incidental to it; indeed, that a people dwells "between certain mountains and rivers" does not a nation make; instead, there is a law "of nature which is much higher," and this involves the idea of a people.

That idea turns on language. Closely following August Wilhelm Schlegel, Fichte argued that the Germans possessed an "original language" relatively untainted by the corruptions of subsequent mixing.[94] This means that unlike other European nations, whose tongue has been corrupted by Latin, the Germans still speak with the voice of their ancestors, and the spirit of these ancestors still speaks through them. Fichte argues here in a very different way than the early humanists, some of whom, like Conrad Celtis, emphasized the sheer ancientness of German as against Latin. Fichte also takes a different tack than the Fruitbearing Society, whose members extolled the special qualities of the German tongue in describing nature. And Fichte differs from Herder, who believed that special qualities inhered in all languages. For Fichte, only German remains an original language because only Germans remained in their original dwelling places, and the Latin world could not conquer them. It was, therefore, their love of freedom that allowed them to maintain their language, and this love of freedom, at the core of what it means to be German, has been communicated across the centuries, only falling into abeyance in the present age. But because the language remained, current corruptions notwithstanding, it was precisely the Germans who were capable of absorbing the new education, fashioning themselves, if they willed it, into a new race of men.

The nation arched back into prehistoric time, but it also stretched endlessly into the future. The sixteenth century already knew the close connection between space and time in two-dimensional renditions of the earth's surface. In Sebastian Münster's first published map, for example, an image of the German nation shared a crowded space with highly

---

[93] Fichte, *Reden an die deutsche Nation*, 216.
[94] On the connection to Schlegel, Leon, *Fichte et son temps*, III, 61–78, and for his place in the history of language more generally, Borst, *Der Turmbau von Babel*, vol. 3, 1551–1553.

intricate dials that allowed the user of the map to calculate when the sun rises and sets, the current position of the zodiac and the ruling planets, the date of Easter, and the days left between Christmas and Lent. Sacral time crowded into national space, but the religious remained paramount. By the late eighteenth century, by the age of Herder, it is historical time that takes precedence, and interiority is conceived, when considering the culture of nations, in terms of origins and development, with linear time and causal sequence defining narrative. But for Herder, the reaching back mattered, initiating a period in which historicism ruled as a dominant form of inquiry. Fichte, however, wrote in a period of immense temporal acceleration and rupture, with the French Revolution bequeathing to contemporaries what Peter Fritzsche has called "an explosive sense of time."[95] Fichte absolutely breathed this "explosive sense of time," with the past of his distant, prehistoric Germans serving as an imagined Eden prefiguring a new Jerusalem. This future orientation was not just a matter of politics and war – the brute fact that Germany lay divided and prostrate. It was also a consequence of Fichte's epistemology, and its turn away from the senses. "The power to create spontaneous images, which are not simply copies of reality, but can become its prototypes, should be the starting point for the molding of a new race," he insisted in his second address.[96]

"One could not hear [the *Addresses*] without being shaken and enthusiastic," the writer Karl August Varnhagen von Ense reported in his memoirs of 1832.[97] Yet the immediate impact of the *Addresses* was limited, reaching a number of important intellectuals and statesmen, among them Baron vom Stein and Friedrich Gentz, but not selling more than 600 copies by the end of 1808.[98] In any case, Fichte's philosophically complex *Addresses* never enjoyed the mass popularity of the great simplifiers of the age, like Ernst Moritz Arndt, whose pamphlets enjoyed print runs ranging between 10,000 and 80,000 copies.[99] Fichte's

---

[95] Peter Fritzsche, *Modern Time and the Melancholy of History* (Cambridge, Mass., 2004), 31.

[96] Fichte, *Reden an die deutsche Nation*, 120.

[97] Cited in Erich Fuchs, introduction to Johann Gottlieb Fichte, *Reden an die deutsche Nation*, 9.

[98] Ibid., 40.

[99] Karen Hagemann, "Francophobia and Patriotism: Anti-French Images and Sentiments in Prussia and Northern Germany during the anti-Napoleonic Wars," in *French History*, 18.4 (2004), 4414, fn.55.

Addresses had few adherents west of the Elbe and fewer still south of the Main.[100] It is true that the correspondences of the time, which were censored by the French occupying forces, reveal a number of references to their impact, but in the end the canonical centrality of the *Addresses* to early German nationalism remains more legend than history.

The legend gathered force in the 1860s, when the shaping power of the state became an article of faith among German nationalists. The hundredth anniversary of Fichte's birth provided the external impetus, but the inner drive stemmed from a generation of nationalists for whom Prussia was the state that would both unify the nation and shape its national culture. The most important of these men was Heinrich von Treitschke, whose "Fichte and the National Idea," published in 1862, set firmly the subsequent image of Fichte as the man who with his *Addresses* fired nationalist passion. In place of Fichte, the founder of an epistemological system, Treitschke enthroned Fichte the nationalist who grasped the power of the state to create the nation.[101] Treitschke was a careful and brilliant reader, and he read Fichte's collected works and his posthumously published essays, fragments, and letters. Yet he screwed Fichte's thinking into the procrustean bed of national politics in the 1860s, even making Fichte into "the first renowned prophet of those ideas, which today Germany's National Party represents."[102] It was the way Fichte married nation and state that mattered, with Treitschke only regretting Fichte's modesty in putting off this marriage until the twenty-second century. In the period of the second Fichte renaissance, circa 1910, Fichte's connection to the assumptions and culture of early Romanticism were in some measure reestablished, but so too was his theory of the Germans as possessing the only "original language." For Fichte, this meant that Germans possessed a privileged access to truth, allowing them "to be superior to the foreigner," and even to "understand the foreigner better than the foreigner understands himself."[103] Put differently, Fichte was pressed first into the service of *Machtpolitik*, then *Kulturpolitik*. In either case, it was a Fichte read back from the present. Modern scholarship

---

[100] Michael Rowe, *From Reich to State: The Rhineland in the Revolutionary Age, 1780–1830* (Cambridge, 2003), 126.

[101] Heinrich von Treitschke, "Fichte und die nationale Idee," in Treitschke, *Historische und politische Aufsätze*, 8th ed. (Leipzig, 1918), 124.

[102] Ibid., 136.

[103] Fichte, "Reden an die deutsche Nation," 155.

has largely followed them in this approach, "looking back on him," as Anthony J. LaVopa has cogently put it, "through the distorting lens of modern ideologies."[104]

V

The main distorting lens has been nationalism itself – but not in the old sense of historians believing, with nationalists, that nations are old as time. Rather, the problem is now more subtle and concerns, one might say, the epistemology of the nation. Pace Fichte, it has now become axiomatic to historians that nations are invented or imagined, and that this process, in which nationalist intellectuals play a central role, occurred at the cusp of modernity, with nations first imagined in the late eighteenth century.

"It is nationalism that engenders nations and not the other way around" – Ernest Gellner memorably asserted, reversing the order of causality, severing nationalism from the history of nations. Tellingly, Gellner adduced as evidence a fictional example, the central European country of Ruritania, made famous in the late nineteenth-century novels of Anthony Hope.[105] But whatever felicity Gellner's analysis may have for his shadowbox nation, its dexterity flags before European nations that had already been "discovered" – surveyed, described, and mapped since at least the sixteenth century. The cultural products of the first discovery were not mass products (a possibility proscribed by the fact of limited literacy), but their presence is not easily reduced to a set of "arbitrary historical inventions," "cultural shreds and patches," as Gellner put it, where any "old shred and patch would have served as well."[106]

The problem is not unique to Gellner. Even in Benedict Anderson's *Imagined Communities*, the early modern nation only exists in a state of non-being. This must surprise given Anderson's powerfully suggestive explanation for how nations represent cultural formations of particular kinds. Yet Anderson takes the "objective modernity" of nations as given, excluding consideration of earlier formations. The exclusion follows from his definition of the nation as "an imagined political

---

[104] LaVopa, *Fichte*, 11.
[105] Gellner, *Nations and Nationalism*, 59.
[106] Ibid., 56.

community . . . both limited and sovereign." A political definition, it fits the age of Fichte, with qualifications the time of Herder, but not the period in which Sebastian Münster thought and wrote. A definition, it bears recalling, does not prove the "objective modernity" of the nation; instead, it simply circumscribes the angle of vision. Anderson's political definition, moreover, vies with his celebrated cultural approach, which asks us to understand nations as "communities distinguished by the style in which they were imagined."[107] But then we must see the nation first as mirror, then as lamp, and only thereafter as positing an identity between individual and nation and rendering that identity as a matter of political sovereignty. To continue to insist that nations are imagined not sensed, posited not given, invented not found, is to remain enmeshed in epistemological coordinates first mapped out by Fichte. More prosaically, it means that modern nationalism still determines our sense of nations. Yet far from making nations, or inventing them, modern nationalism departed from earlier senses of nations: as nations among other nations, as they are on maps, and as they were, however briefly, in Herder's understanding of humanity.

[107] For critical reflections on Anderson, see Thomas Mergel, "Benedict Anderson's Imagined Communities: Zur Karriere eines erfolgreichen Konzepts," afterword to Benedict Anderson, *Die Erfindung der Nation*, 2nd ed., tr. Benedikt Burkard (Frankfurt am Main, 2005), 281–299.

3

ON CATASTROPHIC RELIGIOUS VIOLENCE AND NATIONAL BELONGING

The Thirty Years War and the Massacre of Jews in Social Memory

Entire, more than entire have we been devastated!
The maddened clarion, the bold invaders' horde.
The mortar thunder-voiced, the blood-anointed sword
Have all men's sweat and work and store annihilated.
> Andreas Gryphius, 1636

The hypocritical new love for the Christian religion – God forgive me my sin! – for the Middle Ages, with their art, poetry and faith, stirs up the people to the only atrocity in which it remembers its old liberties – attacking the Jews.
> Rahel Levin Varnhagen, 1819

Individual will, rather than the seemingly hard facts of race or language or natural borders, makes a nation – this was the message Ernest Renan offered in 1882 in his famous address to the Sorbonne, *"Qu'est-ce que'une nation?"* A nation is a daily plebiscite, he memorably told his audience. He also reminded them that for a nation to be a nation, it must have a common past of "endeavors, sacrifice, and devotion." Suffering more than joy unites a people; collective grief is more valuable than a string of triumphs. Yet just as this common past must be remembered, it must also be forgotten.[1] Thanks to a greater scholarly sensitivity to the problems of memory, Renan has recently achieved renewed importance. Yet the kind of memory and forgetting to which Renan referred was very specific; it involved traumatic religious violence: the St. Bartholomew's

---

[1] Ernest Renan, "What is a Nation?," tr. Martin Thom, in *Becoming National: A Reader*, eds. Geoff Eley and Ronald Grigor Suny (New York, 1996), 42–55.

Massacre of 1581 and the thirteenth-century massacres of the Albigensians in the Midi.[2]

Like France, Germany became a modern nation despite a legacy of catastrophic religious violence. It may even be said to have been more scarred than France. Originally a religious conflict, the Thirty Years War laid waste to whole German provinces, especially in the diagonal of destruction from the Baltic coast through Pomerania, Mecklenburg, parts of Saxony, Thuringia, the Palatinate, and Württemberg, with some provinces depleted by half, others by nearly two-thirds of their populations. Similarly ravaged, cities like Magdeburg and Augsburg, Nuremberg and Nördlingen never regained their former luster. Although the complete death toll of the Thirty Years War cannot be known for sure, scholars estimate the antebellum population in the German parts of the Empire at around 16 million people and, at war's end, at roughly 11 million.[3] When measured as a percentage of the population, the Thirty Years War devastated the German population more extensively than the Second World War. And amidst this devastation, the sufferings of the civilian populations proved especially harrowing, as the empathetic etchings of civilian murder in Alsace from the sharp stylus of Jacques Callot attest, and as Andreas Gryphius's poem, "Tears of the Fatherland," bears witness to.

Germany was also a place of catastrophic religious violence for the Jews. This violence began with the devastations of the First Crusade in 1096 and continued through the Rindtfleisch Massacres of 1298 and the scourge of Armleder and his armies of "Jew bashers" from 1336–1339. A decade later, Christian fears associated with the Plague led to killing at a dizzying pace, devastating one Jewish community after the next. Violence against Jews abated thereafter, but hardly disappeared. Between 1350 and 1550, at least forty percent of an estimated 1,038 Jewish settlements in the German lands witnessed either massacre or expulsion. As a result, Jews essentially vanished from most German cities. Significant Jewish communities still flourished in Frankfurt, Worms, Prague, and Vienna.[4] But in the great centers of medieval Jewry, in Strasbourg, Basel, Augsburg, Mainz, Nuremberg, and Regensburg, and

---

[2] Renan, "What is a Nation?," 45.

[3] Johannes Burckhardt, *Der Dreißigjährige Krieg* (Frankfurt am Main, 1992), 236.

[4] Michael Toch, "Die Verfolgungen des Spätmittelalters (1350–1550)," in *Germania Judaica*, vol. 3, eds. Arye Maimon, Mordechai Breuer, and Yacov Guggenheim (Tübingen, 2003),

in countless other cities and towns, absence signaled a history of catastrophic violence.

For violence to be forgotten in Renan's sense, it must first be acknowledged, counted, and mourned, whether as fratricide or as tragedy, in a context that recognizes the humanity of the aggrieved. This recognition is a baseline condition. Yet collective memory easily erases the characteristics of those who suffer or renders suffering invisible, as becomes evident in considering the silence that gathered force after the Holocaust or the complex history of victimhood that marked postwar German memory.[5] These examples also point to another aspect of memory – its relational dimension – the subtle interplay between remembering my victims and forgetting yours.

In what follows, I argue that contrasting histories of memory and forgetting accompanied catastrophic religious violence – among Christians, and between Christians and Jews. The argument turns on three contentions. The first is that a pervasive forgetting followed the violence of the Thirty Years War and remained in place for a century, if not longer. The late W. G. Sebald defined this kind of forgetting, which he called "collective amnesia," as a "means of obscuring a world that could no longer be presented in comprehensible terms," "a tacit agreement, equally binding on everyone, that the true state of material and moral ruin in which the country found itself was not to be described."[6] Sebald told of an amnesia that befell Germany in the last years of World War II and the years immediately after. As historians know, Sebald's insight cannot simply be transposed 300 years back. Yet we can pose the question of how Germans alternately remembered and forgot the violence of their past. The second contention concerns the catastrophic violence suffered by Jews in the medieval and early modern era. Neither Christians nor Jews forgot this violence. In the Christian world, the

2315, 2309; Friedrich Battenberg, *Das europäische Zeitalter der Juden*, 2 vols. (Darmstadt, 1990), vol. 1, 164.

5 From the vast literature on these subjects, see Annette Wieviorka, *The Era of the Witness*, tr. Jared Stark (Ithaca, 2006), who emphasizes that the silence after the Holocaust was not immediate, but instead a product of history. See also Alon Confino, *Germany as a Culture of Remembrance: Promises and Limits of Writing History* (Chapel Hill, 2006); and Robert Moeller, "Germans as Victims? Thoughts on a Post-Cold War History of World War II's Legacies," *History and Memory* 17:1/2 (2005), 147–94.

6 W. G. Sebald, *On the Natural History of Destruction*, tr. Anthea Bell (London, 2003), 9–10.

events that initiated violence, or justified it, became part of a material culture that marked and celebrated the exclusion of Jews – most conspicuously in the form of chapels built upon the ruins of razed synagogues. Jews remembered this violence as well. They recorded the devastations in memory books and recounted them as part of the liturgy. Finally, I contend that these contrasting memories existed in contrapuntal relation. This is surely the most speculative argument, but the importance of bringing the two chords together becomes evident in the transition, circa 1800, to the modern era, when modern nationalism drew from and transformed the possibilities of memory. Christians now remembered and forgot their history of violence. Christians and Jews remembered, if in different ways, the violence between them. But as Germans, at least until the end of the nineteenth century, Jews were only allowed to forget.

I

In the beginning of the Thirty Years War, Lutheran, Calvinist, and Catholic parties mourned their own. By the end of the calamity, they mourned not each other but that so many people on both sides had been killed, and so many cities and towns, "all men's sweat and work and store," ruined.[7] This mourning occurred in the context of an imagined community whose nationness, the "fatherland" of Gryphius, already shimmered through, especially on the Lutheran side, but also more broadly. Etched into the images and messages of newspapers, and into illustrated German broadsides and pamphlets lamenting the duration of the war and the destruction it wrought, this sense of the nation also illuminated the negotiations and final texts of what contemporaries called "a German peace," "*ein Teutscher Frieden.*"[8]

The texts of the Peace of Westphalia remind us that even as Germany was torn and tattered, it was possible to piece together "cultural

---

[7] The translation, here and at the beginning of the chapter, is from George C. Schoolfield, "A Sonnet of Andreas Gryphius: Tears of the Fatherland, Anno 1636," *The German Quarterly*, 25.2 (1952), 110.

[8] See, for example, "Abbild deß hocherwünschten Teutschen Friedens," Nürnberg, 1649, copper engraving. In *Deutsche Illustrierte Flugblätter des 16. und 17. Jahrhunderts*, ed. Wolfgang Harms (Tübingen, 1987), vol. 4, 346–7. Georg Schmidt, "Teutsche Kriege. Nationale Deutungsmuster und integrative Wertvorstellungen im frühneuzeitlichen Reich," in *Föderative Nation: Deutschlandkonzepte von der Reformation bis zum Ersten Weltkrieg*, eds. Dieter Langewiesche and Georg Schmidt (Munich, 2000), 43–51.

artifacts" that in their basic morphology suggested a national frame. This frame depended on peace and the ability to pardon. The peace begins by promulgating a "Christian and universal peace and a perpetual truce" (Article 1). It then commands to forget so that it will be possible to pardon. "That there shall be on the one side and the other a perpetual Oblivion (*Vergessenheit*), Amnesty, or Pardon of all that has been committed since the beginning of these Troubles, in what place, or what manner soever the Hostilitys have been practis'd," states Article II of the Peace Treaty between the Holy Roman Emperor and the King of France and their respective allies.[9] Instead, "outrageous Actions, in Violences, Hostilitys, Damages and Expences, without any respect to Persons or Things, shall be entirely abolish'd in such a manner that all that might be demanded of, or pretended to, by each other on that behalf, shall be bury'd in eternal Oblivion."[10] Forgetting allowed the embers of enmity to cool, but it also marked if by dint of an absence the landscape of Germany. In Lutheran parts of the country, no markers recalling the war were erected; and in Catholic lands, there were only pillars to Maria.[11] For the war as such, for the calamity, the losses, the injustices, the torn families and ruined towns, Germany lacked sites of memory.[12] Between the middle of the seventeenth century and the beginning of the nineteenth, Germany was, as the peace commanded, a landscape of "perpetual oblivion."

A cultural injunction, the insistence on forgetting also had political and religious ramifications. The Peace of Westphalia returned the Lutheran parts of the Empire, except for the Crown Lands and Bavaria, to the status quo of January 1, 1624, and therefore further demanded that the changes that had occurred in the last twenty-four years be erased from memory.[13] The Peace also only recognized three Christian confessions and thus did not extend its appeal to forget to Christian minorities, such as Anabaptists, Mennonites, and Quakers. For Germany's religious

---

[9] *Instrumenta Pacis Westphalicae*, ed. Konrad Müller (Bern, 1966), 103. For the English translation, see the text reproduced in the Yale University Avalon Project: http://www.yale.edu/lawweb/avalon/westphal.htm

[10] Ibid.

[11] Claire Gantet, "Der Westfälische Frieden," in *Deutsche Erinnerungsorte*, eds. Etienne François and Hagen Schulze (Munich, 2001), I, 89.

[12] Ibid., 89–90.

[13] In the Calvinist Palatinate (*Kurpfalz*), 1618 marked the status quo to which the religious constellation returned.

history, the peace was of far-reaching importance. As a result of its reaffirmation of the principle *cuius regio, eius religio (whose rule, his religion)*, the princes of the Holy Roman Empire determined the dominant religion of their state, often expelling populations, such as the Salzburg Protestants, in order to create religiously homogenous zones.[14] At the same time, the state engaged in the social disciplining of its subjects, with no domain untouched, whether school, military, bureaucracy, family, or sexual relations.[15] Yet these processes of enforced religious conformity and social disciplining were never complete, and the peace itself urged circumspection, tolerance. Moreover, curious concessions, cases of belief bowing to history for the sake of reconciliation, riddled the Peace of Westphalia, as later nationalists like Johann Gustav Droysen ceaselessly complained.[16]

The multireligious world of Upper Silesia was, for example, saved by the peace.[17] The Earls of Brieg, Liegnitz, and Münsterberg-Oels, as well as the city of Breslau, remained islands where Protestants could worship; and in the countryside, the Kaiser granted permission to build Protestant churches in the towns of Jauer, Glogau, and Schweidnitz. The "peace churches," as they were called, are monuments not to the war but to the possibilities of reconciliation. A remarkable temple of oak beams with a bell-less spire, the Peace Church in Schweidnitz, for example, evokes a syncretic mixing of Catholic images with Lutheran adoration of the word. Built in 1656, just outside the town walls, the church held more than 6,000 parishioners and soon had to be expanded to a capacity of 7,500. Now hiding from history behind tethered trees and rusted gates of iron, surrounded by the bewildered gravestones of

---

[14] Mack Walker, *The Salzburg Transaction: Expulsion and Redemption in Eighteenth Century Germany* (Ithaca, 1992). For a dated, but perhaps useful entry into this literature, see Helmut Walser Smith and Joel F. Harrington, "Confessionalization, Community, and State-Building in Germany, 1555–1870," *The Journal of Modern History*, 69.1 (March 1997), 77–101.

[15] A useful summary, R. Po-Chia, *Social Discipline in the Reformation: Central Europe 1550–1750* (London, 1989); for the wider context within a history of tolerance, see now Robert Forst, *Toleranz im Konflikt: Geschichte, Gehalt und Gegenwart eines umstrittenen Begriffs* (Frankfurt am Main, 2003), 172–180.

[16] On the nineteenth-century history of reflection on the Thirty Years War, see Kevin Cramer, *The Thirty Years' War and German Memory in the Nineteenth Century* (Lincoln, Neb., 2007).

[17] For an evocation of this world, R.J.W. Evans, *The Making of the Habsburg Monarchy 1550–1700: An Interpretation* (Oxford, 1979).

German families who since the exodus in 1945 no longer live there, the Peace Church of Schweidnitz nevertheless testifies to a remarkable spirit of reconciliation.

There is no such testimony with respect to the Jews. Instead, there are churches built upon the rubble of razed synagogues and markers documenting the alleged crimes of the Jews, the ditches in which they were burned, and the miracles that occurred after they were driven out. In Bavaria, these markers must have seemed especially ubiquitous. One saw them as depictions of host desecration in Heiligenstadt near Altötting, or as a pilgrimage church at Ipfhofen, built in the place where Jews allegedly stabbed the wafer and, when it bled, threw it in a ditch. In Munich, the *Heiliggrabkirche* bore witness to Jewish ritual murder, as it was built upon the ruins of a synagogue of a Jewish community allegedly guilty of the crime. And in Deggendorf, the scene of an alleged host desecration in 1337, the "Jewish altar" of the *Gnadenkirche* informed parishioners that "the Jews were killed by the Christians out of a zeal for justice pleasing to God."[18] The cases extend tediously on. In Passau, Christians constructed the Church of St. Salvator on the spot where once a synagogue stood; the synagogue had been torn down in the wake of the expulsion of 1478, which followed a host desecration charge. In Nuremberg, parishioners built the *Liebfrauenkirche* on the ruins of the razed synagogue in the wake of the expulsion of 1499 (while in the St. Lorenz Church a new stairway was built with Jewish gravestones). And in nearby Regensburg, the New Parish Church stands alienated in the middle of a vast, empty, functionless square, carved out of the rubble of buildings that once housed one of the largest medieval Jewish communities in Germany.[19] In the course of local restorations in the 1980s, it also became evident that many Regensburg citizens of the sixteenth century had plastered the outer walls of their own houses with Jewish gravestones, trophies of the expulsion. While many of these landmarks are no longer extant – the stairs of Jewish gravestones in

---

[18] On Deggendorf, see the groundbreaking work of Manfred Eder, *Die "Deggendorfer Gnad": Entstehung und Entwicklung einer Hostienwallfahrt im Kontext von Theologie und Geschichte* (Deggendorf, 1992).

[19] On Nuremberg, *Germania Judaica*, vol. 3, part 1, eds. Arye Maimon et al. (Tübingen, 1987), 604; for the list, which is far from complete, Romuald Bauerreiss, *Pie Jesu: Das Schmerzensmann-Bild und sein Einfluss auf die mittelalterliche Frömmigkeit* (Munich, 1931).

the St. Lorenz church in Nuremberg collapsed in 1917, for example –
they nevertheless formed part of early modern cityscapes throughout
Bavaria, adorning sacral sites and profane houses alike. Some still exist.
In the Church of St. Kassian in Regensburg, a late eighteenth-century
ceiling fresco details how a miracle happened as the Christians tore
down the synagogue; it depicts shadowy, crafty Jews fleeing the site,
one with a knife used to puncture the sacred host.

If the Bavarian landscape proved especially rich in reminders of the
alleged crimes of the Jews and their subsequent expulsion, it was far
from alone. In the area comprising present-day Baden-Württemberg,
for which we have a close study of the fate of medieval synagogues,
the record is as daunting. Of thirty-four medieval synagogues, twelve
were transformed into secular buildings, and at least nine were made
into churches or chapels; for nine further synagogues, we have no information about how they were used, and for four there is no record of
destruction.[20] Perhaps the most remarkable instances are to be found
along the slim sliver of medieval Jewish civilization that once flourished in northern Baden in the towns along the Main – home, also,
to the Knight Arnold III of Uissigheim, better known as the infamous
King Armleder, who in 1336 initiated the massacres associated with
his name. For hundreds of years, Christians revered him in the village
church of Uissigheim, where Armleder lay buried and believed that miracles emanated from his sepulcher. In the nearby town of Lauda, in
the Chapel of the Holy Blood, built on the ruins of the medieval synagogue, an evocatively painted votive plaque tells the story of how the
Jews stole the host "and brought it home and placed it on a table and
stabbed it with a knife, and the blood flowed plentifully from it."[21] First
made in 1683, then restored in 1791, 1882, and 1956, the plaque also
reminds parishioners that their church stands on the exact spot where
the host desecration occurred. Similarly, in Wertheim the Marian chapel
still now announces that "Anno Domini 1447 is here broken into pieces
and destroyed a *Judenschule* and raised this chapel."[22]

---

[20] Joachim Hahn, *Erinnerungen und Zeugnisse jüdischer Geschichte in Baden-Württemberg* (Stuttgart, 1988).

[21] The votive plaque is reproduced in Hahn, *Erinnerungen und Zeugnisse*, 350. In nearby Gerlachsheim, there is a similar picture of host desecration.

[22] Cited in Hahn, *Erinnerungen und Zeugnisse*, 364.

If concentrated in southern Germany, the heart of Germany's late medieval civilization, the phenomenon of rendering chapels from synagogues was also of a more general central European scope, stretching from Neuss in the Rhineland to Olmütz in Moravia to Neuenkirchen near Vienna. According to the researches of Hedwig Röckelein, at least sixteen of the chapels built on the rubble of torn-down synagogues were dedicated to Maria.[23] Often, a text explained to church visitors that here a synagogue once stood, as is the case in Würzburg, and that it was "to be consecrated and devoted to the Mother Maria," as was the Chapel of "Pure Maria" in Rothenburg ob der Tauber.[24] The text, moreover, did not stand alone. In Rothenburg, miracles accompanied the tearing down of the synagogue, and the new chapel quickly became a pilgrimage site, drawing teeming crowds of the pious, with the throngs of pilgrims so thick that the priests had to hold an average of five masses per day.[25]

Marking the violence of expulsion capped a long-term shift in Christian-Jewish relations. Characterized by a dramatic increase in the proliferation of loathsome images, such as the Jewish pig, the new era spelled the *de facto* and *de jure* marginalization of Jews.[26] This had not always been the case; in the late Middle Ages, Jews often lived in the same streets as Christians, as was the case in Nuremberg, where magistrates complained about the persistence of personal relations between Christians and Jews, especially manifested in gambling, sexual relations, and Christian participation in Jewish wedding ceremonies and Purim festivals.[27] Often Jews lived in Jewish quarters in the center of town, as in Regensburg and Trier. In Cologne, the Jewish street passed directly behind city hall; though soon after the expulsion of 1423, the town

---

[23] Hedwig Röckelein, "Vom Umgang der Christen mit Synagogen und jüdischen Friedhöfen im Mittelalter und am Beginn der Neuzeit." In *Aschkenaz* 5.1 (1995), 32; for more detail, see Röckelein, "Marienverehrung und Judenfeindlichkeit in Mittelalter und früher Neuzeit," in *Maria in der Welt: Marienverehrung im Kontext der Sozialgeschichte*, eds. Claudia Opitz et al. (Zürich, 1993), 279–307.

[24] Cited in Röckelein, "Vom Umgang," 41.

[25] Ludwig Schnurrer, "Rothenburg als Wallfahrtsort des Spätmittelalters," in *Die oberdeutschen Reichsstädte und ihre Heiligenkulte*, ed. Klaus Herbers (Tübingen, 2005), 69–99.

[26] See Gerd Mentgen, "'Die Juden waren stets eine Randgruppe,' Über eine fragwürdige Prämisse der aktuellen Judenforschung," *in Liber amicorum necnon et amicarum: Festschrift für Alfred Heit*, eds. F. Burgard et al. (Trier, 1996), 393–411.

[27] Ibid.

council built its chapel where the synagogue used to be, and between 1450 and 1809 celebrated mass there beneath Stefan Lochner's famous "Altarpiece of the Patron Saints" (now in the cathedral).[28]

Conversely, we do not encounter the first locked ghetto until 1462 – in Frankfurt am Main, as an alternative to expulsion.[29] The yellow badge did not become a common marker until the fifteenth century, in part because the pointed hat had sufficiently differentiated Jews in earlier times.[30] Thereafter, the *gelber Fleck*, or yellow stain, increasingly became part of everyday practice and was codified in the *Reichspolizeiodnung* of 1530, which stipulated, "a yellow ring on coat or cap, not covered over, shall always and publicly be worn by Jews for their identification."[31] In the late autumn of the Middle Ages, the spatial marginalization of Jews began in earnest, with Jews banished to the fringes of Christian society. This banishment occurred in the context of an overall decline in the Jewish population of the German lands, so that by 1600 they comprised an estimated .2 percent of the German population, with most Jews now living in small villages or in the countryside. Christian city dwellers met them, if at all, in the marketplace or on the road.[32]

II

Sites of memory are not synonymous with recollection, though in an age before mass literacy visual markers of catastrophic violence imprinted the consciousness of people far more profoundly than the learned treatise historians are used to citing as evidence. This is in part because of the materiality of markers. Paintings, sculptures, images, or pieces of them, as the sixteenth-century iconoclasts well understood, conveyed, or deformed, something of the divine. They had power and were themselves objects of devotion. As Caroline Walker Bynum has written: "To a medieval pilgrim, theologian, innkeeper, or Markgraf, it was the matter,

---

[28] Julien Chapuis, *Stefan Lochner: Image Making in Fifteenth-Century Cologne* (Turnhout, Belgium, 2004).

[29] *Germania Judaica*, vol. 3, part 1, 347.

[30] Guido Kisch, "The Yellow Badge in History," in Kisch, *Forschungen zur Rechts-, Wirtschafts-und Sozialgeschichte der Juden* (Sigmaringen, 1979), 127.

[31] Ibid., 128, 150.

[32] See Gerd Mentgen, "Die Juden waren stets eine Randgruppe."

the stuff, the object, that was the center of it all – a powerful and dangerous center."[33] Material, especially when it neared the status of relic, was one way to encounter God and to relive the past event in current time. In an age of the mechanical or indeed the electronic reproduction of images, the singular artifact, or relic, has lost much of its power to transfix. But in an earlier time, when "no idea but in things" was already an all-pervasive part of culture, this immediacy struck with more intensity. "To focus on the objects is rather to see the pain and the danger in them," to cite Bynum again: "the blood is still there."[34]

But for memory to stick as collective memory over long stretches of time, it must also be rehearsed, performed, and in this way encoded.[35] The insight is not new. Already in the nineteenth century, Henri Bergson distinguished between memory as recollection and memory as habit.[36] The former can be traced through texts, as when Goethe recalled in *Poetry and Truth* (*Dichtung und Wahrheit*) how in his youth he saw on the Frankfurt Bridge Tower an image of the infant body of Simon of Trent punctured by the awls of Jews.[37] The latter, memory as habit, must however be performed. In the early modern period, celebratory commemorations and holy festivals encoded collective memories, forming habits of mind through ritual. By dint of repetition, formalization of movement and of speech, ritual reinforced memory, if asymmetrically.

The comparisons are again instructive. In the years immediately after 1648, the "Wonder of Westphalia" was widely, if not ubiquitously, celebrated as a great event. Marked by solemn church services, sumptuous court balls, generous banquets, free wine, and spectacular displays of fireworks, these "peace celebrations" were intended to impress. In the midst of a world quieter and darker than ours, the celebrations

---

[33] Caroline Walker Bynum, "The Presence of Objects: Medieval Anti-Judaism in Modern Germany," *Common Knowledge* 10.1 (2004), 20. See also Caroline Walker Bynum, *Wonderful Blood: Theology and Practice in Late Medieval Northern Germany and Beyond* (Philadelphia, 2007).

[34] Bynum, "The Presence of Objects," 20.

[35] Paul Connerton, *How Societies Remember* (Cambridge, 1989), 4–5.

[36] Cited in ibid., 23.

[37] Johann Wolfgang von Goethe, *Aus meinem Leben. Dichtung und Wahrheit*, in *Sämtliche Werke* (Frankfurt am Main, 1986), Series I, vol. 14, 165. On Goethe and the Jews, see Gerhart von Graevenitz, "Das Frankfurtische Karneval: Goethes Bilder des Fremden," in *Der junge Goethe. Genese und Konstruktion einer Autorschaft*, ed. Waltraud Wiethölter (Tübingen, 2001), 25–37.

constituted spectacular events, piercing the routines of the everyday. This was also a world poorer in images, with hardly a picture adorning the walls of even comfortable houses. For this reason, as historians such as Bernd Roeck have argued, the line between the normal and the extraordinary seemed especially sharp, with the extraordinary leaving lasting, profound impressions.[38]

Contemporary descriptions reinforce this sense of grand, vivid, and luminous spectacle, emphasizing its antithesis to the sufferings of war. "The murderous terrible flames/now to the joyous bonfire aims," rhymed Georg Philipp Harsdörffer, "and what in war injured/is now in peace enjoyed."[39] In the period's greatest work of German prose, the story of *Simplicissimus*, first published in 1668, Hans Jakob Christoffel von Grimmelshausen underscored this antithesis by rendering the peace as a victory of God over Lucifer. When Lucifer received a broadside announcing the peace, and heard the "*Gloria in excelsis*" and "*Te Deum Laudamus*" sung in its name, he became so angered that he "rammed his horns against a cliff so that all of Hell trembled."[40] Less imaginatively, if every bit as effectively, local pastors interpreted the war and the suffering it brought as the chastisement of the Lord and presented as evidence the Comet of 1618, which had augured the calamity to come.[41] Easy now to dismiss as superstition, such supernatural explanations at least desisted from assigning earthly blame, and against the vengeful sermons of later centuries, they had the effect of dampening enmity and keeping peace. Finally, local organizers of the ceremonies also paid special attention to children, who it was hoped would value the God-granted peace. In Augsburg and Dinkelsbühl, the children's festival even became the central, if not defining, moment of the peace celebrations.

According to the detailed research of Claire Gantet, there were 204 such "peace celebrations" between 1648 and 1660, of which 181 were in the Empire, and of these 108 in southern Germany, with the greatest

---

[38] Bernd Roeck, "Die Feier des Friedens," in *Der Westfälische Friede*, ed. Heinz Durchhardt (Munich, 1988), 633–659, esp. 635–6.

[39] Cited in Roeck, "Die Feier des Friedens," 645.

[40] Hans Jacob Christoffel von Grimmelshausen, *Werke*, vol. 1 (Frankfurt am Main, 1989), 567–8 (*Simplicissimus*, Book 6, Continuation, Chapter 2).

[41] Roeck, "Die Feier des Friedens," 651.

concentration in Franconia, Württemberg, and Swabia, among Lutherans rather than Catholics, and especially among Lutherans living in the religiously mixed areas.[42] In Coburg and Augsburg, the celebrations became annual celebrations, repeated every year in Coburg until the 1850s, and in Augsburg until the present day. It is, of course, difficult to know what kind of sentiments people felt as they participated in these peace festivals, and it is entirely possible, as in many modern commemorations, that the arrest of daily routine exhausted the emotional response. Yet from detailed studies of communion in late seventeenth- and early eighteenth-century Augsburg, we know that the peace festival counted among the most fervently celebrated holy days of the year, along with Easter, the Pentecost, and Christmas.[43] Leaflets and pictures printed in association with the festival enjoyed special popularity, and many families celebrated the festival with a sumptuous meal.[44]

Celebrations were never integrative in the sense of involving other religious groups – Protestants, to put it simply, rarely celebrated with Catholics. This was true even in cities marked by religious parity, where, far from bringing religious groups together, the peace celebrations shored up the "invisible boundary" of religious denomination. In Augsburg, for example, the celebrations contributed to the internalization of a religious identity that by the end of the eighteenth century "could no longer be separated from the person and belonged," as Etienne François has written, "to the essence of every Augsburg citizen."[45] Perhaps Augsburg represented an exception. Unlike almost all the other cities in the Empire, Augsburg celebrated its "peace festival" not when the peace treaty was signed, but on August 8 – the date in 1629 when Rudolf II expelled Lutheran pastors from the city as the first measure of the Catholic Restitution Edict. But even if we grant Augsburg

---

[42] Claire Gantet, *La paix de Westphalie (1648): Une histoire sociale XVIIe-XVIIIe siècles* (Paris, 2001), 213.

[43] Ibid.

[44] Etienne François and Claire Gantet, "Vergangenheitsbewältigung im Dienst des Friedens und der konfessionellen Identität. Die Friedensfeste in Süddeutschland nach 1648," in *Krieg und Frieden in der historischen Gedächtniskultur: Studien zur friedenspolitischen Bedeutung historischer Argumente und Jubiläen von der Antike bis in die Gegenwart,* ed. Johannes Burkhardt (Munich, 2000), 108.

[45] Etienne François, *Die Unsichtbare Grenze: Protestanten und Katholiken in Augsburg, 1648–1806* (Sigmaringen, 1991), 178–9.

the status of an exception, it must be conceded that in general the peace celebrations were almost exclusively Lutheran and served the ends of Lutheran confessional identity.[46] This may also be true of Stralsund, which belonged to Sweden from 1648 to1815. Here the Lutheran community commemorated its liberation from Wallenstein's siege of 1628 with a yearly church service.[47]

Memory, in Bergson's deeper sense of habit, was thus only extant in a few cities in the Empire.[48] Was the Thirty Years War then forgotten – in the sense that Renan intended the term? This is a more difficult question, for which detailed research remains in its infancy. Yet there are certainly indicators that a kind of forgetfulness descended over the cataclysmic violence that attended the war. According to Konrad Repgen, there were no books written specifically about the Thirty Years War between 1670 and 1748, though subsequent to his counting at least three titles have surfaced.[49] The books that appeared in 1748 were specifically tied to the centennial of the peace, which a number of cities celebrated, typically by minting coins or having odes composed.[50] These books included a Latin-language set of lectures published by a professor at the University of Braunschweig, a catechism-style primer for the schoolchildren of

---

[46] See Gantet, "Das Augsburger Friedensfest im Rahmen der deutschen Friedensfeiern," in *Das Friedensfest: Augsburg und die Entwicklung einer neuzeitlichen Toleranz-, Friedens- und Festkultur*, eds. Johannes Burckhardt and Stephanie Haberer (Berlin, 2000), 218; and in the same volume, Heinz Durchhardt, "Westfälischer Friede und Konfessionelle Erinnerungskultur," 29.

[47] For this information, I thank Dr. Hans-Joachim Hacker, Director of the Stadtarchiv Stralsund.

[48] François and Gantet, "Vergangenheitsbewältigung im Dienst des Friedens," 108.

[49] Konrad Repgen, "Der Dreißigjährige Krieg im deutschen Geschichtsbild vor Schiller," in *Europa im Umbruch 1750–1850*, eds. Dieter Albrecht et al. (Munich, 1995), 210. The first work, pointed out by Repgen himself in an afterword, was Christian Johann Fuestel, *Eine kurtze Erzehlung der vornehmsten Ursachen des Dreysig-Jährigen Krieges... bis auf den Westphälischen Frieden* (Frankfurt/Leipzig, 1736). See also Immanuel Weber, *Lebens-Geschichte, der weyland durchleuchtigst. Chur-Fürsten in der Pfaltz, Friederich des V., Carl Ludwig, und Carl: worinnen die böhmische Unruhe, der dreyssig-jährige Krieg... durch einen gantz kurtzen Begriff annehmlich beschrieben werden* (Cologne, 1693); anon., *Von dem Dreyssig-Jährigen Deutschen Kriege* (Breslau, 1696)

[50] "The Recollection of the Peace of Westphalia," in *1648: War and Peace in Europe: Exhibition Catalogue*, eds. Klaus Bussmann and Heinz Schilling (Münster/Osnabrück, 1999), 430–432. Gantet, "Peace Celebrations," 656, fn. 25 lists the cities and towns celebrating. They include "Münster, Osnabrück, Wittenberg, Aachen, Hamburg, Braunschweig, Amsterdam, Augsburg, Lindau, Dinkelsbühl, Oettingen-Oettingen, Nuremberg, Schwäbisch-Hall, Kaufbeuren, Leutkirch, Lindau, Memmingen, Coburg, Ulm, Fürth."

Augsburg, and a short but serious study of the war.[51] Thereafter, another major work did not appear until 1758–1760, when in the context of the Seven Years War, a Lutheran pastor and schoolteacher, Eberhard Rambach, translated and amended a four-volume work on the Thirty Years War and the Peace of Westphalia by a French Jesuit.[52] Then another two decades passed before further works appeared. It was, it seems, not until the end of the eighteenth century that the Thirty Years War reentered the consciousness of a broader stratum of the population.

This was the effect of Friedrich Schiller's *History of the Thirty Years War*, written between 1790 and 1792, and more decisively of his *Wallenstein* trilogy, staged in Weimar in 1798–1799 and rendered in book form in 1800. For the first time since the seventeenth century, a major author interpreted the Thirty Years War as a religious struggle for "German liberty" with heroic men commanding the stage.[53] Schiller's history followed much of the information contained in the recently published *History of the Germans*, an unjustly forgotten, eleven-volume work from the pen of the enlightened Catholic historian, Michael Ignaz Schmidt.[54] It also benefited enormously from the altered context of the 1790s, when the Empire, as in the early seventeenth century, was in deep crisis, and the possibility of revolution more than just in the air.[55] "In these days we see it crumble/The old fixed form," Schiller wrote in the preface to *Wallenstein* of the 150-year-old peace that followed "thirty woeful years of war."[56] Significantly, Schiller devoted but one page of his

[51] On these three works and their context, see Repgen, "Der Dreißigjährige Krieg im deutschen Geschichtsbild vor Schiller," 193–201.

[52] Guillaume Hyacinth Bougeant, *Historie des dreyßigjährigen Krieges und des darauf erfolgten Westphälischen Friedens*, tr. Friedrich Eberhard Rambach, 4 vols. (Halle, 1758–1760).

[53] On Schiller and Gustav Adolf, see Silvia Serena Tschopp, "Zur Kontinuität von Geschichtsbildern: Friedrich Schiller's *Geschichte des Dreißigjährigen Kriegs*, in *Geschichte(n) der Wirklichkeit: Beiträge zur Sozial- und Kulturgeschichte des Wissens*, ed. Achim Landwehr (Augsburg, 2002), 299–318. Tschopp emphasizes Schiller's reliance on seventeenth-century works based in part on the tendentious pamphlet literature of the time.

[54] On Schmidt, see the excellent article by Michael O. Printy, "From Barbarism to Religion: Church History and the Enlightened Narrative in Germany," *German History*, 23.2 (2005), 172–201.

[55] See the commentary and annotations by Otto Dahn, in Friedrich Schiller, *Werke und Briefe*, eds. Otto Dahn et al. Schiller, *Historische Schriften und Erzählungen*, ed. Otto Dahn (Frankfurt am Main, 2002), 745–787.

[56] Friedrich Schiller, *Wallenstein*, ed. Frithjof Stock in Schiller, *Werke und Briefe*, vol. 4 (Frankfurt am Main, 2000), 15.

History to the Peace of Westphalia, leaving the story of its negotiation to "another person's pen."[57]

No other pen picked it up. The complex stipulations of the peace seemed obsolete in the decade leading up to the strange death of the Holy Roman Empire. And in the wake of the Napoleonic war, it was the nation-tearing experience of the Thirty Years War, not the peace that followed, that interested young intellectuals. Although isolated works of scholarship addressed the Peace of Westphalia, the second centenary of the peace, in 1848, passed without notice, and only one town, Dinkelsbühl, stopped to celebrate it.[58] For a Europe of nations, the non-national peace of 1648 could hardly serve as model.

In the early modern period, in the sphere of literature, a similar period of extended forgetfulness with respect to the Thirty Years War had set in. This claim cannot be absolute, but the fate of Grimmelshausen's *Simplicissimus* may serve as a barometer of the degree of forgetting that occurred. First published in 1668 (but dated 1669 on the front page), the war's grittiest novel was reprinted in 1683 and advertised as "revived and arisen from the grave of oblivion (*Vergessenheit*)."[59] When published again in 1713, the fame of the book had flagged, and when reissued in 1785, it had been cropped down to 180 pages, with its offensive realism trimmed and its rustic edges buffed smooth.[60] Nor was it part of the literary canon. The second edition of Daniel Georg Morhof's *Lessons of German Language and Poetry*, published in 1700, fails to mention *Simplicissimus*, even though the *Lessons* constitutes one of the earliest attempts to place German literature in a European context. In his *Attempt at a Critical Art of Poetry* of 1730, a book programmatic for the style of the early Enlightenment, Johann Christoph Gottsched mentions *Simplicissimus* among pastoral novels "well-known and beloved in their time," but has little else to tell about it.[61] Perhaps most telling is Zedler's massive encyclopedia, the *Großes vollständiges Universal–Lexicon aller Wissenschafften und Künste*, which appeared

---

[57] Friedrich Schiller, "Geschichte des Dreißigjährigen Kriegs," in *Historische Schriften und Erzählungen*, 447–448.

[58] Gantet, "Peace Celebrations," 656, fn. 25.

[59] Volker Meid, *Grimmelshausen: Epoche – Werk – Wirkung* (Munich, 1984), 203.

[60] Meid, *Grimmelshausen*, 209–211; Jakob Koeman, *Die Grimmelshausen–Rezeption in der fiktionalen Literatur der deutschen Romantik* (Amsterdam, 1993), 62.

[61] Johann Christoph Gottsched, *Ausgewählte Werke*, vol. 6, part 2, *Versuch einer critischen Dichtkunst*, ed. Joachim Birke (Berlin, 1973), 474.

in sixty-four volumes between 1731 and 1750; it reports of *Simplicissimus* that "this is a name used in titles of various books as a fictional framework," along with a reference to the 1713 edition.[62] We could extend this list and include the sparse entry for Samuel Greifensohn (the supposed name of the author, whose identity was not discovered until 1834) in Christian Gottlieb Jöcher's otherwise exhaustive seven-volume *General Lexicon of Scholars* (*Allgemeines Gelehrten–Lexikon*) of 1750.[63] There we read of Greifensohn that "he lived in Hirschfeld, and was a musketeer in his youth. More is not known of him, though he wrote various works," including "the *Simplicissimus*, a novel beloved in its time."[64]

That time was clearly another time, and it was left to the Romantic poets to rediscover *Simplicissimus*. Ludwig Tieck initiated the new appreciation, praising in his *Journal of 1789* the style and satirical punch of *Simplicissimus*, especially its ability to portray the "whole of life." Only "now no one reads the old, forgotten book," Tieck lamented.[65] This would change in the coming years. Clemens Brentano, Achim von Arnim, and Joseph Eichendorff read *Simplicissimus* eagerly. So too did Goethe – in 1809 for the first time.[66] A decade later, after the calamity of the Napoleonic Wars, writers and critics would herald *Simplicissimus* as truly German literature, a "healthy, raw, and truthful book," and as an "especially faithful reflection of the horror and infamy of the Thirty Years War."[67]

Finally, in art a similar forgetfulness fell, documenting a significant shift from an intense gaze on the violence of the Thirty Years War to

---

[62] *Großes vollständiges Universal–Lexicon Aller Wissenschafften und Künste* (Leipzig, 1732–1750), vol. 37, 775. Zedler's encyclopedia is revealing for other authors as well. It has a short entry for Andreas Gryphius, but no mention of his "Tears of the Fatherland" or his war poetry. The entry for Martin Opitz is considerably more detailed, but his *Trost-Gedichte in Widerwärtigkeit des Krieges* is not mentioned. Similarly, in the realm of art, there is an extended entry for Jacob Callot, a "famous engraver," but not of his depictions of the horrors of war.

[63] Dieter Breuer, "In Grimmelshausen's Tracks: The Literary and Cultural Legacy," in *A Companion to the Works of Grimmelshausen*, ed. Karl F. Otto Jr., (Rochester, N.Y., 2003), 252–3.

[64] Cited from Johann Christoph Adelung, *Fortsetzung und Ergänzung zu Christian Gottlieb Jöchers Allgemeinem Gelehrten-Lexikon*, 2nd ed. (Leipzig, 1787), vol. 2, 1603.

[65] Ludwig Tieck, *Schriften*, vol. 15 (Berlin, 1829), 338, 350.

[66] Edith Parzifall, *Das Fortwirken des Simplicissimus in der deuschen Literatur* (Berlin, 2001).

[67] Ludwig Wachler, cited in Meid, *Grimmelshausen*, 217.

a blind eye toward its brutality.[68] Nowadays, the carefully staged but evocative etchings of Jacques Callot's *Les misères et les malheurs de la guerre* shapes our visual imagination of the horror of the seventeenth-century war and in particular the often bloody, usually unequal confrontation between soldiers and civilians. But there were other artists, their seeming realism more jarring still, including the anonymous monogramist C. R. (possibly Christian Richter), Rudolf Meyer of Zurich, and Hans Ulrich Franck. A collection of twenty-five military scenes, their order and dating uncertain, Franck's series shave closest to wartime brutality. Against a minimalist backdrop, his etchings place us in the snapshot moment of violence as it occurs, offering little sense of escape or consolation.[69] This angry, despondent mood changed with the peace, as artists from the 1640s to the 1660s etched elaborate allegories of Jupiter's triumph over Mars against the background of a flowering of religion, arts, and letters, with the peasantry returning to the bounty of the land.[70] Even these allegorically sweetened motifs, made popular in countless broadsheets in the mid-seventeenth century, thereafter largely disappear from view. Not until Francis Goya's early nineteenth-century cycle, *Los desastres de la guerra*, which was not published until 1863, would rage again shape how artists rendered the violence of battle, with soldiers freeze-framed as they are about to commit murder.[71]

---

[68] On this subject, see *Von teutscher Not zu höfischer Pracht: 1648–1701*, eds. Franziska Bachner et al. (Cologne, 1998). For music, a similar argument can be made, as the Thirty Years War brought forth a rich harvest of musical lamentations, as well as compositions that expressed longing for peace. The most prominent was Johann Erasmus Kindermann's *Musikalische Friedensseufftzer* (*Musical Suspirations for Peace*) of 1642, which complained of "our dear fatherland, the German nation, virtually inundated with waves of blood, devoid of land and peoples and towns, stripped of population and wealth." As the musicologist Stefan Hanheide writes, "[A]s the Peace approached, and after it, production of these lamentations subsided, in notable contrast" to the Second World War, "which inspired major lamentations even after its end." See Stefan Hanheide, "Musikalische Kriegsklagen im Dreißigjährigen Krieg," in *1648 – War and Peace in Europe: Essay Volume II: Art and Culture*, eds. Heinz Schilling und Klaus Bußmann (Münster/Osnabrück, 1999), 998, 444, 446.

[69] *1648 – War and Peace in Europe: Exhibition Catalogue*, 160.

[70] See Hans Martin Kaulbach, "The Portrayal of Peace before and after 1648," in *1648 – War and Peace in Europe: Essay Volume II, Art and Culture*, 592–603, here 593. See also Reiner Wohlfeil, "Kriegs- und Friedensallegorien," in *Der Krieg vor den Toren: Hamburg im Dreißigjährigen Krieg*, eds. Martin Knauer and Sven Tode (Hamburg, 2000), 349–388.

[71] Susan Sontag, *Regarding the Pain of Others* (New York, 2003), 44. See, in more detail, Bernd Roeck, "The Atrocities of War in Early Modern Art," in *Power, Violence and Mass Death in Pre-Modern and Modern Times*, eds. Joseph Canning et al. (Aldershott, 2004), 129–140.

But Goya remained unique. In Germany, the historical painters, less angry, more willing to render the clichés of heroic battle, took up the Thirty Years War. Daniel Chodowiecki, a Polish Huguenot and lifelong resident of Berlin, was perhaps the first, publishing four prints on the topic in the 1790s. Georg Weitsch followed him, with *Gustav Adolphus outside Berlin*. Presented at the Berlin Art Exhibition in 1800, it was rendered on the order of King Frederick William III to make art serve the "fatherland."[72]

It is, in fact, in the wake of nationalism and in the decades following the Wars of Liberation that Germans began to commemorate the Thirty Years War. Markers and monuments appeared; there were dedications made, chapels built, and crosses erected at the battlefields of Breitenfeld and Lützen. At Lützen, legend recalled that a cavalryman and thirteen peasants placed a rock marking where Gustav Adolph had fallen to his death; in fact, the famous Sweden stone was first inscribed, "G. A. 1632" in 1803.[73] In Perlach, southeast of Munich, a similar "Sweden stone" supposedly marked the place where in 1632 the Swedish general Gustav Carl Horn had fallen. The stone, however, was a product of the nineteenth-century imagination. When a commission of experts examined the matter in 1899, they concluded that Horn, far from being killed in Perlach in 1632, died in Sweden twenty-five years later, and that in any case he lay buried in Stockholm.[74] The 418-meter-high hill called Sweden stone in the West Lausitz has a similar history; before 1832, when it was renamed, it had been called the Gickelsberg. It is true that in Germany one can find an abundance of markers to the Thirty Years War, not the least the nearly ubiquitous Tilly and Wallenstein streets. But these are very likely latter place names, products of the nineteenth, if not the twentieth century. The same may be said of festivals, like the "Wallenstein days" in Stralsund, which celebrates that city's liberation in 1628 from the general's merciless siege; the celebration dates from

[72] Siegfried Müller, "Taking Stock of the Thirty Years War in Nineteenth-Century German History Painting and Genre Painting," in *1648 – War and Peace in Europe: Essay Volume II, Art and Culture*, 658.

[73] The calls for a monument came earlier, however. See anon., "Monument, das dem König Gustav Adolf errichtet werden soll," *Journal von und für Deutschland* 3 (1763): 362–3.

[74] Walter Graßmann, "Der Schwedenstein," in *München im Dreißigjährigen Krieg: Ein universitäres Lehrprojekt*, 1, eds. Gudrun Gersmann and Torsten Reimer. http://www.krieg. historicum.net/themen/m30jk/schwedenstein.htm.

the beginning of the Prussian period, when Stralsund was wrested away from Sweden and Denmark as a consequence of the Congress of Vienna. Other celebrations, like the *Wallensteinspiele* in Memmingen, did not begin until the 1980s.

Whether the Thirty Years War settled in language and was in this way held in memory is more difficult to discern. Over 100 military terms came into German from Romance languages, mainly French, in the period between 1575 and 1648.[75] Perhaps more telling are the terms that speak to the civilian experience of war, with the presence of Swedish troops anchored in topographical imagination. Place names like Sweden field (*Schwedenacker*) denote the locations of buried Swedish soldiers, while Swedish money (*Schwedengeld*) refers to the possibility, found in various folkloric traditions, that Gustav Adolph's soldiers buried their loot. There are, in addition, a number of *Schwedenschanzen* (Swedish fortifications) in Germany, and Sweden streets, where the northern king's armies supposedly passed. The infamous Swedish drink (*Schwedentrunk*), a torture whereby soldiers push a bag of feces and urine down a villager's throat until he reveals the hidden valuables, seems to have remained part of folk memory, passed along via oral tradition.[76] A number of local legends involve small miracles: in Saulgau, the incombustible chapel crucifix that the Swedes could not burn, for example; or in Ellwangen, where in the Palace Chapel an image of Maria struck its Swedish defacer down with a horrible pox.[77] And some "Sweden stones" and field crosses may have been genuine gravesites.

In any case, we may tentatively conclude that in print culture, the Thirty Years War fell from memory, while in popular culture it perhaps found byways. Both propositions will require further research, as the historiography of memory, which has been so fruitful for the study of the nineteenth and twentieth centuries, remains less developed for the early modern period. By the nineteenth century, memory of the Thirty Years War took on new meaning, becoming transformed by the experience of continental-wide war and the emerging sentiment of nationalism. If

---

[75] Peter Burke, *Languages and Communities in Early Modern Europe* (Cambridge, 2004), 130.

[76] Jacob Grimm and Wilhelm Grimm, *Deutsches Wörterbuch*, 16 vols. (Leipzig, 1854–1960), vol. 15, 2385.

[77] Anton Birlinger, *Volksthümliches aus Schwaben*, vol. 1 (Freiburg, 1861), 425, 429–430.

in the eighteenth century, the Peace of Westphalia was the main thing, now the actual war – its destructiveness, its heroes, and the passions they elicited – assumed center stage.

In its embrace of the war and its turn from the peace, the new nationalism proved especially attractive to German Protestants, particularly in Saxony and Prussia, where Napoleonic rule wounded pride more profoundly. A disproportionate number of Germany's early nationalists hailed from this area (the rough triangle between the Elbe, the Oder, and the Swedish Island of Rügen). They included Ernst Moritz Arndt and Father Jahn, Johann Gottlieb Fichte and Jacob Fries, and the poets Heinrich von Kleist and Friedrich Körner.[78] A small group of intellectuals, their views did not represent the sentiments of Prussians and Saxons as a whole, to say nothing of Germans in the Rhineland, or south of the Main, or in the Austrian lands.[79] As historians now understand, nationalism did not fuel the vast and variegated resistance to Napoleonic rule.[80] Yet the early German nationalists set the terms for a discursive shift in thinking about the nation, and while this shift cannot claim sociological depth, it did represent new possibilities. Moreover, its influence on regional elites was more marked than scholars have been willing to admit.[81]

In this context, the rewriting of the Thirty Years War represented a genuine turn, a new narrative that started with the assumption of a lost national-religious unity. For German nationalists, the Protestants in particular, this placed Gustav Adolph back at the center, and his intervention part of a larger religious and national struggle against the enemies of

---

[78] For a social and denominational breakdown of the larger group of nationalist writers (over 300 authors), see Karen Hagemann, *"Mannlicher Muth und Teutsche Ehre": Nation, Militär und Geschlecht zur Zeit der antinapoleonischen Kriege Preußens* (Paderborn, 2002), 151–187.

[79] Ute Planert, "Wessen Krieg? Welche Erfahrung?: Oder wie national war der 'Nationalkrieg' gegen Napoleon?" in *Der Krieg in religiösen und nationalen Deutungen der Neuzeit*, ed. Dietrich Beyrau (Tübingen, 2001), 111–139; Michael Rowe, *From Reich to State: The Rhineland in the Revolutionary Age, 1780–1830* (Cambridge, 2003).

[80] Ute Planert, "From Collaboration to Resistance: Politics, Experience, and Memory of the Revolutionary and Napoleonic Wars in Southern Germany," *Central European History* 39 (2006), 676–705. For more detail, see her *Der Mythos vom Befreiungskrieg: Frankreichs Kriege und der deutsche Süden: Alltag–Wahrnehmung–Deutung, 1792–1841* (Paderborn, 2007).

[81] This point is emphasized throughout Hagemann, *Mannlicher Muth*. See also Jörg Echternkamp, *Der Aufstieg des deutschen Nationalismus, 1770–1840* (Frankfurt am Main, 1998).

German unity. As Kevin Cramer has shown, "Gustav Adolph became the centerpiece of a national narrative founded on the idealization of those Protestant-German virtues that had defied Rome and France for three hundred years."[82] In this sense, the "rediscovery" of the war became part of a religiously inspired interpretation of the German past. Based on Isaac, and therefore on sacrifice, this interpretation posited the suffering of the war as the fulfillment of a covenant between God and his chosen people. "The covenant," in Cramer's words, "promised nationhood; not just in unification but in ascendancy to European and global power."[83]

III

The nineteenth-century way of rethinking the Thirty Years War should not blind us to the significant patches of forgetting that preceded it. No such forgetting took place in the Christian world with respect to violence against Jews. Here there was continuity – but also transformation. The point is not a moral but a structural one. In the context of expulsion, with fewer Jews in German cities and towns, the commemoration of violent episodes became more, not less popular. Our knowledge is most complete for the Deggendorf festival because in the 1980s the Bishop of Regensburg commissioned a study to discern the veracity of the host desecration charge, which had justified the massacre of every Jewish man, woman, and child in Deggendorf in 1337. The resulting work, a remarkable dissertation in theology, concluded that the charge was baseless and laid bare the structure of pilgrimage and piety from which Deggendorf had profited for more than four centuries.[84] For our purposes, especially germane is that the host desecration charge seems to have come thirty years after the massacre, and that it was, in this sense, an invention to justify killing. Moreover, the legend of the host, which retained its form despite being in Jewish hands, gathered force in the sixteenth century; thereafter, festivals in its name burgeoned in the baroque era. As German Christians rehearsed reconciliation, and

---

[82] Kevin Cramer, "The Cult of Gustav Adolphus," in *Protestants, Catholics and Jews in Germany, 1800–1914*, ed. Helmut Walser Smith (Oxford, 2001), 97.

[83] Cramer, *The Thirty Years War and German Memory in the Nineteenth Century* (Lincoln, Neb., 2007), 3.

[84] Manfred Eder, *"Die Deggendorfer Gnad": Entstehung und Entwicklung einer Hostien-wallfahrt im Kontext von Theologie und Geschichte* (Deggendorf, 1992).

concurred in their forgetting of the ravages of the Thirty Years War, more and more Christian pilgrims streamed into Deggendorf to celebrate the miracle. In the eighteenth century, the numbers of annual pilgrims fluctuated between 20,000 and 60,000. For the 400th anniversary of the miracle/massacre in 1737, church authorities tallied a remarkable 140,000 pilgrims. The commemoration thus counted among the most popular devotionals in southern Germany. In the nineteenth century, its numbers abated, but not significantly, suggesting that secularization notwithstanding, the power of the miracle and the allure of the drama continued to attract teeming crowds. The draw, moreover, was anything but local, as pilgrims trekked to Deggendorf from wide areas of Bavaria, Bohemia, and Lower Austria.[85] For Deggendorf, the pilgrimage remained a significant source of economic income well into the twentieth century, finally ending in 1991, when the Bishop of Regensburg put a stop to it.

Deggendorf was not alone, however. The Cult of Saint Simon of Trent, who was allegedly murdered by Jews in 1475, continued to draw pilgrims in large numbers throughout the early modern period and into the nineteenth century, remaining a popular devotional site until 1965, when Pope Paul VI ordered an investigation into the cult and subsequently banned it.[86] The same held true for the cult of Anderl of Rinn, an Austrian village near Innsbruck, where a ritual murder tale, fabricated in the seventeenth century and backdated to the fifteenth, enjoyed considerable popularity. Townspeople even staged renditions of the murder complete with carved figures of blood-lusty Jewish killers.[87] Of such religious dramas, perhaps the most famous was the *Endinger Judenspiel*, which dramatized the "ritual murder" in 1462 of a family in a small town south of Freiburg. First staged in 1610, the play featured a Jewish confession, the occurrence of miracles, and Jews burnt at the

---

[85] Ibid.

[86] Thomas Caliò, "The Cult of Alleged Ritual Murder Victims in the Second Half of the Twentieth Century," in *Ritual Murder: Legend in European History*, eds. Susanna Buttaroni and Stanislaw Musial (Krakow, 2003), 225–245. For a recent review of the scholarship, covering especially German and Italian contributions, see Klaus Brandstätter, "Antijüdische Ritualmordvorwürfe in Trient und Tirol: Neuere Forschungen zu Simon von Trient und Andreas von Rinn," *Historisches Jahrbuch*, 125 (2005), 495–536, and on the resonance of these cults in the seventeenth and eighteenth centuries, esp. 524–8.

[87] Leopoldt Schmidt, *Das deutsche Volksschauspiel: Ein Handbuch* (Berlin, 1962), 304. Stefan Rohrbacher and Michael Schmidt, *Judenbilder* (Reinbek bei Hamburg, 199), 287.

stake.[88] From the surrounding area, the Catholic pious streamed into Endingen to watch the play, and the relics of the slain family became a popular site for pilgrimage.[89]

These examples are drawn from Catholic Germany. In those parts that either became Protestant, or for a time fell under Protestant influence, the recitation of these events had already been snuffed out in the sixteenth century. But memory, like history, has "many cunning passages," and in the early modern period the decimation of the Jewish community remained an act with positive valence and visible consequence. This was especially true at the local level. Sebastian Münster's *Cosmographia*, a sprawling volume claiming to describe the world, contains numerous local histories by humanist scholars trying to augment the luster of their hometowns. First published in 1544, and much expanded by the third edition in 1550, the book includes narrative descriptions of the murder of the Jews in Speyer, Worms, and Mainz during the first crusade; stories of the devastation of the Jewish community in Nördlingen in 1290; and accounts of both the Armleder massacres in Upper Alsace in 1337 and a second wave of murders in 1349, at the time of the Black Death.[90] As the *Cosmographia* boasted superbly etched cityscapes, it also tells us about the architecture of local ghettos – the Jewish towers in Meissen and in Strasbourg, for example, and the *Judenplatz* in Würzburg. With respect to Eger, a Bohemian city now in the Czech Republic, the *Cosmographia* informs us that "there was an old church, called our Lady, which some time ago had been a *Judenschul*," and a *"mordgäßlein* (murder alley), in which the Jews were strangled and beaten."[91]

In the seventeenth century, Matthäus Merian's multi-volume *Topographia Germaniae* served as a similar repository for local knowledge. From its descriptions, we learn about Rothenburg ob der Tauber,

[88] See Winfried Frey, "Das Endinger Judenspiel," *Die Legende vom Ritualmord. Zur Geschichte der Blutbeschuldigung gegen Juden*, ed. Rainer Erb (Berlin, 1993), 201–221. For the genre, Anton Dörrer, "Judenspiel, Endinger, Rinner und Trienter," in *Die deutsche Literatur des Mittelalters*, vol. 2 (Berlin, 1936), 667–717.

[89] R. Po-chia Hsia, *The Myth of Ritual Murder: Jews and Magic in Reformation Germany* (New Haven, 1990), 40. In 1714, the townspeople of Endingen had a new church bell cast, featuring a relief of headless children. *Encyclopedia of Judaism*, 2nd ed., vol. 6. (Detroit, 2007), 403.

[90] Sebastian Münster, *Cosmographia. Das ist: Die Beschreibung der gantzen Welt* (Basel, 1628), 882, 994.

[91] Münster, *Cosmographia*, 837, 1092, 1164, 1314–5.

and how in 1404 a chapel was built on the Milk Market in honor of the Holy Virgin Mary, where before there had been a *"Judenschul"* and a "house of souls." It also tells us that already in 1397, the Jews had been "hunted and then burned alive" on Good Friday, their cemetery confiscated and used for Christians, and their chapel taken and renamed for the Virgin Mary. Rechristened again in 1520, the cemetery and chapel were then torn down in the course of a peasant rebellion.[92] For Regensburg, too, the *Topographia Germaniae* tells us a great deal about local memory. It not only informs us extensively of the Jewish community, "who, along with their forefathers, had been domiciled here next to the Germans"; it also tells of their synagogue, "which was so famous that from faraway places many Jews came here," and of its destruction in 1519 and the subsequent expulsion of the Jews. Moreover, the *Topographia* claims that "there was a stone erected," "where one walks towards St. Kassian in order to memorialize their destruction" (*zum Gedächniss ihrer Ausrottung*).[93] In Überlingen, as the *Topographia* reveals, the citizens commemorated the 1332 burning of all the Jews after an alleged ritual murder with a resolution, incorporated into the town charter and "read aloud every year," that stated "for now and forever one should not allow Jews to reenter."[94]

The Überlingen case suggests an important passage through which memory in the early modern period passed – namely the town charters to which Jewish ordinances were attached. Throughout the cities and territories of a splintered Germany, these Jewish ordinances described in painstaking detail local rules of segregation: where the Jews could live or when they had to leave the town walls, and then how much they had to pay for a day's visit, and whether they had to be accompanied by a guard. Further, they detailed when Jews could sell their wares, where they could worship, and under what conditions they could traffic with Christians. In 1585, the Jewish Ordinance of Hessen-Darmstadt counted as comparatively liberal. It listed thirteen articles circumscribing Jewish worship, the selling of wares, interest on loans, disputations with Christians, Jewish trade, gift-giving to officials, and "disgracing or sleeping

---

[92] Matthäus Merian, *Topographia Franconiae*, 2nd ed. (Frankfurt am Main, 1656), 87–88.

[93] Matthäus Merian, *Topographia Bavariae*, 2nd ed. (Frankfurt am Main, 1657), 87.

[94] Matthäus Merian, *Topographia Sveviae* (Frankfurt am Main, 1643), 192.

with a Christian woman or girl," the latter offense, "to be punished with death."[95] In Cologne, 200 years later, these ordinances continued to define local privilege, which forced Jews to pay a fee for entering the city, to repay that fee daily, to wear special clothes, to be accompanied by a red-suited guard, and then only to specially designated places.[96] Like the rules laid down for beggars and dishonorable people such as executioners, gravediggers, and skinners, these ordinances dyed the fabric of local life with a patterned sense of space, carefully marking the boundaries of separate communities within city walls.[97] They also evinced "an obsessive concern with the avoidance of physical contact."[98] As public law became an internalized order, transgressions polluted, in the sense that Mary Douglas has described, and scratched at the fundamental order of things.

Jews internalized this order, recalling, through recital and ritual, the violence that struck at their community.[99] In Worms, for example, the community recited prayers for the martyrs of the Massacre of 1096 on the seventh day of Passover and throughout the year burned candles in their honor.[100] In Frankfurt am Main, a "second Purim" commemorated the ill-fated Fettmilch Revolt of 1614, an anti-Jewish uprising that ended with its leader, Vincent Fettmilch, quartered and hanged. On the 20th of Adar, shortly after *Purim*, the Jews of Frankfurt heard a Yiddish song, *Megillas Vintz*, which commemorated the revolt.[101] Thick with biblical allusion, *Megillas Vintz* connected the salvation of Esther and the

---

[95] The ordinance is printed in *Judenverordnungen in Hessen-Darmstadt: Das Judenrecht eines Reichsfürstentums bis zum Ende des Alten Reiches: Eine Dokumentation*, ed. Friedrich Battenberg (Wiesbaden, 1987), 66–68.

[96] Shulamit S. Magnus, *Jewish Emancipation in a German City: Cologne, 1798–1871* (Stanford, 1997), 22–23; for Hamburg, see Joachim Whaley, *Religious Toleration and Social Change in Hamburg, 1529–1819* (Cambridge, 1985), 88–93.

[97] Kathy Stuart, *Defiled Trades and Social Outcasts: Honor and Ritual Pollution in Early Modern Germany* (Cambridge, 2000). On the construction of early modern community, see also David M. Luebcke, *His Majesty's Rebels: Communities, Factions, and Rural Revolt in the Black Forest, 1725–1745* (Ithaca, 1997).

[98] Christopher Friedrich, "Jews in Imperial Cities," in *In and Out of the Ghetto: Jewish-Gentile Relations in Late Medieval and Early Modern Germany*, eds. R. Po-chia Hsia and Hartmut Lehmann (Cambridge, 1995), 286.

[99] Yosef Hayim Yerushalmi, *Jewish History and Jewish Memory* (New York, 1989), xxxiv.

[100] *Das Martyrologium des Nürnberger Memorbuches*, ed. Siegmund Salfeld (Berlin, 1898), xxxvii.

[101] Ibid., 46–7.

condemnation of Haman to the more recent hanging of Vincent Fettmilch and the return of the Jewish community to the Frankfurt ghetto.[102] Perhaps Frankfurt was the only major community in the German lands continually to celebrate a "second Purim." Yet some laments composed in the twelfth century for the martyrs of the 1096 massacres survived in the Jewish liturgy and these laments continued to be sung on the Ninth of Av, marking the destruction of the ancient temples of Jerusalem and linking the events in a sacral narrative.[103] Some dirges mention the names of devastated communities, like Mainz, Worms, and Speyer.[104] Others recalled more local and recent events: the expulsion of the Jews from Vienna in 1669, for example. Not all disasters were of Christian making, however, as one dirge lamented the victims of the plague that swept through Prague in 1713.

From extant memorial books, we can surmise that these lamentations played an important role in religiosity. The twelfth-century *Memorial Book of Mainz* became the standard, with many others – like that of Fürth (1592), Trier (1662), and Bonn (1727) – copied from it. By the end of the eighteenth century, memorial books became ubiquitous, with over 150 in Bavaria alone.[105] They often incorporated recent events, like the *Memorial Book of Oberenheim*, which contained descriptions of Jews killed by demobilized soldiers from Louis XIV's Army after the Battle of Nancy in 1698.[106] Others reached deeper into the past. The *Mannheim Memorial Book* included a prayer for those slaughtered in 1349, while the *Memorial Book of the Jewish Community of Minden* listed prayers for those sacrificed in the host desecration persecutions in Sternberg (Mecklenburg) in 1492 and in the Mark Brandenburg in 1510.[107] The lamentations in the German-Jewish tradition of the early modern period never achieved the poetic power of the classics of the earlier eras or of the dirges composed by Spanish Jews in the post-expulsion period.[108] Yet the books ensured the memory of violence. Every year readers recited

---

[102] Ibid., 58, 134, 135.

[103] Ivan G. Marcus, "A Jewish-Christian Symbiosis: The Culture of Early Ashkenaz," in *The Culture of the Jews: A New History*, ed. David Biale (New York, 2002), 463.

[104] Ibid., 464.

[105] Magnus Weinberg, *Die Memorbücher der jüdischen Gemeinden in Bayern* (1938).

[106] *Das Martyrologium des Nürnberger Memorbuches*, xxxv.

[107] Ibid., xxiv.

[108] This was the opinion of Leopold Zunz, *Die Synagogale Poesie des Mittelalters*, 2nd ed. (Frankfurt am Main, 1920), 332.

the names of the murdered, arranged by the towns in which they lived and the violent event that consumed them.[109]

IV

In German history, cataclysmic religious violence, and its overcoming, determined the possibilities of community. On the one side, there was forgetting with recognition of the other. This was the central story of the memory of the Thirty Years War in the early modern period. On the other side was memory twined with disavowal of the other's full humanity – as in Christian violence against Jews. The oppositions are the constructions of the historian, but they also suggest something of what was possible to imagine.[110] One story tells of violence as a scourge and the peace as delivery from it. The other tells of violence as a just act, which can be rehearsed again. In one story, Germans tilled markers recalling catastrophic violence; in the other, they erected them in stone. Among Christians, the causes of violence were forgotten, the insults buried, or at least the attempt was made. With respect to the Christian-Jewish encounter, Christians remembered, reenacted, and ritualized the miracles that accompanied the violence and inscribed the encounter in the "Jewish statutes" of town charters. "The essence of a nation," Renan wrote, "is that all the individuals have many things in common and also that they have already well forgotten some of them."[111] If this is true, then the legacy of catastrophic religious violence enabled Christians throughout the German lands, circa 1800, to imagine community, even a national community, with other Christians, but not with Jews.

But history does not stand still, and the nineteenth century transformed these relationships, arching continuity to one set of memories, while radically transforming the other. Nationalism – not merely the sense of nation – was central to both changes. This is because nationalism attempts, in the words of Clifford Geertz, to raise "settled cultural forms out of their particular context, expanding them into general allegiances, and politicizing them."[112] For the history of Christians and

---

[109] Marcus, "A Christian-Jewish Symbiosis," 464.
[110] Connerton, *How Societies Remember*, 32.
[111] Renan, "What is a Nation?," 45.
[112] Clifford Geertz, *The Interpretation of Cultures* (New York, 1973), 245. Geertz is here writing about the move to national unity.

Jews, this meant raising local traditions of exclusion to a national level and shifting vocabularies in the process. In the course of the nineteenth century, local and religious language ceded to national and political discourses, but slowly, with the coexistence of vocabularies remaining the most salient characteristic of anti-Jewish sentiment. Not until the twentieth century, in the context of war, did German anti-Semitism, as a sentiment widely shared, become predominantly national, political, and murderous. But in the transition from early modern to modern, these possibilities were first thought.

They were thought, moreover, in the context of emerging national-religious ideas, with German nationalists taking up the Old Testament idea of the chosen people and modeling the nation on confessional communities, with political and personal identity one, and boundaries drawn sharp and distinct. Centered on an imagined national-religious community and emphasizing the violence of sacrifice (in the double sense of the German word *Opfer*), this imagined sacred nation, or a secular version of it, would in time fuel exclusionary logics directed with special vehemence against Jews and kindle apocalyptic visions of the nation destined for a final destructive cataclysm.[113]

V

The subsequent story brings us into the religious antagonisms in the nineteenth century; these antagonisms sharpened in the 1830s and again during the liberal era of the 1860s, culminating in the *Kulturkampf*. Initially interpreted in the context of the revolution and the wars of liberation, the Thirty Years War now fell into the crosswind of religious polemics, with hardly an issue – whether the origins of the war, the role of Gustav Adolph and Albrecht von Wallenstein, the trauma of Magdeburg, or the magnitude of the slaughter – left unaffected.

---

[113] The scholarship on this point is now especially rich. See Michael Geyer, "Religion und Nation – Eine unbewältigte Geschichte," in *Religion und Nation: Nation und Religion*, eds. Michael Geyer and Hartmut Lehmann (Göttingen, 2004), 11–34. Greg Eghigian and Matthew Paul Berg, *Sacrifice and National Belonging in Twentieth-Century Germany* (College Station, Texas, 2002); Friedrich Wilhelm Graf, *Die Wiederkehr der Götter: Religion in der Modernen Kultur* (Munich, 2004), 10–132; Wolfgang Altdgeld, *Katholizismus, Protestantismus, Judentum: Über religiös begründete Gegensätze und nationalreligiöse Ideen in der Geschichte des deutschen Nationalismus* (Mainz, 1992); and, most recently, Kevin Cramer, *The Thirty Years War and German Memory*.

Protestant historians and theologians likened the German nation during the Thirty Years War to the biblical Isaac and saw the sacrifice in terms of a national eschatology. The Catholics were not averse to this interpretation but placed the accents differently. Where Protestants, for example, saw Gustav Adolph as liberator, Catholics compared him to Napoleon, a world historical figure eager to tear up the traditional structures of the Holy Roman Empire for the sake of a secular idea. If in the early modern period Germans emphasized the peace, now they underscored the war's catastrophic, indeed apocalyptic qualities. Gustav Freytag, whose *Images of the German Past* (*Bilder aus der deutschen Vergangenheit*) popularized the catastrophic view, claimed that Germany had lost between two-thirds and three-quarters of its population. In his *German History in the Nineteenth Century*, Heinrich von Treitschke similarly asserted that the "horrible war devoured two-thirds of the nation."[114] Adorned with lurid accounts of rape, pillage, and cannibalism, this catastrophic view then found its way into historical novels, patriotic poems, and nationalist songs. The historian Kevin Cramer has recently mapped out this dramatic shift in narration in considerable detail, and he has suggested its importance for structuring German thinking about war well into the twentieth century. Yet for all the historical polemics the nineteenth century brought forth, and the confessional antagonism they engendered, the Thirty Years War remained a national tragedy that recognized the belonging of those who suffered. Indeed, as Cramer argues, it made this suffering into proof of German chosenness, evidence of a special covenant with God.[115]

Christian memory of anti-Jewish violence took a very different turn and evidenced greater continuity with the past. This becomes obvious when we consider the initial reaction to emancipation, which made Jews citizens, and when we consider the possibilities for critical reflection on the violent past.

Jewish emancipation occurred in the context of German defeat and the hope of national rebirth. It is true that the initial discussion derived from a debate initiated by Christian Wilhelm von Dohm's *On the Civic Improvement of the Jews*, published in 1781. *De facto*, however,

---

[114] Cited in Robert Ergang, *The Myth of the All-Destructive Fury of the Thirty Years War* (Pocono Pines, Penn., 1956), 12.

[115] Kevin Cramer, *The Thirty Years War and German Memory*.

emancipation came from Paris. When French troops occupied the Rhineland in 1795, French administrators wasted little time dismantling the special prerogatives of cities. In Cologne, the French commanding general thundered against local intolerance, first of Protestants, then of Jews.[116] By 1797, the French had stripped Cologne of its independent status and declared Jews citizens with the right to reside where they pleased. Over the next decade, Jewish emancipation in cities from Aachen to Worms occurred at gunpoint, and this experience repeated itself as Napoleon's armies occupied, or put under informal control, other parts of Germany as well. While most Germans accommodated themselves to Napoleonic rule, the autonomy of towns and cities crumbled in the process.[117] It was, in fact, by force of arms that the ghettos and endless restrictions placed upon Jews fell. The Rhineland and Westphalia came directly under the rule of Napoleon and his family, but Baden, the Hanseatic Cities, and Frankfurt am Main also felt the pressure of his armies, and this pressure determined the pace of emancipation legislation. In Prussia, military defeat likewise created the conditions for sweeping reforms. Hardenberg's "Jewish Edict" of 1812 remained inconceivable outside of this context; the reform provided Jews with residential rights and occupational freedom; it also made them native-born subjects (*Einländer*) and citizens (*Bürger*), though not without qualification.[118]

Napoleon's armies straddling half the country also conditioned the public discussion. The first phase of this discussion centered on a fulminous tract by a Karl W. F. Grattenauer, *Against the Jews (1803)*, which repeated century-old shibboleths and culminated in the demand that Jews be denied citizenship.[119] Appearing in six editions and 13,000 copies, Grattenauer's pamphlet called forth no less than sixty separate publications, the stream of pamphlets and articles only coming to a halt with strict Prussian censorship.[120] Overwhelmingly anti-Jewish in tone, the debate paid little attention to national arguments. But by 1816, when

---

[116] Magnus, *Jewish Emancipation*, 24–25.
[117] See especially Rowe, *From Reich to State*.
[118] For an introduction, see *German-Jewish History in Modern Times, vol. 2. Emancipation and Acculturation: 1780–1871*, ed. Michael A. Meyer (New York, 1997), 7–49.
[119] Karl W. F. Grattenauer, *Wider die Juden* (Berlin, 1803).
[120] For an astute discussion, see Ulrich Wywra, *Juden in der Toskana und in Preußen im Vergleich* (London, 2004), 155–6.

a second round of discussion occurred, the national rhetoric was decisive, and questions concerning the status of Jews in Germany mixed with a new nationalism besotted by anti-French enmity. Ernst Moritz Arndt, who during the wars of liberation preached "hate of the foreign, hate of the French," proved a revealing transition figure. In 1814, he had opined that "the Jews as Jews do not fit into this world" and constitute "a completely foreign people."[121] This was his theoretical position. In practice, however, he reserved his vitriol for foreign Jews from the east and admonished that they be admitted "under no condition" and with "no exception."[122] For Arndt, the nation rested on a Christian-Germanic basis, and Jews constituted an alien element within it. Yet he abhorred the "severity and horrifying way that they were treated in the Middle Ages," and even now "we may not simply drive them into the ocean or the desert."[123] Instead, he argued, Germans should offer native Jews protection as "German countrymen" and extend to them the "advantages of civil society" commensurate with the interests of the states.[124]

Arndt counts among the first to consider Jewish rights in explicitly national terms, as he grafted a community-based vocabulary onto the nation, which did not yet exist as a political entity. The shuttling back and forth between these two vocabularies was not peculiar to him, however. Instead, it shaped early discussions about citizenship, as these discussions involved the transfer of a series of rights and privileges, including poor relief and the right to practice a trade, from the communal level, where they had been since medieval times, to a centralized state.[125] These were not just abstract matters: they touched on material issues, and these material issues, especially after the economic downturn of 1816, fueled not so much subsequent debate as the popular reaction to it.

The subsequent debate began with Friedrich Rühs's pamphlet, *The Rights of Christianity and the German People*, first published as a

[121] On Arndt, see Hagemann, *Mannlicher Muth*, 262–4; Arno Herzig, "Ernst Moritz Arndt und der Diskurs um die Emanzipation der Juden," in *Ernst Moritz Arndt weiterhin im Widerstreit der Meinungen*, ed. Karl-Ewald Tietz (Greifswald, 2003), 86–99.

[122] Ibid.

[123] Ernst Moritz Arndt, *Blick aus der Zeit auf die Zeit* (n.p., 1814), 190.

[124] Ibid.

[125] In the complicated arrangements of the Holy Roman Empire, for example, there was no definition of an imperial subject. See Andreas Fahrmeier, *Citizens and Aliens: Foreigners and the Law in Britain and the German States, 1789–1870* (New York, 2000), 18.

journal article in 1815. "Every nation that wishes to develop and sustain its uniqueness and worth must seek to remove and expel all alien parts," the Berlin professor and historian insisted, while denouncing the Jews as "a nation within the nation," even a "state within the state."[126] Here the new language of nationalism, first articulated by Arndt, turned inward. Rühs thinks the possibility of expulsion, but balks at the measure. "It would be terrible now if one were to completely expel them or persecute them with violence," he wrote. Instead, he suggested special laws detailing the relationship of Jews to Germans. He also advocated restrictions on immigration and easing the conditions for conversion. The Jews, in this sense, would be "a tolerated nation" (*ein geduldetes Volk*).[127]

For the Heidelberg philosopher Jacob Friedrich Fries, Rühs did not go far enough. A follower of Kant and Fichte, a nationalist with considerable influence on the German youth, not least through the fraternity movement, Fries argued against the "love of humanity" that in the last forty years "had led especially Prussian thinkers, contrary to the sentiments of the people, to be the advocates of the Jews."[128] This elevated sentiment was based on misunderstandings: first, that Christians had unjustly persecuted Jews beyond what was already part of the raw and brutal atmosphere of previous epochs (with Jews more than others often the beneficiaries of protection); and second, a mixing of categories, Jews with Judaism. "We are not declaring war on Jews, our brothers," Fries wrote, "but on Judaism."[129] Like the plague, Judaism was "an atavism of an unenlightened prehistoric era, which one should not limit but exterminate."[130] For the first time in the modern era, an intellectual applied the word "extermination" to Judaism, in explicit juxtaposition to Dohm's vocabulary of "civic improvement."[131] Fries did not intend to kill Jews, but to eradicate their supposedly harmful characteristics.

---

[126] Friedrich Rühs, *Die Rechte des Christenthums und des deutschen Volks* (Berlin, 1816), 5, 32–3.

[127] Ibid., 32–3.

[128] Jacob F. Fries, *Über die Gefährdung des Wohlstandes und Charakters der Deutschen durch die Juden* (Heidelberg, 1816), 9.

[129] Ibid., 10.

[130] Ibid.

[131] Paul Michael Rose, "Extermination/Ausrottung: Meanings, Ambiguities and Intentions: German Antisemitism and the Holocaust, 1800–1945," in *Remembering for the Future: The Holocaust in the Age of Genocide*, eds. Yehuda Bauer et al. (New York, 2001), 731.

Moreover, he employed the word exterminate (*ausrotten*) again in the text and insisted that "this caste should be exterminated root and branch" (*diese Kaste mit Stumpf und Stiel ausgerottet werde*).[132]

The text echoes the nation-making efforts of the French Revolution – which, according to the historian David Bell, implied "an intense political and spiritual union of like-minded citizens."[133] For German nationalists of the early nineteenth century, this "intense political and spiritual union" demanded the unconditional assimilation of Jews and the complete eradication of Judaism. Fichte had already proffered a similar position in his *Contributions to the Understanding of the French Revolution*, published in 1793, where he had remarked in a footnote that it would be necessary "to cut off all their heads in one night and replace them with others in which there was not a single Jewish idea." As this was not possible, it made sense "to conquer their sacred land for them, and send them all there."[134] Fichte wrote these words in his pre-national period; they, therefore, do not derive from German national ideas *per se* and are better understood in the context of the French debate about the difference between human rights (which Fichte insisted on for the Jews) and civil rights (which he thought impossible so long as Jews remain Jews).[135] Yet Fichte transposed his earlier ideas onto the nation in his *The Republic of the Germans in the Twenty-Second Century (1806)*, where he posed the alternative, radical assimilation or expulsion, for Jews as well as for Poles.

Fries's radical position likewise derived from a separation, already evident in the Jacobin phase of the French Revolution, between the claims of humanity and the claims of citizenship. Jews may be protected according to the dictates of the former (humanity) even as they are not part of the community (citizenship). Moreover, the community – in this case the nation – was obliged to protect itself from the allegedly injurious effects of the Jews. Fries urged a halt on Jewish immigration, an easing of the conditions of emigration, closer control over marriage practices,

---

[132] Fries, *Über die Gefährdung*, 18.

[133] David A. Bell, *The Cult of the Nation in France: Inventing Nationalism, 1680–1800* (Cambridge, Mass., 2001), 200.

[134] Johann Gottlieb Fichte, "Beitrag zur Berichtigung der Urtheile des Publikums über die französische Revolution," in Fichte, *Gesamtausgabe*, vol. 1, part 1, eds. Reinhard Lauth and Hans Jacob (Stuttgart, 1964), 293.

[135] The most sophisticated discussion of Fichte and the Jews is to be found in Anthony J. LaVopa, *Fichte: The Self and the Calling of Philosophy* (Cambridge, 2001), 131–149.

banishment from the countryside (where he believed Jewish influence especially deleterious), and strict rules with respect to Jewish residency. Unlike Rühs, who still believed Jews could be "a tolerated nation," Fries thought about the state in purely secular terms and argued that it cannot tolerate "a race in the nation that can never achieve the full rights of citizenship." Not tolerance, Fries insisted, but complete assimilation, and if assimilation cannot be achieved, expulsion. "If they cannot melt with the Christians into a civic community," he wrote, "so their rights as citizens should be annulled, and one should, as was once the case in Spain, forgo protection and send them out of the country."[136] In this way, Fries returned to the late medieval and early modern concept of expulsion, which like Arndt he now grafted onto the nation.

Rühs and Fries represented two strands of a discourse, one Romantic, the other Fichtian, which twined in a series of pamphlets and articles published between 1816 and 1819. The two strands also found their way into a pamphlet written by Thomas August Scheuring in May 1819, and this pamphlet, which argued against the return of Jews to Würzburg, helped ignite the Hep Hep Riots.[137] The first supra-local, anti-Semitic riots in the German lands since the medieval period, these riots occurred in cities and towns and explicitly focused on Jewish transgressions of the spaces marked out as off-limits in earlier periods. We will consider these riots in more detail in the context of anti-Semitic violence in German and European history during the long nineteenth century. Suffice here to note the convergence between the learned debate and popular protest. In this convergence, the heritage of anti-Semitic violence, with its internalized rules of exclusion, came full circle as social memory mixed with modern nationalism and transformed local segregation into a wider discourse. But in 1819, the relationship between nationalist ideology and local violence was not causal. The rioters of Würzburg reacted to the concrete results of emancipation legislation, not to Scheuring's nationalist arguments. Anti-Jewish violence continued to center on the perceived rights of the community to restrict Jews, not on nationalist positions as such; and these communal rights had accrued in the late medieval and early modern era. In this sense, the popular violence of 1819 looked back, even as the elite discourse legitimizing it looked portentously forward.

---

[136] Ibid., 23.
[137] Jacob Katz, *Die Hep-Hep-Verfolgungen des Jahres 1819* (Berlin, 1994), 25–28.

VI

In 1818, Leopold Zunz published "Regarding Rabbinical Literature" ("Etwas über die rabbinische Literatur"), a founding document of *Wissenschaft des Judentums* (the scholarly study of Judaism). Zunz argued that the lure of secular German culture meant the demise of Hebrew literature, and that philology, the patient reconstruction and interpretation of texts, was the key to the preservation of the Jewish past.[138] But when Zunz looked back, he discovered that lamentations pervaded the tradition that he hoped to salvage, and in his greatest single work, *Die Synagogale Poesie des Mittelalters* (1855), he attempted to explain the pleading, desperate tone of these medieval and early modern expressions of grief.[139] To this end, he became a historian, chronicling one after another occurrence of anti-Jewish violence. Even after the Holocaust, with our sense of what is possible in human affairs dismayingly cynical, his sense of urgency is arresting. For Zunz, *Wissenschaft* was a powerful tool of counter-memory.[140]

For German nationalists, however, this counter-memory posed a problem. Precisely that Jews had not forgotten became evident proof that they could never be counted as fully German. This cannot be a full and sweeping generalization, as the nineteenth century was a period of immense contradictions. As a generalization, however, it holds true for crucial German nationalists, especially after the founding of the Second German Empire, which in 1871 granted the Jews full emancipation. And it holds true for the most influential intellectual of the age, Heinrich von Treitschke. In November 1879, he published a famous article in the *Preussische Jahrbücher* entitled "Our Prospects," which touched off the so-called "Berlin Anti-Semitism Debate" of the next two years. The "scars of many centuries of Christian tyranny are deeply embedded," he asserted, and these scars rendered German Jews "in terms of experience

---

[138] Leopold Zunz, "Etwas über die rabbinische Literatur," in *Gesammelte Schriften* (Berlin, 1875), 1–31. On Zunz, see Nils Roemer, *Jewish Historical Scholarship and Culture in Nineteenth-Century Germany: Between History and Faith* (Madison, 2005), 24–46. For the importance and the explosiveness of this essay, see also Leon Wieseltier, "Etwas über die Jüdische Historik: Leopold Zunz and the Inception of Modern Jewish Historiography," *History and Theory*, 20.2 (May, 1981), 135–149.

[139] Zunz, *Die Synagogale Poesie des Mittelalters*.

[140] For this argument with respect to *Wissenschaft* and the historical Jesus, see Susanah Heschel, *Abraham Geiger and the Jewish Jesus* (Chicago, 1998).

disproportionately strange to the European and especially to the German essence."[141] As evidence, he cited Heinrich Graetz's *History of the Jews*, the standard work of Jewish history, as full of "fanatical fury" against Christianity and the "purest and strongest representatives of German essence."[142] A central document of the "second foundation" of the German Empire, Treitschke's article moved in the uneasy grey zone between integral nationalism ("for we do not want that after a millennium of German customs, that a period of German-Jewish mixed culture should follow") and a principled racism ("there will always be Jews, who are nothing but German-speaking Orientals").[143]

The response was swift, especially from Jewish authors. In Berlin, within two weeks of the appearance of Treitschke's essay, Moritz Lazarus delivered a speech entitled "What is National?" in which he emphasized the cultural dimension of the nation, its roots in language and in a subjective sense of belonging, against what he took to be Treitschke's emphasis on blood. Soft in tone, Lazarus's essay was a hymn to the German nation written to a Herderian score. Along with Heymann Steinthal, Lazarus had founded in 1859 a journal called the *Zeitschrift für Völkerpsychologie und Sprachwissenschaft* in which the editors, both Jewish, propagated a cultural understanding of nation as the integration of individual minds into a larger collectivity.[144] Far from homogenous, that collectivity drew its strength from its pluralism.[145] Against the state-centered, academically established journal, *Die Preussische Jahrbücher*, edited by Treitschke and Heinrich von Sybel, Lazarus and Steinthal advanced a cultural nationalism that was an unmistakable progenitor of Renan's daily plebiscite.

It was more of a progenitor than historians have conventionally assumed. In the first order, as we know, Renan's address of 1882 must

---

[141] Heinrich von Treitschke, "Unsere Aussichten," in *"Der Berliner Antisemitismusstreit" 1879–1881: Eine Kontroverse um die Zugehörigkeit der deutschen Juden zur Nation*, ed. Karsten Krieger, 2 vols. (Munich, 2003), vol. 1, 11.

[142] Ibid., 12.

[143] Ibid., 12, 15.

[144] On Lazarus, see Ulrich Sieg, "Bekenntnis zu nationalen und universalen Werten: Jüdische Philosophen im Kaiserreich," *Historische Zeitschrift*, 263 (1996), 609–639; Till van Rahden, "Germans of the Jewish Stamm: Visions of Community between Nationalism and Particularism, 1850 to 1933," in *German History from the Margins*, eds. Neil Gregor, Nils Roemer, and Mark Roseman (Bloomington, 2006), 27–48.

[145] Moritz Lazarus, "Was heißt national?," in *"Der Berliner Antisemitismusstreit" 1879–1881*, 37–89.

be understood against the background of the struggle between Germany and France over Alsace-Lorraine. If the nation is a daily plebiscite, then the people of those provinces would surely have voted for France; as such, they were French. The textual references supporting this interpretation are unmistakable. Renan criticizes a Germanic theory according to which "the right of the Germanic order over such-and-such a province is stronger than the right of the inhabitants of that province over themselves."[146] Moreover, many of the arguments Renan advanced in 1882 he had first put forward in 1871 in a letter exchange with David Friedrich Strauss, like Renan more known for his historical *Life of Jesus* than for his understanding of nationality. In the shadow of French humiliation, and in ire over the loss of Alsace-Lorraine, Renan emphasized that "the individuality of each nation is without doubt constituted by its race, language, history and religion, but as well by something much more tangible, by current consent, by the will of the different provinces of the state to exist together."[147] Yet in the 1882 lecture, a significant thrust of the essay attacks the confusion of race with nation, and this suggests a second, chronologically more proximate context, the wave of anti-Semitism that crested across Europe from the pogroms of Czarist Russia, to the German anti-Semitism debates of 1879 to 1882, to the crisis caused by the vainglorious General Boulanger in France. A further lecture, held in the following year in the Cercle Saint Simon and entitled "Judaism as Race and Religion," underscores this context. Here too Renan argued against a confusion of terms, contending that while Judaism started as a national religion, it had taken on so many different ethnic admixtures over the years that the characteristic was no longer apt. The nineteenth century, he concluded, had been the century in which ghetto walls were torn down and to raise them again would be to impede the progress of mankind.[148]

The connection between German debates, which Renan closely followed, and the formulations of "*Qu'est-ce qu'une nation?*" may, indeed, be literal. According to the posthumous *Memoirs* of Lazarus (admittedly put together by his wife Nahida and Alfred Leicht, a pupil, and thus

---

[146] Ibid., 47.

[147] This letter is reproduced in Ernest Renan, *Qu'est-ce qu'une nation? et autres écrits politiques*, ed. Raoul Girardet (Paris, 1996), 211.

[148] Ernest Renan, "Das Judentum als Rasse und Religion," in *Was ist eine Nation und andere politische Schriften* (Vienna, 1995), 173.

unabashedly laudatory), Lazarus claims to have given Renan a copy of his 1880 lecture, "What is National?" Through Lazarus' nephew in Paris, who handed him the manuscript personally, Renan supposedly replied that he "is completely versed" in the thought of Lazarus and Steinthal and that "the Jewish question, which interests all thinkers greatly, concerns him actively because of the terrible movements, which have in various places broken out."[149] Yet Renan never mentioned Lazarus in his lecture, "*Qu' est-ce qu'une nation*," even though, in the formulation of Lazarus's posthumous memoir, the lecture "is completely based on Lazarus."[150]

But whether or not based on Lazarus, Renan's idea that a nation is a daily plebiscite, a question of will and culture, subjective not objective, was not new in 1882. As Siegfried Weichlein has convincingly argued, it had its origins in a European-wide debate from the 1860s and 1870s about nationality statistics, in which the proponents of a subjective understanding, ranging from the Hungarian liberal Joseph Eötvös, to the German publicist Julius Fröbel, to the Württemberger Gustav Rümelin, advanced a notion of nation remarkable for its affinity to the later Renan. "My people is that which I regard as my people," Rümelin wrote in 1872, "the one to which I feel myself bound with indissoluble bonds." In the context of this debate, the notion of "cultural nation" stood in opposition to objective criteria for national ascription, whether geography, or race, or religion.[151]

The voice of Lazarus and central European intellectuals who argued for a cultural nation based on subjective not objective criteria reminds us that the conventional wisdom, which posits a distinction between a German idea of nation based on ethnicity and race and a French conception based on culture and will, is not entirely tenable, as both conceptions existed within each political culture.[152] Whether culture or

---

[149] Moritz Lazarus, *Lebenserrinnerungen*, eds. Nahida Lazarus and Alfred Leicht (Berlin, 1906), 261.

[150] Ibid., 262.

[151] Siegfried Weichlein, "Qu'est-ce qu'une nation?" Stationen der deutschen statistischen Debatte um Nation und Nationalität in der Reichsgründungszeit," in *Demokratie in Deutschland. Chancen und Gefährdungen im 19. und 20. Jahrhundert* (Munich, 1999), 71–90. Rümelin quoted on p. 78.

[152] Dieter Gosewinkel, "Staatsangehörigkeit in Deutschland und Frankreich während des 19. und 20. Jahrhunderts – ein historischer Vergleich" in *Staatsbürgerschaft in Europa: Historische Erfahrungen und aktuelle Debatten*, eds. Christoph Conrad and Jürgen Kocka (Hamburg 2001), 165–181.

ethnicity was the measure depended, in the end, not just on a national tradition, but on perspective and on politics. For Jews, it also depended on the peculiar legacy of the cataclysmic violence they were asked to forget.

This becomes evident in the second response to Heinrich von Treitschke, which came from the more caustic pen of Heinrich Graetz, and the debate that ensued. If Lazarus had barely mentioned anti-Semitism, Graetz steadfastly defended his evocation of medieval anti-Semitism, "the thousands of bloody, merciless persecutions" – though he denied that they left scars making it impossible for Jews to be Germans. "I was not writing about the present but the past," he insisted, reminding his fellow historian that to forget the past ought not to mean to expunge it.[153] Treitschke's response to Graetz proved telling: "Can such a man, who thinks and writes in this way, count as a German?" Treitschke asks. "No, Mr. Graetz is a foreigner on the soil of the country he was coincidentally born in, an oriental who neither understands nor wants to understand our people."[154] Treitschke further maintained that Graetz advocated a nation within the nation and for this, Treitschke opined, "[T]here is only one solution: emigration, the founding of a Jewish state somewhere else."[155]

The exchange shows us that memory and forgetting were at the heart of the matter, though not so simply as Renan supposed. Within integral nationalist categories of belonging, the erasure of memory, for which forgetting is a euphemism, was not for the minority a question of will, a daily plebiscite, but the *sine qua non* of inclusion. In 1882, many Jewish intellectuals surely felt this and accordingly distanced themselves from Graetz.

Yet thereafter the story takes a complex, if one-sided turn. Thanks to the proliferation of Jewish lending libraries, reading societies and book clubs, Graetz's works, his critics notwithstanding, reached an ever wider Jewish audience, making him the popular nestor of Jewish historiography. This turn brought about and signaled a changing German-Jewish relationship to the persecutions of the past. In the early nineteenth century, during the founding years of *Wissenschaft des Judentums*, Jewish

---

[153] Heinrich Graetz, "Erwiderung an Herrn von Treitschke," in *Der "Berliner Antisemitismusstreit*," 99.

[154] Heinrich von Treitschke, "Herr Graetz und sein Judenthum," in ibid., 125.

[155] Ibid.

historians had pointed to these persecutions in order to emphasize the great gulf between the modern and early modern period; but in the latter half of the nineteenth century, as Nils Roemer has argued, they were more concerned to elicit compassion with the Jews of the past and thus to solidify a Jewish identity through historical memory.[156]

This was a historically important moment for the complex relation between Christians and Jews in Germany. Yet non-Jewish historians of Germany did not take it up, and it would be nearly a century, with two world wars and the Holocaust in the middle, before non-Jewish historians addressed the question of Jewish persecution with anything but an accusatory eye. This is even true of highly reflective works, such as Friedrich Meinecke's *The German Catastrophe*, published in 1946 and perhaps the first work by a historian attempting to pick up the shattered pieces of the past. Meinecke accorded great significance to the Nazi rejection of Christianity, but only one paragraph to the problem of anti-Semitism in the pre-war period, placing the blame for it on the Jews, "who aroused resentment of various sorts."[157] Of the major German historians of the early postwar years, only Martin Broszat had written on the subject directly – in a 1953 dissertation that tellingly remained in manuscript form.[158] But in 1969, Karl Dietrich Bracher published his *German Dictatorship*, a synthetic history that attempted to explain the crimes of the Third Reich not as an accident of German history but as a product of it. And for the first time, there existed a major work that placed the persecution of Jews and the history of anti-Semitism in the center of a synthetic, if pointed, German history as such. Much criticized at the time for insufficiently appreciating the structuring force of capitalism, Bracher's *German Dictatorship* nevertheless illuminated the deep continuities of German history, and helped inaugurate a long overdue change in the culture of history and memory in Germany.

---

[156] Nils Roemer, *Jewish Scholarship and Culture in Nineteenth-Century Germany* (Madison, 2005), 147–148.

[157] Friedrich Meinecke, *The German Catastrophe*, tr. Sidney B. Fay (Cambridge, 1950), 15.

[158] Karl Dietrich Bracher, *The German Dictatorship* (New York, 1970). See the Introduction by Peter Gay.

4

FROM PLAY TO ACT

Anti-Jewish Violence in German and European History during the Long Nineteenth Century

I

Long ignored by historians, the history of anti-Jewish violence has witnessed a remarkable surge in scholarly interest.[1] This new work, which has illuminated both medieval and modern manifestations of anti-Jewish violence, allows one to conceptualize the tradition of violence and to ask questions about its patterns and significance. As we know from the standpoint of an interpretive study of culture, group violence, no matter how appalling, is almost never senseless, but instead expresses meaning and remains for the historian one of the most promising if disheartening avenues into the popular imagination. Similarly, speech said in the midst of violent acts (a specific category of speech act) represents an opening for a cultural history of anti-Semitism that takes seriously both its diachronic dimension and its contemporary context.

Historians are just now beginning to put this story together. Although the history of anti-Semitism is a rich field, it has tended to ignore the problem of violence, and, where it has not ignored the problem, it has tended to concentrate on explaining the causes of violence as opposed to discerning the significance and meaning, in an anthropological sense, of violent acts and words. Until recently, this was even true of major

---

[1] The starting place is John D. Klier and Shlomo Lambroza, *Pogroms: Anti-Jewish Violence in Modern Russian History* (Cambridge, 1992). For Germany, see Christhard Hoffmann, Werner Bergmann, and Helmut Walser Smith, eds., *Exclusionary Violence: Anti-Semitic Riots in Modern German History* (Ann Arbor, 2002); for Poland, see the early and groundbreaking appreciation of the problem, Frank Golczewski, *Polnisch-jüdische Beziehungen 1881–1922* (Wiesbaden, 1981). An adequate study of the problem in the Austro-Hungarian Empire remains a *desideratum*; the same may be said of Rumania.

nation-tearing events, like the Dreyfus Affair. In 1998, Pierre Birnbaum could write in the introduction to *The Anti-Semitic Moment*:

A great deal is known about the Dreyfus Affair: the power of propaganda, the inventiveness of artists and writers, the frenzy of the press, the passion of the politicians, and the extent of the prejudice, which existed even without the institutions of the Republican government. But virtually nothing is known about the streets, the demonstrations, the parades, the marches, the racket, or the burned effigies during the affair. Nothing is known about the vociferous and out-of-control mobs, their screams, their slogans, their songs, or about the intermittent attacks on merchants who were Jewish or taken for Jewish, or about the rage to destroy their shops or break down the doors of synagogues.

The problem Birnbaum discerned is by no means limited to French historiography, even if that historiography had for a long time considered the problem of collective violence without theorizing the place of anti-Jewish or ethnic violence within it.[2] The historiography of eastern Europe is hardly different, though for the Russian Empire and Poland we now have fine studies of the pogroms. Yet even these studies rarely address with sufficient seriousness the symbolic and theatrical dimension of mass violence, interrogating, in William H. Hagen's words, "violence's ritualized forms of staging, the social and cultural scripts it followed, and the messages it conveyed."[3] The situation is still less satisfactory for Rumania, the early-modern Ukraine, and even for the history of the Austro-Hungarian monarchy. Nevertheless, when we bring the new research together, and supplement it with the reports of contemporaries, a new and more comprehensive image of anti-Jewish violence emerges.

What follows is a preliminary attempt to sketch this image across the long nineteenth century. To discern the contours of anti-Jewish violence, however, it is first necessary to place this violence in its early modern context; only then can we trace the transformations that occurred and see its affinity to, but also difference from, the mass murder that

---

[2] See Charles Tilly, *The Contentious French* (Cambridge, Mass., 1986), where the problem goes unmentioned. For the above citation, see Pierre Birnbaum, *The Anti-Semitic Moment: A Tour of France in 1898*, trans. Jane Marie Todd (New York, 2003), 4.

[3] William W. Hagen, "The Moral Economy of Popular Violence: The Pogrom in Lwów, November 1918," in *Anti-Semitism and Its Opponents in Modern Poland*, ed. Robert Blobaum (Ithaca, 2005), 125. See also Hoffmann et al., *Exclusionary Violence*, 8–11, and Helmut Walser Smith, *The Butcher's Tale: Murder and Anti-Semitism in a German Town* (New York, 2002), 165–186.

occurred in the Holocaust. These transformations, I argue, are of three kinds. The first is from anti-Jewish violence centered on the community (the *Gemeinde*) defending its perceived rights to exclude Jews to anti-Jewish violence whose rationale was nationalistic, culminating in the accusation that Jews were traitors to the nation. In European history, this latter claim, which in terms of anti-Jewish violence (as opposed to polemics) emerged at the end of the nineteenth century, harbored the possibility, and soon the reality, of murderous violence. The transition from the threat of murder to actual murder, from word to deed, speech to act, bounded ritual to bloody ritual – this constitutes the second great change in the history of anti-Jewish violence. Throughout much of the early modern period and deep into the nineteenth century, anti-Jewish rioters threatened murder and evoked the massacres of the past, but rarely crossed the threshold of actual murder. By the end of the nineteenth century and certainly by the beginning of the twentieth century, this changed dramatically. Why? The answer is that the script of anti-Jewish violence changed and that these changes had partly to do with the national justification for violence, partly with the more general context of violence in which the massacres occurred. The murderous turn, for which the Kishinev pogrom of 1903 stands as a marker, ushered in a period, first in Russia, then in central Europe after World War I, in which the ritual boundaries of anti-Jewish riots were habitually broken, with mass murder following. The murderous turn was enabled, and then furthered, by the state. This is the third major transition that occurred across the long nineteenth century. Throughout most of the early modern period, and the nineteenth century as well, European states controlled anti-Jewish violence by deploying armed forces. When states proved unable to exert that control, violence of apocalyptic dimension usually followed. In the modern history of anti-Jewish violence, a still more decisive step occurred when states exploited anti-Jewish violence for their own ends. Then the dam of inhibition broke.

II

In incidence and intensity, the anti-Jewish violence was something new, even if in form it represented an archaic mode of protest. At the end of the eighteenth century, anti-Jewish violence of significant moment had not been a central part of Christian-Jewish relations in northern central Europe for a century, arguably even longer. "In the philosophical century [the eighteenth], the bloody persecutions gradually came to an end," admitted Leopold Zunz in his ardent recounting of anti-Jewish violence in *The Synagogal Poetry of the Middle Ages*, written in 1854.[4] For Germany, he could have extended his insight back further still. One of the last major anti-Jewish uprisings had occurred in Frankfurt in 1614. Beginning as a reaction of the guilds against the economic policy of the city council, it soon turned violent, with rioters plundering the Jewish Street. Rather than spiral into a massacre, the Fettmilch Uprising ended with Jews finding shelter in Christian homes and the leader of the uprising, the baker Vincent Fettmilch, hanged on the gallows. A similar event in Worms in 1615 ended likewise.[5] Thereafter, incidences of anti-Jewish violence involving looting soldiers punctured the Thirty Years War, but these are difficult to separate from the extremely common lot of subjects throughout the Empire in the midst of the most destructive war ever fought on German soil. Similarly, a wave of anti-Jewish violence accompanied the Turkish Siege of Vienna in 1683–4, with the most violent episode occurring in 1683 in the context of the Kuruc wars, when soldiers descended on Ungarisch Brod (Hungary) and slaughtered all the Jews of the town.[6] Sporadic incidents of violence occurred in the decades thereafter. We know, for example, of incidents of the plundering of Jewish property in the countryside around Bamberg in 1699; and we know of a similar incident in 1772 in the Kronach area in the Franconian Forest. In both cases, anti-Jewish excesses led to attacks on noble estates and the intervention of local military forces.[7] There are also scattered reports of "an atmosphere of violence" at the time of Holy Week,

---

[4] Leopold Zunz, *Die Synagogale Poesie des Mittelalters*, 2nd ed. (Frankfurt am Main, 1920), 349. Zunz was quick to point out that other kinds of discrimination continued unabated.

[5] Mordechai Breuer, "The Early Modern Period," in *German-Jewish History in Modern Times*, ed. Michael A. Meyer, vol.1 (New York, 1996), 93–94. Christopher R. Friedrichs, "Politics or Pogrom? The Fettmilch Uprisings in German and Jewish History," *Central European History*, 19.2 (1986), 186–228; Friedrichs, "Anti-Jewish Politics in Early Modern Germany: The Uprising in Worms, 1613–1617," *Central European History*, 23, 2–3 (1990), 91–52.

[6] David Kaufmann, "Die Verheerungen von Ungarisch-Brod durch den Kuruzzen-Ueberfall vom 14. Juli 1983," in: *Jahresbericht des Priv.-Gymnasium zu Ung. Brod*, 1894.

[7] Robert von Friedeburg, *Ländliche Gesellschaft und Obrigkeit* (Göttingen, 1997), 174. On these cases, see also Stefan Rohrbacher, *Gewalt im Biedermeier: Antijüdische Ausschreitungen in Vormärz und Revolution, 1815–1848/9* (Frankfurt, 1993), 53–61, who argues cogently against the notion that the episodic violence of the early modern period represented a "permanent pogrom."

and occasionally these tensions broke out into violent "excesses," as they did in Schwabach in Franconia in the years 1727–1729.[8]

The violence of the early nineteenth century was also new in the rest of non-Ottoman Europe, though here significant qualifications are necessary. The first qualification concerns Poland. Catholic ascendancy in early modern Poland came paired with the constant vilification of Jews. In pamphlets, sermons, theology tracts, and sacral art, the Church denigrated the Jews, rendering them a distinct other to a Polish national-religious identity.[9] Moreover, a great number of ritual murder accusations and trials plagued Christian-Jewish relations in the Polish-Lithuanian Commonwealth. Between 1574 and 1787, Polish courts executed some 200–300 Jews for this alleged crime, with the executions often highly public and very gruesome.[10] Perhaps a relation exists between these highly structured and public judicial murders and the lack of popular violence against Jews. But this lack may also be explained by the Polish nobility's protection of the Jews in Poland and by the weakness of cities and towns in the Polish-Lithuanian Commonwealth.[11] The one important incident of anti-Jewish violence in the eighteenth century, the Warsaw Riots of May 1790, focused on precisely this tension between the "traditional" rights of towns and guilds to keep Jews out on the one side and the power of the *Szlachta* and the presence of the Jews in an urban economy on the other.[12] The Warsaw Riots remained, however, an "isolated incident."[13]

---

[8] Rohrbacher, *Gewalt im Biedermeier*, 55.

[9] This story is now told in Magda Teter, *Jews and Heretics in Catholic Poland: A Beleaguered Church in the Post-Reformation Era* (New York, 2006).

[10] Zenon Gulden and Jacek Wijacka, "The Accusation of Ritual Murder in Poland, 1500–1800," in *Polin*, 10 (1997), 139–40.

[11] Instructive is Golczewski, *Polnisch-jüdische Beziehungen*, 22–24.

[12] Krystyna Zienkowska, "'The Jews have killed a Tailor': The Socio-Political Background of a Pogrom in Warsaw in 1790," in *Polin*, 3 (1988), 78–101. Rioters damaged property, but in a highly specific sense of targeting and destroying Jewish residences that actually belonged to the nobility. Some evidence suggests that lower levels of occasional violence bedeviled Jewish-Polish towns, especially during market days, fairs, and Christian holidays. In the town of Opatów studied by the historian Gershon David Hundert, for example, the local magistrate "ordered that each guild have four full flails in readiness. If a tumult arose, a guard was to beat on a drum, and the artisans were to assemble and 'smash the rebels.'" Gershon David Hundert, *The Jews in a Polish Town: The Case of Opatów in the Eighteenth Century* (Baltimore, 1992), 43.

[13] Ibid. Hundert only reports one incident of anti-Jewish violence, a riot in 1639, in which the Jewish cemetery was desecrated.

The second qualification concerns Italy, where since the sixteenth-century Jews had been compressed and confined in ghettos. As the counterreformation deepened, anti-Jewish policies sharpened further, as did the general atmosphere of violence, with physical attacks common during Holy Week.[14] Yet major outbreaks of violence appear to have been less numerous, with the most destructive in the seventeenth century being Padua in 1684, when a mob attacked the Jewish community because of a rumor that the Jews of Buda aided and abetted the Turks. Not until the 1790s did large-scale violence again become salient. Popular riots against Jansenist reforms quickly turned against the Jews in Tuscany and in Florence; in Livorno, they ended in a pitched battle between demonstrators and 400 regular troops.[15] Then, as Napoleon withdrew his occupying forces in 1799, a series of anti-Jewish rampages occurred in which Italians, incited by the Catholic "*Viva-Maria*" movement, massacred hundreds of suspected "*Giacobini*" and stormed the Jewish quarters of a number of towns, including San Savino and Arezzo. The violence also reached Siena, where rioters beat ten Jews and burned them on a pyre in the central square. An account of this massacre, by Enzo Antonio Brigidi in 1882, likely documents the first use of the Greek word "Holocaust" for the sacrificial burning of Jews.[16] But the massacre in Siena was not portentous for this reason – but rather because it suggested the possibility for bloodshed where state authority – in this case retreating French troops – proved fragile.[17]

The major and most remarkable exception to the general tenor of the quiet years in terms of anti-Jewish violence was, however, the Ukraine, where the uprising led by Bogdan Khmelnytsky against the Polish regime in 1648 occasioned the massive murder of Jews. Jewish chronicles vividly describe the massacres, rendering them constitutive

[14] Alessandro Guetta, Michele Luzzati, and Roni Weinstein, "Italien," in *Handbuch zur Geschichte der Juden in Europa*, vol. 1, eds. Elke-Vera Kotowski, Julius H. Schoeps, and Hiltrud Wallenborn (Darmstadt, 2001), 356.

[15] Ulrich Wyrwa, "Sozialer Protest und antijüdische Gewalt: Die Unruhen in der Toskana von 1790," in *Zeitenwende: Herrschaft, Selbstbehauptung, und Integration zwischen Reformation und Liberalismus*, eds. Jörg Deventer, Sussanne Rau, and Anne Conrad (Münster, 2002), 129–142.

[16] Ulrich Wyrwa, *Juden in der Toskana und in Preußen im Vergleich* (Tübingen, 2003), 170; for more detail, Wyrwa, "'Holocaust': Notizen zur Begriffsgeschichte," *Jahrbuch für Antisemitismusforschung*, 8 (1999), 300–311.

[17] David A. Bell, *The First Total War: Napoleon's Europe and the Birth of Warfare as We Know It* (New York, 2007), 216.

for the Jewish experience of early modern eastern Europe. Recent investigations based on carefully tabulated demographic data suggest, however, that the massacres were not as ubiquitous as previously supposed, and that many Jews survived. Still, the total number of Jews killed ranged close to 20,000, half the Jewish population.[18] These massacres occurred in tandem with massacres of Poles, whom the Ukrainians perceived as allied with the Jews, and in Cossack chronicles, the Poles, not the Jews, were singled out and focused upon as the enemy. While traumatic for the Jewish populations, the larger context of the massacres was the conflict between the Polish nobility and the Cossack elite on the borderlands of the Polish-Lithuanian Commonwealth and the inability of the commonwealth to integrate Cossack elites into a stabile political order.[19] Similarly, the Haidamak raids and rebellions plagued Jewish communities in the Ukraine throughout the eighteenth century and culminated in butcheries in 1734, 1750, and 1768. Here too brigandage and borderland conflicts ended in devastating massacres of Poles and Jews.[20] Where the state lacked a monopoly of violence, the threat of brutality and murder hung in the air.

The bloody events in the Ukrainian borderlands contrasted with the relative quiet throughout the rest of Europe.[21] Torn by war in the seventeenth, exhausted in the eighteenth century, Europe also witnessed the rise of standing armies that rendered popular violence significantly more dangerous from the standpoint of the participants. These armies accompanied the growth in the power of dynastic states, a power that came at the expense of towns and cities, the historical home of anti-Jewish violence. The relative quiet was not just a matter of force, however; it also suggested the formation of disciplined subjects and the slow inculcation of the rule of law. The reluctance to externalize anger in the form of violence was a central part of this disciplining and self-disciplining

---

[18] Shaul Stampfer, "What Actually Happened to the Jews of the Ukraine in 1648," *Jewish History*, 17 (2003), 207–227.

[19] Natalia Yakovenko, "The Events of 1648–1649: Contemporary Reports and the Problem of Verification," *Jewish History*, 17 (2003), 165–178. Timothy Snyder, *The Reconstruction of Nations. Poland, Ukraine, Lithuania, Belarus, 1569–1999* (New Haven, 2003), 112–117.

[20] Z. Kohut, "Myths Old and New: The Haidamak Movement and the Koliivshchyna (1768) in Recent Historiography," *Harvard Ukrainian Studies*, 1.3 (1977), 359–378.

[21] The other exception one might consider is Spain and Portugal, which in the context of the Inquisition continued to persecute forcibly baptized Jews. See Jonathan Israel, *European Jewry in the Age of Mercantilism, 1550–1750* (Oxford, 1985), 220–221.

process, and while our understanding of the history of emotions remains in its infancy, one may speculate about the connection with respect to anti-Jewish violence.[22] More prosaically, the ascendancy of territorial states, centered on mercantilist economies, had good economic reason to protect Jewish communities and even encourage settlement. "Between 1570 and 1713," Jonathan Israel has forcefully argued, "the recovery of European Jewry was due to the fundamentally secular pressure of *raison d'État* and mercantilism."[23] Not a change of heart in towns and cities, but a European-wide political shift occasioned the period of relative stability, allowing a limited number of Jewish communities to flourish and confining Christian-Jewish violence to episodic and inconsequential outbreaks. Significantly, Johann Eisenmenger, whose *Judaism Discovered (Entdecktes Judentum, 1713)* was the most scathing anti-Jewish tract of the period, advocated neither the physical harm nor the expulsion of the Jews. A Jewish community sufficiently degraded and meek, he believed, was positive proof of the veracity of Christianity.[24]

It is against this backdrop of relative Christian-Jewish peace that one must measure the significance of the Hep Hep Riots that swept through Germany in 1819. The first major outbreak of sustained anti-Jewish violence in Germany since the expulsions of the late Middle Ages, the Hep Hep Riots constitute a starting point for charting incidences of significant anti-Jewish violence in modern European history.

Let us define "significant" as requiring the intervention of the military to quell. A subjective measure, it reflects the will and ability of states to keep order and protect Jews as much as it reveals the vehemence of popular violence. Yet it is a remarkable if unexplored fact of nineteenth-century military history that European states, including the Russian Empire, regularly dispatched troops to put an end to anti-Jewish riots that targeted Jewish property and people. Taken together, these incidences disclose a pattern that allows historians to see the wide arc of anti-Jewish violence. We can thus begin to connect events of anti-Jewish

---

[22] See, in this context, Edward Muir, *Mad Blood Stirring: Vendetta in Renaissance Italy* (Baltimore, 1993), xxiv–xxv.

[23] Israel, *European Jewry*, 219

[24] Jacob Katz, *From Prejudice to Destruction: Anti-Semitism, 1700–1933* (Cambridge, Mass., 1980), 20–21. Israel, *European Jewry*, 192–3. In her careful analysis of the vocabulary of early modern anti-Jewish texts, Nicole Hortzitz finds little evidence that authors called for the physical harm of Jews. See Hortzitz, *Die Sprache der Judenfeindschaft in der frühen Neuzeit (1450–1700)* (Heidelberg, 2005), 570.

violence in the long and rebellious nineteenth century and to consider the relation between these events and those of the cataclysmically violent twentieth century.

III

The Hep Hep Riots of 1819 erupted in early August and eventually engulfed some forty cities and towns. Economic downturn and the impoverishment of the artisan classes certainly fueled these riots, but economic fluctuations were not new to the cities and towns of central Europe. New was the widespread violence targeting the Jews, and this targeting reflected popular chagrin at the return of Jews to the towns and cities that had expelled them and that had preserved, at least until the Napoleonic Wars, an elaborate set of rules and ordinances governing the movement and practices of Jews within city walls. The Hep Hep Riots thus represented the first uprising in Germany against emancipation, and especially against that part of emancipation that affronted local privilege.

This becomes evident when we consider the remarkable degree to which the rioters targeted specific symbols of a crumbling order of local exclusion. In Würzburg, where the riots first broke out, angry mobs initially targeted the house of the Hirsch family, the first Jews to acquire a residence permit since the expulsions of 1642; the crowd then went after Jewish shops with signs.[25] After the seventeenth-century expulsions, Jews could store their wares in Würzburg but not sell them openly or advertise; when the provisions fell in 1816, the signs became symbols marking the end of the era of exclusion, and three years later rioters targeted them with fervor. The rioters in Frankfurt am Main, who imitated the violence in Würzburg, selected a similarly precise series of highly symbolic targets. On August 10, a week after the Würzburg riots, rioters shoved Jews off the main promenade and attacked Jews in the post office. The promenade had become a symbol of resistance to Jewish integration, especially after 1796, when the ghetto walls had crumbled during a French assault on the city; Jews suddenly enjoyed freer access to the city, with the promenade, until 1806, the city's last

---

[25] Stefan Rohrbacher, "The Hep Hep Riots of 1819: Anti-Jewish Ideology, Agitation and Violence," in Hoffmann et al., eds., *Exclusionary Violence*, 31.

prohibited place. Likewise, the post office had been off limits to Jews; and only a special "Jewish mailman" could bring letters back to the ghetto. After initial skirmishes on the night of August 8, the riots in Frankfurt escalated, as hundreds of men pushed their way into the Jewish quarter, breaking windows and roughing up Jews.[26] Realizing that they could not control the situation, the city magistrates called upon the militia for help, and by the end of three days, the military quelled the riots. Although considerable destruction of property occurred, there were no fatalities.

If the rebellions started in the cities of southern and middle Germany, where anti-Jewish exclusionary practices had an especially long tradition, they soon spread north. The Prussians were quick to quell anti-Jewish violence, but in Hamburg, then home to Germany's largest Jewish community, a more significant outbreak of violence occurred. Like Würzburg and Frankfurt, the outbreak in Hamburg started by targeting symbolic refuges of Christian townsmen – in Hamburg, the coffeehouses that had been banned to Jews until 1798. Young people entered the coffeehouses, demanded that the Jews leave, and physically assaulted a number of them, including one Jewish man supposedly wearing a medal of courage from the Wars of Liberation.[27] After the tumult in the coffeehouses, the rioters stoned Jewish houses outside the traditional Jewish quarter; and only thereafter did the violence expand to encompass the Jews of Hamburg more generally.[28] The Hamburg Senate replied with military intervention, and within a week the violence in Hamburg subsided. Many Jews had, meanwhile, fled to nearby Altona, then part of Denmark, which granted Jews full emancipation in 1814; soon rioting started in Copenhagen, where rumors suggested that the Jews of Hamburg would settle. The military repressed this rioting too.

Did these riots spring *de novo* from an otherwise quiet history of German-Jewish relations? The rioters' focus on communal rights tells us otherwise and suggests instead continuity back to earlier periods of time. This continuity has been worked out in detail by Robert von Friedeburg. In the case of Hessen, he argues, anti-Jewish protest, lodged

---

[26] Jacob Katz, *Die Hep-Hep-Verfolgungen des Jahres 1819* (Berlin, 1994), 47.
[27] Ibid., 60–61.
[28] Rohrbacher, *Gewalt im Biedermeier*, 144–147; in considerable detail, Katz, *Hep-Hep-Verfolgungen*, 57–71.

in a tradition of peasant politics, centered on the community, and this "communal anti-Semitism," as he calls it, reached back into the eighteenth century, deriving its sustenance from local resistance to allowing Jews to reenter towns after centuries of expulsion. Friedeburg is careful not to claim direct lineage, as territorial cities, unlike imperial cities, did not ordinarily possess the right to expel Jews on their own accord.[29] In this sense, the claims made by early modern communities constituted the imaginative grafting of traditional corporate rights onto the problem of reintegrating Jews into Germany's urban spaces. This imaginative grafting placed early modern communities in constant conflict with territorial lords, as well as serving as the backdrop for the emergence of a communal anti-Semitism with an anti-state inflection.[30]

The local issue of reintegration backshadowed the larger anti-Jewish uprisings of the first half of the nineteenth century and provided emotional élan for popular antipathy to emancipation legislation, with townsmen reserving their special ire for legislation that allowed Jews to live where they had previously been forbidden and to participate in communal life where they had hitherto been shut out. To understand the magnitude of the issue, it helps to recall how late many cities in central Europe accepted Jews back into their walls as residents with rights. Augsburg, Cologne, Nuremberg, and Strasbourg did not harbor Jewish communities until the end of the eighteenth century, though, as in the case of Nuremberg, the nearby community of Fürth ensured constant traffic in and out of the city. In the towns and cities of the Lake Constance region, such as Ravensburg, Lindau, Schaffhausen, Überlingen, and Constance, there was not a Jewish presence until the 1860s – a near-permanent consequence of the expulsions following a ritual murder trial in Ravensburg in 1431. In Tübingen, there were no Jews until 1848; in Naumburg, not until 1859; in Rothenburg ob der Tauber, not until 1870; and in Passau, not until the end of the nineteenth century. This list could be easily extended, and not just for cities that became part of the German Empire. Colmar did not readmit Jews until after the French Revolution; there were no Jews in Graz or Trent or Zurich until the nineteenth century; Eger in Bohemia did not have a Jewish community until 1848; Olmütz not until the 1860s; and Budweis not

---

[29] Friedeburg, *Ländliche Gesellschaft*, 171.
[30] Ibid., 189.

until the second half of the nineteenth century.[31] Some cities, like Bremen and Lübeck, had to house Jews at the time of French occupation, but expelled them thereafter.[32] After "liberation" from French rule, the magistrate of Cologne tried to limit the scope of the emancipation legislation that Napoleon had forced upon the city. But after 1815, Prussia, to which Cologne now belonged, did not tolerate this relic of Rhenish exclusion.[33]

The local tradition of *de non tolerandis Judaeis* – this *is what* sent townsmen to the streets. Even in the cities and towns that had readmitted Jews in the course of the seventeenth and eighteenth centuries, a battery of restrictions remained and had come to constitute a central pillar of a communal sense of "we" and "they." The dissolution of these communal privileges, laws, and rights fired the first wave of significant anti-Jewish uprisings in the nineteenth century and bound the larger outbreaks of the first half of the nineteenth century back to earlier forms of communal anti-Semitism. The Hep Hep Riots of 1819 explicitly drew their meaning from this context. In Rothenburg ob der Tauber, for example, the "sworn townsmen" gave public notice that "the local swindlers (the Jews are meant) have to leave the town within eight days; or it will come to a fire."[34] In Fulda, one flyer stated that now that the citizens of Frankfurt and Würzburg have acted to expel their Jews, "so we think it good and should use this opportunity to beat the Jews out of town." A day laborer then told a Jewish merchant that "if the Würzburger stuff starts here, I'm going to split your head open."[35] But rioters came with stones, not axes; they smashed mainly windows, in very few cases doors; they rarely looted and seldom plundered. In the major cities, rioters initially spared synagogues and holy sites. In Würzburg, they killed two people; elsewhere, they spared lives. Even personal injuries remained an exception.

---

[31] The source of this listing is *Germania Judaica III, 1350–1519*, ed. Arye Maimon, 2 vols. (Tübingen, 1987).

[32] Rainer Erb and Werner Bergmann, *Die Nachtseite der Judenemanzipation* (Berlin, 1989), 97–106.

[33] Erb and Bergmann, *Nachtseite*, 108. Shulamit Magnus, *Jewish Emancipation in a German City: Cologne, 1798–1871* (Stanford, 1997), 75.

[34] Cited in Friedeburg, "Kommunaler Antisemitismus, Christliche Landgemeinden und Juden zwischen Eder und Werra vom späten 18. bis zur Mitte des 19. Jahrhunderts," in *Jüdisches Leben auf dem Lande. Studien zur deutsch-jüdischen Geschichte*, eds. Monika Richarz and Reinhard Rürup (Tübingen, 1997), 164.

[35] Cited in Friedeburg, *Ländliche Gesellschaft*, 372.

The rioters played with past forms of persecution, especially expulsion and murder, and this serious play lent anti-Jewish riots in the modern period their particular ability to threaten. Play implies rules, and the specificity of the targets as well as the predictable course of the riots suggests that the rioters operated within a bounded structure.[36] In some cases, leaflets told the rioters where to go and when to show up.[37] Once underway, the rioters did not act mindlessly but at least on the first day stuck to the main targets. Only thereafter did riots become more general and threatening. Typically, young people, schoolboys, and journeymen started the riots and were soon joined by more established and older groups – though in the case of the Hep Hep Riots our knowledge of the social composition of the rioters remains scanty. The rioters had a sense of the legitimacy of their cause, as they were, in fact, defending rights and privileges, and these rights and privileges were central to their own understanding of community. Their sense of right offended, the rioters also expressed outrage against the state, which had forsaken them and their communities.

One is tempted to compare this sense of right to the notion of just price that lay at the center of the moral economy of the crowd, especially as revealed in countless food riots in eighteenth- and nineteenth-century Europe.[38] The Hep Hep Riots bore a family resemblance to these limited protests, with both kinds of riots remarkable for their target specificity, defense mentality, and insistence on protecting the old way against the new. They also rarely became murderous. Like the desperate plea for a moral as opposed to a market economy, the anti-Jewish demand for a return to the "old way" signaled that local power was slipping away, that the rights were in decay, and that a battle was being lost.[39] Yet there is another possible comparison – with the "rites of violence" that marked the religious violence of sixteenth-century Europe and before.

---

[36] On play and rules, Johann Huizinga, *Homo Ludens: A Study of the Play Element in Culture* (London, 1950).

[37] Katz, *Die Hep-Hep-Verfolgungen*, 53.

[38] Thompson, "The Moral Economy of the English Crowd in the Eighteenth Century," in Thompson, *Customs in Common: Studies in Traditional Popular Culture* (New York, 1993), 185–258.

[39] Charles Tilly, Louise Tilly, and Richard Tilly, *The Rebellious Century, 1830–1930* (Cambridge, 1975), 284. Although the authors did not address anti-Semitic riots (a more than curious omission), their characterization of the "reactive form" of rebellion, which "aims for the retention of established rights in the face of a challenge," remains apt.

Table 4.1. *Anti-Semitic Violence, 1819–1870*

Year	Place	Trigger	Riots	Fatalities
1819	Würzburg, Frankfurt Hamburg, Copenhagen	Emancipation	40*	2
1819	Dormagen/Rhineland	Ritual murder	1	0
1825	Werl/Westphalia	Emancipation	1	0
1830	Baden/Hessen/Franconia	July Revolution	30*	0
1832	Alsace	New synagogue		
June/August 1834	Neuenhoven/Bedburdyck	Ritual murder	2	0
1835	Hamburg	Emancipation	1	0
1846	Buchau	Emancipation	1	0
1848	Central Europe	Revolution	180+	2
1866	Bohemia	Social/nationality conflicts	?	
1866	Laudenbach, Franconia	Emancipation	1	0

* Numbers drawn from Stefan Rohrbacher, *Gewalt im Biedermeier* (Frankfurt am Main, 1993) and tabulates incidents of violence, not military interventions.
+ Numbers from Manfred Gailus, "Anti-Jewish Emotion and Violence in 1848," *in Exclusionary Violence: Antisemitic Riots in Modern German History*, eds. Christhard Hoffmann et al. (Ann Arbor, 2002), 50, and likewise tabulates incidence of violence, not military interventions.

This was violence based on conviction, on the sense that "the other" was dangerous and defiling, and not fully human. Intended to purify the religious community, this violence sought to expel if not extinguish the other.[40] As Natalie Zemon Davis has shown, it also bore the markings of ritual, even as it crossed a threshold into full-blown massacre.[41] The subsequent anti-Jewish riots, at least in the nineteenth century, oscillated between these two poles – remaining limited, specific, and bounded, like the riots of the moral economy, but gesturing to the general, the religious, the ethnic, and lethal.

IV

The year 1819 marks the start of a significantly increased anti-Semitic violence with central Europe as its epicenter. Table 4.1 marks out the major incidences of this violence, which until 1881 were almost always

[40] Natalie Zemon Davis, "The Rites of Violence," in Davis, *Society and Culture in Early Modern France* (Stanford, 1975), 152–187.
[41] Ibid.

triggered by the general violence of revolution, issues of local inclusion (i.e., emancipation), and the charge that Jews committed ritual murder. Rarely did fatalities occur. Between the German Hep Hep Riots of 1819 and the French July Revolution of 1830, there were two outbreaks of violence: one following a ritual murder accusation in Dormagen, but not completely separate from the Hep Hep Riots of the previous month, and another an isolated incident in the Westphalian town of Werl. Not until the general disturbances of the July Revolution of 1830 did another wave of anti-Semitic riots break out. Economics and politics motivated most of the German uprisings associated with the July Revolution in France. But in a number of areas, their proximate cause and symbolic targets suggested an anti-Jewish impetus as well. The riots in Hamburg, for example, started out as anti-Semitic riots (and focused, again, on Hamburg's coffeehouses), and there was a discernible anti-Jewish element to the riots in Breslau, Hanau, and Karlsruhe, as well as to those in a series of towns and villages in Hessen. In Franconia and Baden, rioters almost exclusively targeted Jews.[42]

Thereafter, intermittent bouts of regional violence continued to mar the social and political landscape of central Europe. The slow, fitful transition from a feudal to an industrial economy, and from an agrarian to an urban world, constituted the wide frames of these protests. But the proximate causes, the specific grievances, as well as the more precise symbolic targets of the rioters continued to be focused on specific aspects of Christian-Jewish relations, whether ritual murder charges or communal rights. In Alsace, in 1832, for example, a food crisis constituted the general background for the anti-Jewish riots of Ittersweiler and Bergheim, but the incident began when Christian farmers drove their cattle into a Jewish procession meant to celebrate a new synagogue. The riots ended in the destruction and plunder of Jewish houses in both towns and in the intervention of the Army, which resulted in five fatalities and a number of wounded.[43] Two years later, in 1834, a ritual murder accusation in the Rhineland led to considerable violence – first in Grevenbroich in July, then again in the village of Bedburdyck in August. In both cases, there was significant destruction of Jewish

[42] Rohrbacher, *Gewalt im Biedermeier*, 160–161.
[43] Zosa Szajkowski, *Jews and the French Revolutions of 1789, 1830 and 1848* (New York, 1970), 1029.

property, including the Grevenbroich synagogue; and in both cases, it required the intervention of the military to quell the violence. Finally, the specific question of communal rights vexed the local populations in a series of anti-Semitic incidents in the pre-March period. This was true in Werl in Westphalia in 1825, when the violence turned on Jewish inclusion in a local shooters' club; in Hamburg in 1835, when the rioters again targeted coffeehouses that served Jews; and in Buchau in Württemberg in 1846, when the issue concerned whether Jews had the right to vote in local elections.[44]

But these were small incidents compared to the magnitude of violence unleashed during the Revolution of 1848. In the wake of the revolution's sesquicentenary, scholars have gained a richer sense of the "sheer size, multiplicity, and complexity of the events of 1848 on a European scale," as Jonathan Sperber has put it.[45] This sense entails a greater appreciation for the part played by the peasantry and small-town actors, as against an older focus on major cities, with its attendant inflation of the role of industrial workers.[46] Instead, historians now emphasize the range of anti-feudal violence in the countryside, which included subsistence riots, communal unrest, and general revolutionary protest. Often overlooked by historians focusing on the middle-class character of 1848, these smaller "excesses" and "tumults" numbered well over 1,000 in non-Habsburg Germany. They no doubt propelled the revolution forward. But they also furthered traditional demands, especially as they drew from a "moral economy" of immediate grievance, with protesters proving less interested in the political future than in the defense of traditional rights.[47] "Rather than a bourgeois revolution,"

---

[44] Rohrbacher, *Gewalt im Biedermeier*, 161–164, 248–256.

[45] See Sperber's preface to the English-language version of Dieter Dowe, Heinz-Gerhard Haupt, Dieter Langewiesche, and Jonathan Sperber, eds., *Europe in 1848: Revolution and Reform*, trans. David Higgins (New York, 2001), xiv. See also Dieter Langewiesche, "Revolution in Germany: Constitutional State – Nation State – Social Reform," in ibid., 120–144, where this complexity is underscored for the German case.

[46] For the emphasis on local experience and the "heterogeneity" of the revolution, see Christian Jansen and Thomas Mergel, eds., *Die Revolutionen von 1848/9: Erfahrung – Bearbeitung – Deutung* (Göttingen, 1998), especially Jansen's and Mergel's introduction, 7–13. On symbolic politics, Manfred Hettling, *Totenkult statt Revolution: 1848 und seine Opfer* (Frankfurt am Main, 1998).

[47] Manfred Gailus, *Strasse und Brot: Sozialer Protest in den deutschen Staaten unter besonderer Berücksichtigung Preußens, 1847–1849* (Göttingen, 1990), 500–501.

as one historian has recently argued, the events of 1847–1849 can "more plausibly be characterized as the last great rebellion of wide classes on the basis of pre-industrial goals and anti-capitalist norms and values...."[48]

This "great rebellion" is also the most plausible context for understanding the anti-Semitic violence of the revolution. In most areas, exclusively anti-Semitic violence remained rare, except for northern Baden where it became a dominant form of rural unrest, and even here it was motivated by a mix of economic, social, and political circumstances.[49] Nevertheless, in one counting, there were at least 180 separate communities in which attacks on Jews occurred; and in non-Habsburg Germany, there were at least 100, with flashpoints including Baden, Hessen, Bavaria, and Posen – all areas of small-town Jewish settlement where Christians and Jews lived in close proximity.[50] According to Manfred Gailus, the historian who has conducted the most exhaustive study of popular uprisings during the Revolution of 1848, three factors motivated the violence: traditional Christian anti-Judaism often centered on the blood libel, the widespread criticism of Jews as usurers injurious to the local economy, and resistance to Jews becoming equal members of the local community. Like other acts of violence during the revolution, and as with the Hep Hep Riots of 1819, anti-Jewish riots focused on highly-charged symbolic targets and often involved acting out revenge, typically by smashing the doors and windows of houses. Theft also occurred, as greed twined with the righteous sense that the Jews had extorted "the people."[51] Finally, there were physical attacks on particular Jews, though the only Jewish fatalities occurred in Posen, where Jews were caught in the midst of an anti-Prussian uprising.

It was, instead, the threat of serious violence, not only to property but also to persons, that distinguished the anti-Semitic uprisings that

[48] Ibid., 516.
[49] Gailus, "The 1848 Crisis of German Society," in Hoffmann et al., eds., *Exclusionary Violence*, 44–45. Stefan Rohrbacher, *Gewalt im Biedermeier*; and, on Baden, Rainer Wirtz, *"Widersetzlichkeiten, Excesse, Crawalle, Tumulte und Skandale": Soziale Bewegung und gewalthafter sozialer Protest in Baden, 1815–1848* (Frankfurt am Main, 1981).
[50] Gailus, "The 1848 Crisis of German Society," 50.
[51] Ibid., 55.

occurred in the context of the Revolution of 1848, and these threats harkened back to earlier devastations. Manfred Gailus writes:

What stands out in anti-Jewish unrest is the perpetrators' distinctive fantasies of collective violence, and their extremely aggressive threats within the context of the conflict. The rhetoric of anti-Jewish letters and fliers, rumors, and public speeches incorporated a graphic, symbolic language of gestures and often expressed the use of direct physical violence to the point of physical annihilation: bloody revenge for crucifying the Savior, death and misfortune, physical punishment, dismembering adults and children, pillaging, arson, hanging, slitting of throats. Such was the dreadful language of late medieval or early modern pogroms.[52]

These threats were not mere markers of identity or cultural codes in the precise sense of the term. Rather, they were speech acts uttered in the context of violent ritual. They referred not to contemporary politics, democratic or otherwise, but to the entangled and violent history of Christian-Jewish relations. The rioters recalled past memories of persecution and reenacted them, not literally in the sense of killing again, but figuratively in the sense of rehearsing a murderous drama.

The drama, or serious play, had consequences for both sets of primary actors – for both Christian rioters and the Jews in danger. First, there is the emotional dimension of serious play, the unique quality of yelled speech and bodily assault that makes it difficult to imagine the active participants as not being in a state of emotional arousal, of, at the moment, not fully and with the force of their bodies believing in what they were saying and doing. Put plainly, fighting for a cause does not just derive from a thing, it causes belief in it. Second, speech acts such as "Jews out" or "beat the Jews to death" forged a momentary kinship of rioters and sympathizers, who were bound in a collective denial that Jews belonged to their community. This ritual exclusion occurred, moreover, just as Jews were fighting for civil rights and political inclusion. Violence, in this sense, became part of a public struggle for what community meant and how rights and privileges would be defined.

These questions of community cut to the central issue dividing Christians and Jews in the nineteenth century. The evidence for this comes not only from anti-Semitic violence during the Revolution of 1848, but also

[52] Ibid., 56.

from one of the most popular petitions of the mid-nineteenth century. In Bavaria in December 1849, the lower house of parliament passed a bill granting equal rights to Christians and Jews and immediately faced a groundswell movement of massive proportions. According to the research of James Harris, there were at least 552 separate petitions from 1,762 Bavarian localities. The petitions made it clear that the Christians in Bavaria feared the results of Jews being allowed to become full-fledged members of their communities and that they would no longer have the status of foreigners. Many and variegated reasons fueled this fear, with economic, political, and cultural motivations mixed. But as Harris underscores, "anti-Semitism was the most important," and this anti-Semitism was historically rooted, both thematically and in terms of form.[53] It was anchored thematically because the petitions emphasized old grievances about how Jewish business practices impoverished the local population, and about how Jews hated Christians. Harris sees this anti-Jewish animosity as having developed new forms in opposition to enlightened efforts at Jewish integration; for this reason, he insists on the term anti-Semitism, which Wilhelm Marr would not coin until 1879.[54] Although religious in inflection, the anti-Semitism that inhered in the Bavarian petitions mainly drew its venom from peasant and small-town bitterness over the results of Jewish emancipation. The anti-Semitic petitions were rooted in terms of form because "the overwhelming majority of the petitions were communal rather than personal in nature," and "the communities perceived the central government as infringing on their central rights."[55] Concretely, these "central rights," as articulated in 140 separate petitions, involved the communal privilege, extant from the ancient regime, to veto the admission of Jews to their hometowns.[56] They also involved the question of Jewish participation in the traditional rights of communities, and these most often concerned usage of common land and wood. Not surprisingly, the last local uprising in pre-unification Germany, which was of sufficient gravity as to require military intervention, occurred in the small town of Laudenbach in

[53] James F. Harris, *The People Speak!: Anti-Semitism and Emancipation in Nineteenth-Century Bavaria* (Ann Arbor, 1994), 2, 214.
[54] Ibid., 214.
[55] Ibid., 2.
[56] Ibid., 140.

Franconia in 1866 and turned centrally on just such questions of communal equality.[57]

V

A powerful tradition of liberal historiography has focused on the explicitly political dimensions of anti-Semitism at the turn of the century, seeing it in the context of a brief but portentous flare of populist politics. Within this tradition, debate turned on the continuities linking the political manifestation of central European anti-Semitism in the late nineteenth century to the genocidal dynamic of the twentieth. This link constituted one set of questions. Another concerned the form anti-Semitism took. Political cultures, historians argued, encouraged either archaic or modern forms of anti-Semitism; the former lead to pogroms, the latter to the Holocaust. In schematic terms, France and Austria witnessed especially virulent forms of political anti-Semitism, but this anti-Semitism did not lead directly to the Holocaust. In the Russian Empire, by contrast, archaic forms of anti-Semitism prevailed. Yet it was in Germany, marked by a weak anti-Semitic movement, that the Holocaust emerged, and this fact has strongly suggested a tenuous connection between political anti-Semitism prior to World War I and the anti-Semitism of the Nazi period. Shulamit Volkov's "Anti-Semitism as Cultural Code" may be seen as an attempt to solve this paradox by recognizing that by the 1890s political anti-Semitism had already plunged into disarray while shifting the burden of continuity to political culture more generally. In any case, the decisive chronological marker for the revival of a more widespread radical anti-Semitism is placed later. Most historians then argue that the new quality of anti-Semitism in World War I became decisive or that anti-Semitism remained a marginal factor in Hitler's rise to power; and only in the Third Reich did Germans learn how to be anti-Semites. Even then, popular forms of violence are not central to the story. The riots of Crystal Night, it is maintained (following the Germany Reports of the Social Democratic Party), were "severely

---

[57] James F. Harris, "Bavarians and Jews in Conflict in 1866: Neighbors and Enemies," *The Yearbook of the Leo Baeck Institute*, 32 (1987), 103–119. A second riot in nearby Wiesenfeld, while equally threatening, did not result in military intervention.

criticized by the majority of the German people."[58] Moreover, the grim violence of the Holocaust occurred in the east, far from the view of ordinary Germans, even if, in the last analysis, ordinary men carried it out. Decisive for this line of reasoning, which minimizes anti-Semitic violence in the explanation of the Holocaust, is the concentration on political history, or at least political culture, and on the national parameters of anti-Semitic politics.

But if we consider popular violence as symbolic acts, and set these acts within a transnational frame, then the landscape looks very different, with the years 1880 to 1900 riven with popular violence directed against Jews and the violence stretching in a band from the Russian Empire through the lands of the Habsburg Monarchy to the German Empire and France. When taken together, the dimensions of this violence are significant, occurring in two major waves, the first from 1881 to 1884, the second between 1898 and 1903. A third wave, starting with the destructive pogrom of Kishinev in 1903 and continuing through the far bloodier massacres of Jews that occurred during the Revolution of 1905, remained confined to the Russian Empire. Table 4.2 documents outbreaks in continental Europe of anti-Semitic violence between the pogroms of Elisavetgrad and Kishinev that were of sufficient moment as to necessitate military intervention; it also underscores the major waves of violence and suggests their transnational connections across Europe. Furthermore, the table suggests the mixing of archaic and modern elements, with ritual murder accusations and the traditional violence of Easter persisting as triggering events alongside the increasing incidents of labor disputes and problems centered on nationality and the nation-state. Finally, the table shows that although outbreaks often involved many thousands of rioters, fatalities remained rare, with most riots remaining ritually bounded.

The first wave of violence began in 1881, when urban pogroms in southern Russia and the Ukraine spilled out into the towns and villages; in all, there were over 250 separate outbreaks of violence, directly affecting some 60,000 Jewish families, with 20,000 families rendered homeless, and many beaten and injured. According to various estimates, as

---

[58] Cited in Wolfgang Benz, "The November Pogrom of 1938: Participation, Applause, Disapproval," in Hoffmann et al., eds., *Exclusionary Violence*, 147.

Table 4.2. *Anti-Semitic Violence between the Pogroms of Elisavetgrad and Kishinev*

Year	Place	Trigger	Riots	Fatalities
1881	Elisavetgrad	Ritual murder	250	ca. 50
1881	Pomerania	Synagogue fire	30	0
1881	Warsaw	Church fire	1	0
1882	Balta (Podalia)	Easter week		
1882	Tisza-Eszlar (Hungary)	Ritual murder	?	0
1883	Tisza-Eszlar	Ritual murder trial		
1883	Ekaterinoslav			
1884	Nizhnii Novgorod	Ritual murder	1	yes
1884	Neustettin	Synagogue fire trial	1	0
1884	Galicia (Borysław Wars)	Fight over debt	2	0
1885	Brusturoasa (Rumania)	Land ownership	1	yes
1891	Xanten/Rhineland	Ritual murder	ca. 15	0
1891	Corfu	Ritual murder		
1892	Lodz	May day/labor strikes	1	0
1892	Iuzovka (Donbass)	Cholora measures	1	
1893	Kolin/Czech.	Ritual murder	3	0
1897	Pilsen/Prague	Language decrees	6	0
1897	Schodnica, Galicia	Labor Unrest/Pentecost	1	1
1897	Bukarest	Jews in the Army	1 (?)	
1898	France	Dreyfus Affair	30	2
1898	Western Galicia	Social/electioneering	32	0
1899	Nachod/Czech.	Ritual murder/labor	1	0
1899	Nikolajew am Bug	Easter week	1	0
1899	Jassy/Rum.			
1899	Prague/Holleschau	Ritual murder/Badeni	ca. 15	0
1900	Konitz/West Prussia	Ritual murder	30	0
1900	Odessa	Soldiers en route	3	yes
1900	Dwinsk (Kowno)	Religious agitation	7	yes
1902	Czsestochowa	Market conflict	1	0
1902	Lvov	Labor dispute	1	0
1903	Kishinev	Ritual murder	1	47

many as 225 women were raped and forty Jews killed.[59] Triggered by a ritual murder accusation during Holy Week, the pogroms of 1881 represented an explosion of the annual tension that had long bedeviled Christian-Jewish relations; they were not, as previous generations of historians assumed, planned and instigated by the Czarist government.

[59] Klier and Lambroza, *Pogroms*, 328. I. Michael Aronson, *Troubled Waters: The Origins of the 1881 Anti-Jewish Pogroms in Russia* (Pittsburgh, 1990), 61.

Pogroms, in fact, were comparatively new to this part of the world. The early modern killings of Jews in the Ukraine – the Kmelnytsky massacres of the seventeenth century and the Haidamak slaughters of the eighteenth – involved borderland conflicts in which Jews were not the only, or even the primary, victims. But 1881, to cite John D. Klier, "reversed the model of past episodes of violence in East Europe" with "pogrom violence directed primarily against Jews."[60] In the nineteenth century, those pogroms that existed remained confined to the new city of Odessa, a hotbed of multi-cultural competition and conflict, which in 1821, 1849, 1859, and 1871 witnessed significant anti-Jewish violence, more often of ethnic Greek than of ethnic Russian origin. Each time the violence started during Holy Week and involved brawling and the damage of property. Absent was the cold-blooded murder of Jews; instead, the ritual remained bounded, reluctant to cross a murderous threshold.[61] The pogroms of the early 1880s, by contrast, crossed this threshold, even if by twentieth-century standards the scale of violence remained limited. And in this crossing lay their significance. In fact, they seemed to become more violent with ritual recurrence. The first "anniversary" of Elisavetgrad was marked during Easter 1882 by a pogrom in Balta (Podalia Province) that was, according to the historians John D. Klier and Shlomo Lambroza, "notorious for the brutality and destructiveness of the *pogromshchiki*." Then there was a violent outbreak at Ekaterinoslav in 1883, marking the second anniversary. The third, in 1884, was distinguished by a pogrom in Nizhnii-Novgorod that turned out to be an "especially vicious one, with its victims dispatched with axes and thrown from rooftops."[62]

The murderous, threshold-crossing violence of the pogroms unleashed a wave of emigration, with large numbers of refugees emigrating to the United States and a smaller number fleeing to the German and Austro-Hungarian Empires. In the German Empire, foreign Jews counted no more than 22,000 by 1890; similarly in the Habsburg Empire, large-scale immigration proved more phantom than reality. Yet in both Empires, petitions circulated to limit the influx of poor Jews from the east. In this transnational context of human movement, real

[60] John D. Klier, "The Pogrom Paradigm in Russian History," in Klier and Lambroza, eds., *Pogroms*, 13–15.

[61] Klier, "The Pogrom Paradigm," 15–24.

[62] Klier and Lambroza, eds., *Pogroms*, 42.

and imagined, animus against eastern Jews deepened and more violence ensued.

Pomerania and West Prussia in the German Empire, and Hungary in the Habsburg Monarchy, comprised the two principal sites of this animus. In 1881, local tensions and anti-Semitic agitation in the city of Neustettin led to the burning down of a synagogue and the subsequent eruption in the summer of a series of anti-Semitic riots, the worst outbreak of anti-Semitic violence in Germany since the Revolution of 1848. During the revolution, rioters had taken advantage of the collapse in state authority in order to unleash their wrath on Jews whom they perceived as unprotected oppressors. In 1881, the dynamic was somewhat different. Caused by economic strain and its exploitation by anti-Semitic agitators from Berlin, the eruption of violence occurred in the context of a new anti-Semitism with its attention turned eastward. Like the Russian pogroms, the anti-Semitic riots in Pomerania were fueled by the belief, incorrect as it turned out, that Bismarck supported their anti-Semitic actions (when, in fact, he had only replied to a letter of praise concerning his tariff policies).[63] To the south, in eastern Hungary, the death of a Christian girl in the town of Tisza-Eszlar led to a ritual murder accusation in spring 1882, with riots continuing throughout the summer. Concentrated in western Hungary, these riots soon spread eastward and likewise took the intervention of the Army to bring under control.[64] Ignited by similar riots in Pressburg (Bratislava) in Slovakia, the riots in Hungary flared up again in October.[65] When in the following year, the Jew accused of ritual murder at Tisza-Eszlar was acquitted, there was renewed violence, this time affecting at least thirty-two separate counties and continuing on in Budapest for five days, with rioters shouting "hep hep" as they chased Jews through the streets.[66]

Taken together, the violence of the early 1880s was anything but a marginal phenomenon. The Russian pogroms set off the greatest exodus

---

[63] *Jüdische Presse* 12.33(8/18/1881): 350–351. *Allgemeine Zeitung des Judentums* 45.35 (8/30/81): 570. On Bismarck, Gerd Hoffmann, *Der Prozeß um den Brand der Synagoge in Neustettin* (Schifferstadt, 1998), 25. On the case, see Christhard Hoffmann, "Political Culture and Violence against Minorities: The Antisemitic Riots in Pomerania and West Prussia," in Hoffmann et al., eds., *Exclusionary Violence*, 67–92.

[64] Robert Nemes, "Hungary's Antisemitic Provinces: Violence and Ritual Murder in the 1880s," *Slavic Review*, 66.1 (2007), 16.

[65] Ibid., fn. 39.

[66] Ibid., fn. 44.

in Jewish history; and the riots following the trial of Tisza-Eszlar constituted the largest outbreak of street violence in Hungary prior to World
War I. While contained in the northern parts of Pomerania and West
Prussia, the riots in Neustettin similarly constituted an unsettling outbreak of popular violence. The outbreaks also came very close on the
heels of full Jewish emancipation and raised the possibility that emancipation, even if inscribed in law, could still be revoked. Bismarck's
expulsion of foreign Jews and Poles in the mid-1880s did little to allevi-
ate that anxiety and much to embolden anti-Semitic demands. Finally,
these outbreaks of violence expressed a new kind of demagogic politics and accelerated the penetration of this demagogy into the countryside.[67] In the Russian Empire, the restrictive May laws and the intol-
erant politics of official nationality gathered force after, not before, the
pogroms. In Hungary, the Tisza-Eszlar trial contributed powerfully to
the development of an organized anti-Semitic press and the growth of
anti-Semitic political parties. And in Germany, the violence in Neustettin
fanned agitation against eastern Jews and furthered the cause of nascent
anti-Semitic organization. Violence also taught governments about the
sagacity of swift reaction. When in 1884 in the German town of Skurz,
near Danzig, a murder led to a blood libel, the government avoided violence because anxious officials sent in reinforcements before the rioting
began.

VI

Anti-Jewish violence calmed thereafter, with intermittent flare-ups
throughout the 1890s. These flare-ups were concentrated in central
Europe, not eastern Europe, with the important exceptions of a devastating pogrom in Corfu and the continued deterioration of Christian-
Jewish relations in Rumania, which flared into violence in 1897 and
1899 before erupting into a major conflagration in 1907, when a massive peasant revolt began by targeting Jews.

In European terms, 1898 represents the start of a second wave of
anti-Semitic violence, with outbreaks of anti-Semitic riots in France and

---

[67] David Blackbourn, "The Politics of Demagogy in Imperial Germany," in Blackbourn,
Populists and Patricians: Essays in Modern German History (London, 1987), 217–245.
James Retallack, "Fishing for Popularity," in Retallack, *The German Right, 1860–1920:
Political Limits of the Authoritarian Imagination* (Toronto, 2006), 76–107.

in western Galicia inaugurating a new climate. At first sight, France seemed like an unlikely place for violent eruption. The Jews of France were highly integrated into the economy, and even into the offices of the state, where many had pursued successful careers. The anti-Semitic movement was comparatively weak, and it enjoyed little support from established figures of the republic. Yet the Dreyfus Affair, which had begun in 1894 and reached its culmination in the riots of January and February 1898, changed all of that.

For good reason, the Dreyfus Affair belongs to the most thoroughly researched events of modern European history; it was a decisive marker not only for gauging anti-Semitic attitudes but also for the emergence of a class of critical intellectuals on the left and radical thinkers on the right. In *The Origins of Totalitarianism*, Hannah Arendt accords the Dreyfus Affair a central place in her analysis – precisely because the political right came to identify the good of the nation not with the action of the state but with the chants of "the mob," and the mob, far from being merely a threat to order, became for the new right a "living expression of virile and primitive 'strength.'"[68] In this way, the events of 1898 foreshadowed twentieth-century developments, even if "it was not in France that the true sequel to the affair was to be found."[69]

Arendt also understood that France had been shaken by street violence, though she discerned bourgeois attitudes toward Jews as the real crux of the problem. "While the mob actually stormed Jewish shops and assailed Jews in the streets," she wrote, "the language of high society made real, passionate violence look like harmless child's play."[70] Historians, similarly, have tended to consign "real, passionate violence" to "harmless child's play," precisely, one suspects, because most of the violence was ritually bounded; while crowds chanted "death to the Jews," they did not actually kill them, except in Algiers, where the forces of order watched passively as a crowd killed two Jews.[71] Yet even if

---

[68] Hannah Arendt, *The Origins of Totalitarianism* (New York, 1949), 112.

[69] Ibid., 93.

[70] Ibid., 107.

[71] The two major exceptions are Stephen Wilson, *Ideology and Experience: Antisemitism in France at the Time of the Dreyfus Affair* (London, 1982); and now Pierre Birnbaum, *The Anti-Semitic Moment: A Tour of France in 1898*, tr. Jane Marie Todd (New York, 2003). For a helpful overview of the new research, see Paula Hyman, "New Perspectives on the Dreyfus Affair," *Historical Reflections/Reflexions Historiques*, 31.3 (Fall 2005), 335–350.

bounded, popular demonstrations remained impressive. According to police reports, more than 4,000 people assembled in Angers and Marseilles, more than 3,000 in Nantes, 2,000 in Rouen, and more than 1,000 in Saint-Die, Bar le Duc, and Saint-Milo.[72] There were sixty-nine outbreaks of violence in fifty-five separate places, mainly in the north and east, with the crowd's sympathies with the position of the army as evident as their ire against Emile Zola, whose *J'Accuse* had just been published. Yet local reports emphasize the preponderance of more ordinary kinds of anti-Semitism and a significant role for anti-Semitic journalists and agitators. The actions of the crowd, which consisted of students, artisans, shopkeepers, even the *bourgeois*, also pointed to the banality of anti-Semitic sentiment. Rioters shouted anti-Jewish epithets, like "down with the Jews" and *"mort aux Juifs"*; they threw rocks through the windows of Jewish homes and, in many cases, damaged Jewish stores; and they beat people with sticks.[73] In thirty places, the situation had become sufficiently threatening that troops had to be called to aid the police, and in a string of cities the demonstrations lasted for days. In the countryside, too, there was considerable agitation, suggesting that, like the Russian pogroms of 1881, the anti-Semitic violence started in the cities, but worked its way into rural areas as well.[74]

The dimensions of this violence made the Dreyfus Affair a traumatic experience – not quite "a St. Bartholemew's Day Massacre for the Jews," but the peril of it nevertheless. "For the Jews of France, death – so frequently present in shouts and insults – remained a virtual threat," Pierre Birnbaum concludes in his microhistorically, sharp-focused account, "so many angry crowds, so many out-of-control demonstrations, so many stirred-up populations, so many knives brandished, so many wounded . . . "[75] Birnbaum, too, sees as significant that "death did not have its way."[76] If Jews were burned, they were burned in effigy – the killing was enacted, and the act was a sign, not the thing itself.

[72] Stephen Wilson, "The Anti-Semitic Riots in 1898 in France," *Historical Journal*, 16.4 (1973), 792.

[73] Ibid., 794–7.

[74] For the contrary view, see Michael Burns, *Rural Society and French Politics: Boulangism and the Dreyfus Affair, 1886–1900* (Princeton, 1984), 136, 171, who emphasizes the distinctiveness of the rural reception.

[75] Birnbaum, *The Anti-Semitic Moment*, 333.

[76] Ibid.

If traumatic, the violence was also transformative; it signaled the emergence of a new kind of politics that mixed the economic distress of peasants and the lower middle class with the nationalist ideologies of more settled groups in society; in short, it made anti-Semitism a force in modern politics. Anti-Semitism, in this interpretation, was not a secondary phenomenon, or a cultural code, "a familiar and conventional symbol, ... a short-hand label," to cite Shulamit Volkov's famous definition of the code, "for an entire set of ideas and attitudes having little if anything to do with direct affection or dislike of Jews."[77] Rather, it provided the emotional élan for the demonstrations that engulfed France, as hundreds of thousands of people, some active, others passive, assumed roles in nationwide, locally staged street dramas. These street dramas involved scripts concerning the nation itself, with rioters acting out xenophobia. For historians used to thinking about the French peasantry as more concerned with their regional folkways, Birnbaum's conclusions must surely give pause: they suggest the depth of anti-Semitic sentiment in both city and country, and they imply broad participation in anti-Semitic rites of violence.[78] Finally, the Dreyfus Affair also transformed politics in a more ordinary but fateful sense. Henceforth, anti-Semitism became a discursive monopoly of the political right, and when combined with nationalism, it constituted a politically explosive program.

After Dreyfus, the epicenter of anti-Semitic violence returned to central Europe – to the Habsburg and German Empire. There had been intermittent outbreaks of smaller moment in both empires during the 1890s: in Germany in the Rhenish town of Xanten following a ritual murder accusation in 1891, and in the Habsburg lands in the Czech town of Kolín on the Elbe in April 1893, where only the early arrival of extra forces kept the mob, which had assembled in the Jewish quarter after a rumor that there had been stab wounds on the body of a young girl (suggesting ritual murder), from a violent rampage.[79] The violence then spread to other towns and, while not bereft of anti-Semitic impulse,

---

77 Shulamit Volkov, "Antisemitism as a Cultural Code: Reflections on the History of Anti-semitism in Imperial Germany," *Leo Baeck Institute Yearbook* XXIII (1978), 35.

78 For the older view, see Eugen Weber's classic *Peasants into Frenchmen: The Modernization of Rural France, 1870–1914* (Stanford, 1976).

79 Michael A. Riff, "Czech Anti-Semitism and the Jewish Response Before 1914," in *Wiener Library Bulletin* 29.39, 29, 40 (1976), 9. Hillel Kieval, *The Making of Czech Jewry: National Conflict and Jewish Society in Bohemia, 1870–1918* (New York, 1988), 66;

became intertwined with labor unrest and demonstrations for universal suffrage, the growth of social democracy, and the emergence of the Young Czechs.[80] Increasingly, the Jews of the Habsburg Empire became caught between the fronts of nationality, one of the anti-Semitic politicians even suggesting that the cause of the violence was the "provocation of German-speaking Jews."[81] A still more significant outbreak occurred in November 1897, on the occasion of the resignation of the Austrian Prime Minister, Count Badeni; these outbreaks were similarly caught in Czech/German nationality conflicts, as they began with fighting between Czech and German students in Prague. Soon, however, the violence got out of hand; Czech students went after Germans and Jews alike, and by the third day of rioting the military was called in to quell the situation.[82]

The major, and for many Jews shocking, event was, however, the west Galician Peasant Uprising of 1898, which soon turned explicitly anti-Jewish and violent, "causing the police," as one report put it, "to declare a state of emergency in half of Galicia."[83] The Galician peasant uprising is both interesting and important for the larger story. It is interesting because hitherto, anti-Semitic violence in the lands of partitioned Poland had been exclusively urban and local. The Warsaw Riots of 1790 remained an isolated incident; there had been modest collateral violence during the Peasant Uprisings of 1846, and again in Posen and in Galicia in 1848.[84] But in 1848, the anti-Semitic thrust of the revolution had been farther to the west, and the Polish Insurrection of 1863 passed without anti-Semitic violence – indeed with considerable Polish-Jewish cooperation.[85] When pogroms broke out in the southwestern provinces of the Russian Empire in spring 1881, most Poles found the violence shocking and attributed it to what they perceived as the low cultural

---

Kieval, *Languages of Community. The Jewish Experience in the Czech Lands* (Berkeley, 2000), 188.

[80] Riff, "Czech Anti-Semitism," 9–10.

[81] Cited in *Mitteilungen aus dem Verein zur Abwehr des Antisemitismus*, 3 (5/14/1893), 211 (hereafter MVAA).

[82] Riff, "Czech Anti-Semitism," 11–12.

[83] *Im deutschen Reich*, 6–7 (June 1898), 345–6. *Im deutschen Reich*, 8 (August 1898), 386 "Die Lage in Oesterreich."

[84] For the view that there had been "no anti-Jewish outrages," see the classic work by Artur Eisenbach, *The Emancipation of the Jews in Poland, 1780–1870*, ed. Antony Polonsky, trans. Janina Dorosz (Oxford, 1991), 349. For the revision, see Gailus, "The 1848 Crisis of German Society," in Hoffmann et al., eds., *Exclusionary Violence*, 57.

[85] Eisenbach, *The Emancipation of the Jews in Poland*, 479.

level of the Ukrainian peasants.[86] In the Polish provinces of the Russian Empire, by contrast, there was no imitative violence – until Christmas of that year, when in the heart of Warsaw a pogrom erupted, lasting three days and causing significant damage to Jewish houses and shops. The pogrom started when someone had yelled fire in a church, and in the subsequent panic at least twenty people lost their lives and many others were badly injured. A rumor soon surfaced that a Jew had falsely cried fire, and the next day riots began. Mostly young workers and artisans, the rioters tore through the Jewish district and terrorized the Jewish population, rich and poor, for three days. No one was killed, and some reports even suggest that women and children were especially spared. There were over 2,600 arrests and appeals by the church and various citizens' committees to stop the violence. The pogrom remained confined to Warsaw, despite attempts to incite violence in a number of other Polish towns as well as in Krakow.[87] Most Poles and Jews nevertheless saw the Christmas pogrom as a watershed, showing that something had gone awry since the Polish-Jewish cooperation that marked the insurrection of 1863. Subsequently, isolated pogrom-like incidents occurred in the Galician Oil Fields between workers and Jews in 1884 (the Boryslaw Wars) and again in 1897.[88] In Lodz in 1892, violence against Jews resulted from labor strikes directed, in part, against Jewish employers. Nevertheless, Polish-Jewish coexistence during the long nineteenth century had not been marked by the periodic recurrence of anti-Semitic violence to the same degree as Germany since 1819.

It is against this background that one must see the Galician Peasant Uprising of June 1898. The violence started south of Krakow on the eve of Corpus Christi day and fanned out in its first wave into twenty-three separate districts. Rioters looted Jewish property and destroyed taverns – synagogues and prayer houses, by contrast, remained largely untouched.[89] The almost exclusive focus on taverns, distilleries, and Jewish stores in June suggests the degree to which the Galician violence

---

[86] Theodore Weeks, *From Assimilation to Anti-Semitism: The "Jewish Question" in Poland, 1850–1914* (DeKalb, Ill., 2006), 74.

[87] Golczewski, *Polnisch-jüdische Beziehungen*, 42–44, 50–51.

[88] Alison Fleig Frank, *Oil Empire: Visions of Prosperity in Austrian Galicia* (Cambridge, 2005), 129–133.

[89] Keely Stauter-Halsted, "Jews as Middleman Minorities in Rural Poland: Understanding the Galician Pogroms of 1898," in Robert Blobaum, ed., *Antisemitism and its Opponents in Modern Poland* (Ithaca, 2005), 47.

of 1898 was motivated, as Keely Stauter-Halsted has recently argued, by "the rising economic tensions that characterized rural and small-town Poland."[90] Yet within this economic tension, distinguished by near-famine conditions for Polish peasants and debilitating Jewish poverty, there was a decisive political element: a newly founded peasant party that pursued unmistakably modern and demagogic politics in the form of an explicitly anti-Semitic campaign. The infusion of this political dimension was itself a result of the extension of the franchise embodied in the Austrian Electoral Law of 1896, which gave a fifth curia to males above twenty-four years of age, with some restrictions and within a slanted electoral system. The extension meant that in Galicia electoral politics pushed into the village, and this politics, as we will see, was anti-Semitic and violent.

Encouraged by an initially sluggish reaction from the authorities, violence and destruction broke out in no less than thirty-two separate towns.[91] In some places, like the market town of Kolaczyce, it devastated the whole Jewish community – breaking, according to one report, 800 windows in houses and stores. When the forces of order intervened, the troops were pummeled with stones.[92] Throughout western Galicia, rioters ruined thousands of stores, and with them the economic livelihoods of countless Galician Jews. If centered on economic grievances, the revolt also constituted a political baptism for rural Polish Catholics into modern politics and into the exclusionary logic of ethnic anti-Semitism.[93] This was politics in a new and violent key, outside the controls of church and nobility, indeed against the clergy, the landowners, and the Jews.[94]

In Polish Galicia, the newspaper of the peasant party of Father Stojalowski spread suggestions to the effect that "if 10,000 Jews were slaughtered, the situation would be better"; while other propagandists peddled a rumor that "the Jews must be beaten to death because they

---

[90] Ibid., 40.

[91] *Die Welt* 2.24 (6/17/1898).

[92] *Dr. Bloch's Oesterreichische Wochenschrift* (6/17/1898).

[93] The Jewish monopoly derived from the fact that prior to the emancipation of the peasantry, wealthy landlords sold concessions only to people not in servitude. On economic competition between Poles and Jews in the region, see Keely Stauter-Halsted, *The Nation in the Village: The Genesis of Peasant National Identity in Austrian Poland, 1848–1914* (Ithaca, 2001), 134.

[94] MVAA 8 (6/25/1898), 204. Golczewski, *Polnisch-jüdische Beziehungen*, 76.

were trying to take the Kaiser's life."[95] A fantasy of elimination was in this way tossed into a social tinderbox, and a conflagration ensued. It is not easy here to separate inside from outside, peasants in the villages from middle class instigators, nor is it a simple matter to sort out before-the-event motivation from after-the-fact justification. But violence is not just a structure; it is also a process, and by the end of the first wave of violence, as one observer reported, "in nearly every community the firm conviction predominated that the murder of the Jews had been ordered from Vienna."[96] This aspect of the riots is worth pausing upon – for it suggests the degree to which the rioters needed, or believed they possessed, legitimacy. "We will beat the Jews, we have a decree," one rioter claimed, while another said, "the Kaiser allowed it."[97] Tellingly, the appeal was to the Habsburg Crown, not to the Polish nation. Peasant animosity did not yet funnel into nationalist byways. If violence hardened religious/national opposition, it was the line between Poles and Jews, not Poles and the Empire.[98]

The revolt did, however, suggest something about the relationship between street violence and state power. Although the demonstrators decimated houses and shops, no Jews were killed despite various rumors that murder had been ordered. Perhaps, as one commentator remarked, this is because "no Jew dared go out on the street and instead sought diverse holes and hiding places."[99] Perhaps, also, it is because the military, although slow to intervene, eventually put a stop to the rampage. But the uprising was itself ritually bounded – in the tradition of revolts limited in their violence and specific about their targets. The Imperial German Consul in Lwów understood this fact with unique clarity. "The anger of the peasants is directed especially against the Jews, and in particular against their property," he wrote, "without threatening their lives."[100]

The importance of this fact is easy to overlook, especially as the revolt left a stricken landscape in its wake. One correspondent, who visited Western Galicia, reported hordes of homeless men, women, and children

---

[95] *Die Welt*, Heft 25 (6/24/1898), 10.
[96] *Die Welt*, Heft 25 (6/24/1898), 10.
[97] Cited in Golczewski, *Polnisch-jüdische Beziehungen*, 73–74, 77.
[98] Ibid., 78.
[99] *Die Welt*, Heft 24 (6/17/1898).
[100] Cited in Golczewski, *Polnisch-jüdische Beziehungen*, 79.

huddled at train stations in shattering scenes reminiscent "in miniature of what the Russian persecution offered writ large."[101] Whole towns resembled military camps, "the railway crossings guarded by Hussars, the bridges taken by the military, the country roads patrolled by the cavalry, and in front of the train station a patrol of police and infantry with armed weapons."[102] In the end, the military crackdown meant that scores of rioters were killed, and 3,500 people arrested. More than 1,000 people, Christians and Jews, were forced to stand trial for a series of offenses associated with the uprising, including attempted murder, assault, looting, and arson.[103]

Jews in the Habsburg Monarchy saw the Galician Uprising as foreshadowing worse to come. Leo Herzberg-Fränkel, who had long catalogued the history of the Jews in his native Galicia, believed that the uprisings cast a dark shadow over the future of Jews in the Monarchy and urged more unity among Jews, lest "the persecution reach the heights that it had in 1881 in the neighboring monarchy."[104] The Uprising also contributed to an enduring climate of violence. Already by Holy Week of the following April, anti-Semitic violence flared up anew – this time in the textile city of Nachod, and in connection with an ongoing strike. The riot, which commenced on the evening of April 5, and involved the plundering of stores and the shattering of windows, was quelled the next morning by a battalion of 300 military troops from nearby Josefstadt.[105] Yet the "Nachod excess," as it was called, paled before the problems thrown up by two ritual murder accusations, one in the Bohemian town of Polna, and the other farther east in the Prussian town of Konitz. As both trials and accusations have been the subject of intensive investigation, it will here suffice to note that each was followed by severe anti-Semitic violence, arrested only by the intervention of military troops.

The violence following the ritual murder accusation in Polna did not occur until October 1899, when Leopold Hilsner, the Jewish vagrant accused in the case of ritually murdering a Christian girl, was erroneously found guilty of the crime. The uprisings also ran parallel with

[101] *Dr. Bloch's Oesterreichische Wochenschrift*, Heft 26 (7/1/1898).
[102] Ibid.
[103] Keely Stauter-Halsted, "Jews as Middleman Minorities," 40.
[104] In *Dr. Bloch's Oesterreichische Wochenschrift*, 6/17/1898.
[105] *Die Welt*, 1899, Heft 15 (4/14/1899), 7.

the nationality concerns of the Young Czechs following the retraction of the Badeni Language Decrees (which insisted that communications with local governments be conducted in the native tongue of citizens – thus if an inquiry was written in Czech, its response was to be in Czech). In this sense, the new uprisings mixed an archaic motif with very modern concerns about belonging in a national polity.

The center of the uprisings was not Polna itself but Moravia, where Jews, more so than in Bohemia, were German speaking, with only seventeen percent (as opposed to fifty-four percent in Bohemia) declaring Czech their language of daily use.[106] Czech anti-Semitic violence had, in this sense, a double-edged sword. The violence started on October 2, 1989, in the industrial town of Holleschau, which had a population of 7,000 people, with 1,000 of them Jews. The proximate cause of the violence remains unclear, yet observers spotted signs of at least local organization. One tavern placed a picture of Hilsner in the window with a light on it. Some agitators distributed a rendition of the ritual murder while others handed out leaflets demanding that the Jews be expelled by the beginning of the year. In familiar fashion, demonstrators tore through the streets at night chanting, "beat the Jews to death." They smashed windows and plundered stores, tossing crates of soap, rolls of linen, colonial articles, lamps, and other wares onto the street, even auctioning them off – an act reminiscent of early modern bread riots. Finally, some rioters broke into the houses of the Jews of Holleschau, who were forced to huddle in hiding places.[107]

Breaking into houses crossed a threshold in one way. But what distinguished the events in Holleschau was the clash with authorities. This clash proved deadly for demonstrators, as military troops fired into a crowd, killing five and wounding at least twenty others.[108] The next week a similarly violent confrontation in the town of Wsetin also ended with bloodshed, as the army opened fire on the crowd, made up mainly of workers and apprentices.[109] In addition to the main scenes of

---

[106] Kieval, *Languages of Community*, 33.

[107] Erwin Rosenberger, "Holleschau," *Die Welt*, Heft 43 (10/27/1899), 3. "A Jew who today builds a house," one commentator noted, "should never forget about building such hiding places. Secret doors, underground rooms, are as necessary in a Jewish house as hearth and kitchen."

[108] Ibid.

[109] *Die Welt*, Heft 44 (11/3/1899), 8–9.

anti-Jewish demonstrations, there were many more in the small towns of Moravia and Bohemia, including in Polna itself, where a crowd of 200–300 people came together and marched through the street, smashing windows and shouting anti-Semitic slogans.[110] The Polna Affair has become an important part of Czech history because of the intervention of Thomas Masaryk, who cogently argued against the ritual murder charge and for Hilsner's innocence, and in this way influenced Kaiser Joseph II to commute his sentence. Yet even when the question of Hilsner is settled, it remains to integrate the anti-Semitic violence, which represented a broader base of Czech sentiment and to see the way in which the affair polarized Czech-Jewish relations.

Six months after the rioting in Polna, an eerily similar ritual murder charge in the West Prussian town of Konitz unleashed the largest outbreak of anti-Jewish violence in Wilhelmine Germany. Contemporaries not only noticed but remarked upon its connections to Polna. They also saw wider affinities: the likeness to ritual murder accusations of bygone eras and the structural similarity of the new ritual murder charges to outbreaks across Europe in the last two decades of the nineteenth century. Since the Xanten case in 1891, the liberal Defense League Against Anti-Semitism had compiled a running list of these accusations and counted over 100, even if the real number (excluding obviously demagogic attempts to incite accusations by the anti-Semitic press) was closer to eighty.[111] Still, by the turn of the century, more accusations had been made in Europe than in any other period. There was, however, a crucial difference. The medieval accusations proved more violent, while the violence that accompanied modern ritual murder accusations (if one excludes the pogroms of Russia) remained reluctant to cross this significant threshold. They involved threats, stone throwing, beating with sticks, but not murder. This was also true of Konitz, which witnessed some thirty separate anti-Semitic demonstrations, the largest with crowds of over 1,000 people in a town of 10,000. Konitz was the last significant incident of anti-Semitic violence in Germany until the Weimar Republic, when riots in the *Scheunenviertel* occupied the police of Berlin in 1923. It was also the last major blood libel accusation in

---

[110] Ibid.

[111] Helmut Walser Smith, *The Butcher's Tale: Murder and Anti-Semitism in a German Town* (New York, 2002), 123.

Germany that came from the population, as opposed to the government (as would be the case in the Nazi years).

When taken together, the incidences of public violence of the last two decades of the nineteenth century represent events of extraordinary magnitude. In the first wave, from 1881 to 1884, there were over 300 outbreaks of anti-Semitic violence, if one counts the many non-fatal pogroms in Russia, Hungary, and Prussia. There were also a handful of fatal pogroms. Then, after intermittent if often significant outbreaks, a second wave followed between 1898 and 1900; it started with the Dreyfus Affair in France and was followed by the events in Galicia, Moravia, and West Prussia. The high incidence of popular violence undermines a facile division of Europe between east and west, just as it suggests that the nation-state was not a self-evident container of violence. It cautions us, too, against considering anti-Semitism too narrowly within the scope of politics nationally conceived. While politics in the ordinary sense was hardly incidental to these eruptions, they cannot be reduced to the language of party politics as such.

How, then, do we consider the phenomenon of anti-Semitic violence in the last two decades of the nineteenth century in its larger dimension? One influential approach for assessing the wider phenomenon draws from the pioneering work of Hans Rosenberg and posits a connection between Jewish integration during the years of economic upswing between 1849 and 1873 and the reaction against it during the years of the Great Depression between 1873 and 1896.[112] The insight, innumerable caveats notwithstanding, remains powerful, especially for explaining the initial emergence of anti-Semitism in the late 1870s and early 1880s. It is less persuasive for the second wave of violence, between 1898 and 1900, when economic indicators point in a positive direction and, in terms of Kontradieff's long waves, suggest a general upswing. It is possible to conceive of the Galician Uprisings as the revolt of backward provinces and to posit an economic explanation for them nevertheless. Contemporaries had already seen it this way; even Zionists like Joseph Bloch believed that "the Galician uprisings had 'a specifically social character.'" Yet neither the Dreyfus Affair nor Polna, nor the uprisings in Konitz can be put into this economic matrix.[113]

---

[112] Hans Rosenberg, *Grosse Depression und Bismarckzeit* (Berlin, 1967), 88–117.
[113] Birnbaum, *The Anti-Semitic Moment*, 4.

The second wave was instead inextricably tied to questions of community in a wider sense, with the pattern of violence providing a key. Despite the considerable number of uprisings across central and western Europe, only two Jews were killed in them (in Algiers); generally, the rioters targeted highly symbolic symbols of property. In Galicia, rioters even went out of their way not to ruin synagogues. In other places, Jews were not so fortunate. Even where attackers charged into the households of Jews or beat them on the street, the attacks were not fatal. It may seem callous to pause on this matter, yet it tells us something about the relation between speech and act. "Beat the Jews to death" was not a command. Rather, it was an evocation of past acts, when Jews were, in fact, beaten to death, or an echo of the Russian pogroms, where, at least in some of the uprisings, the threshold of murder was crossed. In the context of these anti-Semitic uprisings, "beat the Jews to death" was not an instruction to kill, or a statement about what would soon happen, but speech enunciated in "a ritual of denigration," one that asserted supremacy and acted out a violent drama of Christian-Jewish relations. This acting out occurred outside established structures, in liminal time, and indeed challenged these structures. Many anti-Semitic demonstrators claimed loyalty to the state, yet they ended in pitched battles with the forces of order. Confrontation with the state was not the motivation behind the uprisings, but a function both of the state's imperative to maintain order and the liminal situation of the violence itself. It is characteristic of liminality that a reintegration into structure must thereafter occur; but this reintegration is always into a changed structure. And the change, at least from the standpoint of those who participated in the violence, involved a redefinition of who belonged and who was deemed outside. The shouts "beat the Jews to death," far from instructing to kill, had their primary effect in this redefinition. And this was true of the Dreyfus Affair, which changed French politics, even if it barely dented the actual status of Jews working in the government; as of the Galician Uprisings of 1898, which saw a precipitous decline in Polish-Jewish relations thereafter; as of the violence following Polna and Konitz.

VII

The murderous world of Kishinev was, however, of a different order, even if the anti-Semitic riots that started in this Bessarabian city seemed at first glance to follow the same logic as outbreaks across Europe in the previous two decades. The economic context of the outbreak included poor harvests in 1902–1903 and subsequent unrest in rural areas of Russia; rising unemployment in urban areas also fueled an increase in street demonstrations and political strikes.[114] A local anti-Semitic paper, *Bessarabets*, the only daily newspaper in the province, fed the non-Jewish population with a steady stream of anti-Semitic invective of a particularly provocative kind, including incitements such as "Death to the Jews" and calls to start a "Crusade against the Hated Race." Repeated requests by the Jewish community to various levels of Czarist officialdom to censor *Bessarabets* fell on deaf ears, despite attempts in other parts of the Russian Empire to snuff pogroms out before they started. Kishinev was then a city of 147,000 people, with 50,000 Jews and 50,000 Moldavians, and 8,000 Russians, the rest an assortment of nationalities from southeastern Europe, and a small community of Germans.

A ritual murder accusation, which surfaced during Holy Week, triggered the pogrom. On April 19, Jews celebrated the last day of Passover while Christians observed the first day of Easter: that night, a Sunday, the rioting began, at first with boys throwing rocks at windows, then with workers breaking into Jewish stores and looting the wares. A Jewish defense force, organized after the Czestochowa pogrom of the previous year, confronted the mob in an effort to defend people and property. The opposite happened, and violence escalated. By the end of the first night, twelve Jews had lost their lives, and close to 100 were gravely injured. The threshold had been crossed. But it would not end there. The next day the rioters returned – this time more organized, and with incomparably greater brutality, inflicting untold atrocities on the Jewish population of Kishinev. By the end of the second day, forty-seven Jews were killed and more than 400 wounded; 700 houses had been burned and 600 shops looted. In a mere two days, the Kishinev pogrom approached the total destructiveness of the pogroms of 1881. And still the military had not intervened and would not until the third day. Why this is the case is difficult to discern. The mob dramatically outnumbered the police, and there is some evidence for state collusion

---

[114] Here I follow the account of Schlomo Lambroza, "The Pogroms of 1903–1906," in Klier and Lambroza, eds., *Pogroms*, 195.

with the rioters at the provincial level. In any case, the lack of military intervention surely convinced the rioters that the state was on their side. The rioters had, one may recall, read nothing but anti-Semitic invective in the previous months. It was, moreover, the beginning of Holy Week, so one might surmise the confluence of archaic religious notions with modern demagoguery. The pogroms started soon after Easter services, and there are reports that spikes were driven through the hands, feet, and even heads of Jews.[115]

Kishinev represented the terrible transmutation of words into literal acts. Here the call "beat the Jews to death" was something other than a reenactment of past persecutions; it was the thing itself. The shift, rendered possible by the confluence of ideology (religious and secular) and the seeming neutrality if not support of the state, meant that the dam of inhibition, which had marked the pogroms of the last twenty years, had been broken. In Russia, this dam would remain in disrepair. In Gomel, a city in the northern Pale (now in White Russia) with a majority population of Jews, a pogrom broke out in September 1903, after a marketplace scuffle in which a peasant was killed. There were concerted efforts at Jewish self-defense, and the military attempted to quell the violence. But the violence again crossed the threshold, though not as decisively as at Kishinev, a result, perhaps, of the Jewish Bund's defense efforts, which had become extensive after Kishinev. Indeed, Gomel "was more a fight than a pogrom," as one newspaper put it.[116] But if the Jews may have won the fight, it was unclear that subsequent battles could as easily be won. And this is because anti-Semitic violence was thereafter taken up by the nationalist right and integrated into the ordinary practice of radical nationalism. The trials of the pogromists of Kishinev and Gomel evidenced this turn. In the Kishinev trial, the sentences handed down to the pogromists were startlingly mild, despite the magnitude of the killing; and in the trial after Gomel, the state attorney argued that it was the Jews who had started an anti-Russian pogrom. If the latter argument did not convince the courts, it received a sympathetic ear at the highest levels of government, including at the court of Nicholas II and the Czar himself. Although the government did not plan the pogroms,

---

[115] Ibid., 205.
[116] Cited in ibid., 209.

it seemed increasingly clear that the government condoned them. This condoning was a license to kill.

Pogroms now became an increasingly lethal part of the Russian political landscape. In 1904, there were thirty-four pogroms in the Russian Empire, most of which were in some way connected to the Russo-Japanese War. In the first pogrom of that year, in Bender, south of Kishinev, the anti-Semitic newspaper *Bessarabets* had incited the crowd with the claim that the Jews were aiding and abetting the Japanese. It was also preceded by the circulation of anti-Semitic pamphlets. The wording of one of these pamphlets, as Shlomo Lambroza in his finely etched study of Kishinev shows, suggested the temper of coming violence. "The people must arise and help in this war of annihilation," the pamphlet insisted, "let us show the Jews our Russian might, and destroy them wherever they live. Kill them. No quarter. Every single one is a foe and traitor... God is with us and the Czar is for us."[117] By the end of the year, there had been forty-five pogroms in 1903–04, including Kishinev and Gomel, with 93 Jews murdered, and over 4,000 severely injured.[118] A shift had occurred, but it was not to end there: the pogroms of 1905 and 1906 proved more cataclysmic still, with the vast majority occurring in the months after Prime Minister Sergei Witte issued the October Manifesto, which in the wake of the Revolutions of 1905 established the outlines of a constitutional monarchy. Demonstrations of support for the reforms were followed by counterrevolutionary protests. These protests were increasingly organized by the Black Hundreds, radical nationalists who blamed the Jews for the revolution. The struggle for rule, the persistent drum of anti-Semitic propaganda, the increasing organization by radical nationalists, and the collusion of local officials – this is the mix that proved volatile. According to Lambroza's estimate, 674 pogroms occurred in Russia in the first two weeks following the October Manifesto; these constituted more than eighty percent of the pogroms of 1905–1906; in all these pogroms killed over 3,000 Jews and wounded 17,000 more. A quarter of the Jews killed were women. The scale of violence was unprecedented; the dam collapsed.

This breaking is an important part of the larger story of anti-Semitic violence in Europe. Hitherto, with the exception of the pogroms of 1881,

---

[117] Cited from the *New York Times*, April 4, 1904, in ibid., 214.
[118] Ibid., 218.

anti-Semitic violence remained bounded by a speech act that evoked the possibility of killing without murder actually happening. It may again seem callous to point out, but even the pogroms of 1881 did not often cross the threshold. Most of the more than 200 pogroms that wracked the Pale of Settlement targeted property, not people. Even now historians place the death toll between thirty and fifty, which, given the magnitude of the disturbances, does not fully constitute the breakdown of inhibition. The pogrom wave that started at Kishinev dramatically changed this – now the numbers killed mounted into the thousands. Why?

Considered from the history of violence in the longer term, Kishinev and the pogroms of 1905 and 1906 displayed several novel features, and these features combined to change the pattern of anti-Semitic violence. The first is that Jews fought back – at Kishinev, and still more effectively at Gomel. Perhaps lives were as a result saved, but the historic pattern of anti-Jewish violence demanded submission, huddling in houses, a passive acceptance of the script of a ritual drama. This script was not a Russian script but a European one, and in the modern period it had been rehearsed dozens of times throughout the zones of Christian-Jewish settlement. A similar script demanding passivity in the face of violence was in operation in other supremacist societies, whether the American south or colonial societies, with the response of dominant groups to "fighting back" often a release of extreme cruelty. Put differently, the Jews of Kishinev and Gomel provided the Russians with what Peter Gay called an "alibi for aggression," and this alibi covered not just property but people; it was, in short, an alibi for murder. But this was not the only change.[119]

A second change involved the increased level of popular violence in society. This too was a European story with a Russian dimension. In the long nineteenth century, anti-Semitic violence of significant moment had often been correlated with higher levels of violence generally. In central Europe, this had been true of the violence accompanying the revolutions of 1830 and 1848, but also the increasing levels of national-ist violence in the Habsburg Monarchy in the wake of the Badeni Crisis of 1898. Even the outbreaks of anti-Semitic violence in Pomerania in 1881 and in Hungary in 1882 occurred in the heightened atmosphere of

---

[119] Peter Gay, *The Cultivation of Hatred* (New York, 1993), 35–36.

violence during the Russian pogroms. Historians fixed on the social and economic causes of violent outbreaks have tended to assume that what caused the large revolution must have caused the anti-Semitic components of it as well. Yet violence, its rhythms and intensities, was itself a factor. As we have seen, violence often occurred in waves, and these waves did not always respect political borders. The 1905–06 pogroms in Russia happened in the context of the largest outbreak of revolutionary violence since the French Revolution. Not all of this violence was cut of a clean labor union cloth; much of it was disorganized, muddled, and common. A U.S. consul reported that Russia "is permeated with sedition, and reeking with revolution, racial hatred and warfare, murder, incendiarism, brigandage, robbery and crime of every kind."[120] As thresholds lowered, all forms of violence increased, especially on the periphery of the Empire, where anti-Russian sentiments ran strong, and centralized control remained weak.

A corollary to the general violence was the fact of the specific violence associated with the Russo-Japanese War, whose repercussions on a global scale historians are just now starting to understand as the first world war of the twentieth century.[121] It may be recalled that following the pogroms of Kishinev and Gomel there were forty-three pogroms in 1904, and more than half of them had to do with mobilization for war.[122] Not usurious practices or ritual murder was at issue, but traitorous collaboration with the Japanese. It is important to underscore the novelty of this claim and its association with anti-Semitic violence. The Napoleonic Wars, the Crimean War, the Wars of Unification – these, with the possible exception of Jacob Fries's mention of avaricious Jewish suppliers in Prussia's struggle against France, and minor Czech violence against pro-German Jews in Bohemia in 1866, did not culminate in the accusation that Jews were traitors to the fatherland.[123] In Russia, the disaster of the war, and the revolution it brought forth, tightened the connection, especially in Army circles and on the political right. Here the

[120] Cited in Orlando Figes, *A People's Tragedy: The Russian Revolution, 1891–1924* (New York, 1996), 188.
[121] Jonathan Steinberg et al., eds., *The Russo-Japanese War in Global Perspective: World War Zero* (Leiden, 2005).
[122] Lambroza, "The Pogroms of 1903–1906," 213–216.
[123] Jacob Fries, *Über die Gefährdung des Wohlstandes und Charakters der Deutschen durch die Juden* (Heidelberg, 1816), 11–12.

notion of community, transposed onto the national level, operated in increasingly Manichean terms. The alleged traitorous nature of the Jews, first centered in a public debate during the Dreyfus Affair, now became associated with the broad anti-Semitic polemics of the European right. It is perhaps a coincidence that the *Protocols of the Elders of Zion*, first published in full in St. Petersburg in 1903, has its origins in France – but common is the focus on conspiracy. In Russia, however, the association of Jews and conspiracy had come to the fore in the midst of a war in which Russia met disastrous defeat at the hands of a non-European foe. The context of war and defeat, not some timeless urge of pogrom violence, made the murderous difference.

War, defeat, revolution – and counterrevolution. Perhaps the most portentous development after the 1905 October Manifesto, which was followed by a concentrated whirl of pogroms, was the founding of the Union of Russian People, or the Black Hundreds as their opponents called them. Established in order to return authority to the Czar and the government to an autocracy, the Black Hundreds became a mass movement with over 1,000 branches and 300,000 members. Like the *Action Française* and fascist movements throughout inter-war Europe, the Black Hundreds fused conservative blood-and-soil ideology with a modernist glorification of the transformative energy of violence. They had a direct or indirect hand in instigating or organizing a number of the pogroms of October 1905, in which over 30,000 Jews were killed. In places like Odessa, where the death toll was appallingly high, the Black Hundreds had worked closely with the police, who were often sympathetic to them, and this created the not-altogether-incorrect illusion that the government supported the killing. This governmental support was something new. It is true that anti-Semitic rioters had in the past evoked the consent, even the support of authority. In Elisavetgrad in 1881, they had claimed the Czar was on their side; in Galicia in 1898, rioters had even asserted that the destruction was ordered by the Crown Prince. But beginning with Kishinev, the claim was no longer fanciful. If the Russian government did not itself organize pogroms, its complicity was now by design. Moreover, it became clear that anti-Semitism would be at the center of the defense of monarchy – and during the Russian Civil War this would have terrible consequences. While a left-right scheme of politics does little to illuminate the trajectory of anti-Semitic violence during the long nineteenth century, after the Revolution of 1905 radical nationalists and authoritarian regimes put forward the possibility of plunder and of murderous pogroms in order to cultivate support among the peasants and the lower middle classes. Perhaps the Polish-Lithuanian poet Czseslaw Milosz was right to cite Joseph Conrad's Kurtz scribbling "horror" on the margins of a report about the Congo as the beginning of the climb into the twentieth century.[124] But with the horror of truly murderous anti-Semitism, the climb began as well.

VIII

In the twentieth century, the context that brought about significant violence against the Jews of Europe was essentially the same: war, defeat, revolution – and counterrevolution. With the exception of Rumania, the pogrom furies that had plagued Europe had fallen silent in the years before World War I.[125] During the war, the Russian Army had expelled whole Jewish towns and villages in areas of combat, essentially tearing up large stretches of eastern Galicia and the Pale of Settlement and eventually displacing more than 500,000 Jews. Although justified with arguments of military necessity, the expulsions of 1915 came with unjustified accusations that Jews were traitors to the Russian cause. Especially in Galicia, they also came with brutal assaults, including looting, rape, and murder, often papered over with talk of the removal of unreliable ethnic elements and the cleansing of the area of military operations.[126] Still, the expulsions and degradations were not citizen pogroms in the usual sense.

It was, paradoxically, when the guns of August ceased to fire that the real trouble began, and it began in earnest in the shatter zones of

---

[124] Czeslaw Milosz, "A Treatise on Poetry," tr. Robert Hass (New York, 2001), 9.

[125] In Rumania, a massive peasant rebellion directed against landlords and Jews led to a genuine war between the state and the populace, with some 11,000 people killed and the army literally bombarding villages in order to regain control over the countryside. See Keith Hitchins, *Rumania 1866–1947* (Oxford, 1994), 178. On p. 177, Hitchins writes that "the uprising was not an anti-Semitic outbreak" and that "its causes were broadly social and economic, and no distinction was made between Christian and Jewish 'oppressors.'" This may be true in the same sense that the revolutions of 1830, 1848, and 1905 were not anti-Semitic in origin, but they, like the Rumanian Peasant Uprising of 1907, unleashed significant waves of specific anti-Semitic violence.

[126] Alexander Victor Prusin, *Nationalizing a Borderland: War, Ethnicity, and Anti-Jewish Violence in East Galicia, 1914–1920* (Tuscaloosa, 2005), 24–64.

collapsed Empires, first with viciousness in the fallen Russian Empire, where, as John Klier and Shlomo Lambroza have written, there was "Jewish suffering which was unparalleled in Eastern Europe before the Holocaust itself."[127] Then, albeit on a smaller scale, violence visited parts of the torn-asunder Austro-Hungarian Monarchy, especially in Galicia, but also in the Hungarian, Czech, Slovakian, Sudeten-German, and Ruthenian areas of the former Empire. There were two epicenters of this violence. One was the Ukraine, the other Poland, where the birth of the new nation, to cite a Galician Jew who experienced those days, was "accompanied by rivers of Jewish blood."[128]

It cannot be the purpose of this chapter to recount in detail the dimensions of this story, whose pieces are only now being put together. Suffice to say that in the shatter zone the inhibition against murder had fallen with impunity. Even Kishinev must appear to belong to another age when compared with Proskurov, a Ukrainian village in which some 2,000 innocent Jews were simply murdered within three hours by the troops of the bloody-minded Ukrainian nationalist leader, S. V. Petlura. If Proskurov was the best documented of the massacres, it also stood *pars pro toto* for hundreds of others, some of similar magnitude, many smaller, that decimated the Jews of the Ukrainian countryside.[129] An utter absence of centralized governmental authority and a corresponding lack of any kind of monopoly of violence characterized the frame in which these murders took place. Chronologically, the frame stretched from September 1917, when the Germans separated the Ukraine from Russia, to 1921, when the Bolsheviks reestablished enduring rule in the Ukraine. The pogroms of this period not only assumed new viciousness, but focused on killing.[130] This killing was carried out now by Red Army units, now by Cossacks, now by the Ukrainian Volunteer Army. But in the history of anti-Semitic violence, a special place of infamy must be reserved for the disciplined troops of General Anton Deniken. When his Volunteer Army carried out the killings, which reached a crescendo in late 1919 and the early months of 1920, there was for the first time,

---

[127] Klier and Lambroza, eds., *Pogroms*, 292.

[128] Joachim Schoenfeld, cited in Marsha L. Rozenblit, *Reconstructing a National Identity: The Jews of Habsburg Austria during World War I* (New York, 2001), 136.

[129] David Vital, *A People Apart: The Jews in Europe, 1789–1939* (Oxford, 1999), 716.

[130] Peter Kenez, "Pogroms and White Ideology in the Russian Civil War," in Klier and Lambroza, eds., *Pogroms*, 302.

perhaps since the Khmelnitsky massacres of the seventeenth century, the spectacle of a well-organized Army carrying out a pogrom as if it were a military operation, and this with a great deal of ideological conviction.[131] Anti-Semitism now mixed with anti-Bolshevism and with a kind of stab-in-the-back explanation for defeat in war, and it became an increasingly central part of the worldview of both officers and enlisted men. Moreover, far from evincing sympathy for Jews, killing created new solidarities among the perpetrators, much as it would for Germans two decades later. The comparison is neither willful nor original. David Vital, in his passionately but soberly argued *A People Apart*, has suggested the comparison as well. "The term 'genocide' had yet to be coined," he writes, "but no sane contemporary observer of the scene in the Ukraine at the time of the Russian Civil War could doubt that *that* – crudely and imperfectly, to be sure – was what was being attempted."[132]

The situation in Poland and in a number of areas of the former Habsburg Monarchy were not destructive on the same scale, but they too became emblematic for the era. "Can it be," asked Isaac Babel of the Jews in 1920, "that ours is the century in which they perish?"[133]

In November 1918, there were over 100 incidents of anti-Semitic violence in Galicia, precisely marking the twentieth anniversary of the Galician Peasant Uprising of 1898. There were additional pogroms in what had been Russian Poland and in Lithuania. Yet the pogroms of 1918 were different in important respects from Galician predecessors. They occurred amidst greater uncertainty about political sovereignty, in particular along the Polish-Ukrainian ethnic borders, and nationalism, indeed the nationalization of the borderlands, was at their core.[134] Jews, in this situation of uncertainty, could not easily opt for one or the other national identity; and in the ethnic *bellum omnium contra omnes* that marked the collapse of Empire, neutrality was not a simple option either. As in Russia in 1905, and with increasing vehemence during the war, the question of national allegiance became tantamount, and the suspicion that Jews were traitors now to the Polish, now to the Ukrainian cause, grew apace. But what especially distinguished the Galician pogroms of 1918 from their predecessors is that they were lethal.

---

131 Ibid.
132 Vital, *A People Apart*, 726.
133 Cited in ibid., 728.
134 Very instructive is Prusin, *Nationalizing a Borderland*, 1–12, 75–91.

In the history of anti-Semitic violence in the modern era, murder, as we have seen, was a threshold seldom crossed. Murder had been held in check by legitimate governmental authority and by a ritual injunction to reenact expulsion and killing but to stop short of actually doing it. Operative even when peasants believed that the Kaiser had ordered the Jews killed, and even as rioters had run through the streets shouting "*mort aux Juifs*," the threshold had collapsed only once before Kishinev: namely during the Russian pogroms of 1881 that began in Elisavetgrad. Even here, the number of deaths, measured against the number of pogroms, must be counted as small – certainly by twentieth-century standards. That there was something new in 1918 was now evident. Sizing up what was happening in central Europe, one German commentator sensed a new relationship between speech and act. "In our day, when human life isn't worth a straw," he wrote, "it's only a hair's breadth from incitement to the deed."[135] This hair's breadth refers to the ability of demagogues to incite hatred and violence, but we may also take it to refer, in the more exact sense, to anti-Semites who in the midst of riot do what they say.

The most deadly pogrom occurred in Lwów in November 1918. In the course of three days, Polish rioters murdered seventy-five Jews, injured more than 400, burned down thirty-eight houses, and caused an enormous amount of damage to Jewish property. For the first time in the modern era, Poland witnessed a pogrom on the scale of Kishinev. As William W. Hagen has astutely shown, the pogrom was a highly scripted and ritualized event, even, or especially, in its killing. "These stages and scripts," he argues, "constituted the pogrom as a communal act whose carnivalesque elements were central to its character and purpose."[136] That the pogrom remained a communal act underscores its ties to the tradition of communal violence against Jews; that the ritual now crossed the threshold into murder suggests the new conditions in which it occurred. Part of the historically new involved the cheapening of life as a result of war and ethnic violence. New as well was an exclusive understanding of community in terms of nationality – an understanding still alien to the Galician peasants of 1898, but already

---

[135] William W. Hagen, "Murder in the East: German-Jewish Liberal Reactions to Anti-Jewish Violence in Poland and other East European Lands, 1918–1920," *Central European History*, 34.1 (2001), 9, 28.

[136] Hagen, "The Moral Economy of Popular Violence," 125.

evident during the Dreyfus Affair, and certainly part of the counterrevolutionary ideology of the Black Hundreds in 1905. A further context involved collapse and defeat, and from the Polish standpoint "loss of mastery" in the city over both Ukrainians and Jews. Significantly, much of the emotional élan of the pogrom derived from the belief that Jews had sided with the Ukrainians in the fight for the city and that they had taken up arms against the Poles. As in Kishinev and Gomel, this constituted a breach of a ritual agreement, according to which Jews were to remain passive, and, as in those pre-War Russian pogroms, it provided Polish attackers with an alibi for murderous fury.[137]

IX

Ludwig Geiger, chief editor of the Berlin-based *Allgemine Zeitung des Judentums*, believed that Jews had entered a "pogrom era" but carefully pointed out that, fears of imminent violence in Germany notwithstanding, the pogroms occurred "in other lands."[138] Although also a collapsed Empire, the loser of a devastating war, the site of significant governmental disarray between 1918 and 1923, and the heir to a significant tradition of anti-Semitism (including, as we have seen, anti-Semitic violence), Germany did not devolve into a pogrom landscape. This fact must both be taken seriously and rendered more precise if we are to connect the history of anti-Semitic violence in the long nineteenth century to the catastrophe that marked the twentieth.

First, there is the undeniable difference in the stability of the government and its perceived monopoly of violence. For all its chaos, the early Weimar Republic did not become the Ukraine of the Russian Civil War. Instead, demobilization proceeded successfully, an immense accomplishment given that six million men remained under arms at the end of the war.[139] Perhaps a murderous *Endkampf*, its outlines already apparent, was merely postponed.[140] In the short run, however, historical compromises and artificially high levels of employment prevented

---

[137] Ibid. See also Prusin, *Nationalizing a Borderland*, 75–91.
[138] Cited in Hagen, "Murder in the East," 8.
[139] Richard Bessel, *Germany after the First World War* (Oxford, 1993).
[140] Michael Geyer, "Endkampf 1918 and 1945: German Nationalism, Annihilation, and Self-Destruction," *No Man's Land of Violence*, eds. Alf Lüdtke and Bernd Weisbrod (Göttingen, 2006), 47.

demobilization from devolving into mayhem.[141] For Jews, the "notorious" telephone deal struck between the Socialist Friedrich Ebert and Army Quartermaster-General Wilhelm Groener, whatever deleterious long-term consequences this may have had, nevertheless prevented Germany from falling into the condition of lawlessness that encouraged the eager executioners of Deniken's armies.[142] Related to this is the attitude taken up by Gustav Noske, charged with the security of Prussia, but best known for his severe persecution of the radical left. For Noske, it remained imperative that the republic quash at the outset all "anti-Semitic propaganda and incitements to pogroms."[143] He had an easier time of it than the Bolsheviks, since unlike the Russian Black Hundreds, the German right did not pursue pogroms as politics by other means.[144] Even Theodor Fritsch, among the most radical and bloody-minded of German anti-Semites, renounced pogrom-like violence as a legitimate tool of politics. "Educated enemies of the Jews reject any acts of violence against the Jews," he wrote in an open letter to Gustav Noske, insisting instead that Jews be subject to special laws.[145] Second, violence focused on German borders did not continue indefinitely. By 1921, international pressure and a democratically legitimized plebiscite settled the boundaries of Upper Silesia, the most violently disputed border.[146] The international dimension is significant. More than was possible with the Ukraine, Germany remained under the watchful eyes of an international community, and when in 1923 the country threatened to come undone, international powers and a complex weave of corporatist arrangements assured that it held together.[147] Finally, the tradition of anti-Semitic violence in

[141] On the problem of postwar stability, Charles S. Maier, *Recasting Bourgeois Europe: Stabilization in France, Germany, and Italy in the Decade after World War I* (Princeton, 1975) remains of fundamental importance. For Germany, see also Bessel, *Germany after the First World War*; Gerald Feldman, *The Great Disorder: Politics, Economics, and Society in the German Inflation, 1914–1924* (New York, 2003).

[142] See, most recently, and with further references, but a different perspective, Geoff Eley, *Forging Democracy: The History of the Left in Europe, 1850–2000* (Oxford, 2002), 167.

[143] Dirk Walter, *Antisemitische Kriminalität und Gewalt: Judenfeindschaft in der Weimarer Republik* (Bonn, 1999), 41.

[144] Ibid., 41.

[145] Cited in ibid., 41–2.

[146] See T. Hunt Tooley, *National Identity and Weimar Germany: Upper Silesia and the Eastern Border, 1918–1922* (Lincoln, Neb., 1997).

[147] Maier, *Recasting Bourgeois Europe.*

Germany had not, as it had in the Pale of Settlement (but not in Poland or Hungary), crossed the threshold of murder before. Instead, anti-Semitic violence enacted expulsion and threatened murder.

This was the intention of the *Scheunenviertel* Riots of November 1923, the largest outbreak of popular violence in the history of the Weimar Republic. Thousands of rioters looted shops, smashed windows, destroyed property, tore through the streets, assaulted Jews (most of them poor, often refugees from the Galician horrors of the war and its aftermath), and shouted, "beat the Jews to death" and "out with the Eastern Jews."[148] The police reacted sluggishly, but soon brought the rioting under control. No Jews were killed, but there were three fatalities among the rioters.

Yet violence against Jews, as Dirk Walter has shown, increased significantly during the Weimar Republic, keeping apace with the twining of violence and politics generally. Mainly, this violence manifested itself in symbolic acts. Between 1923 and 1932, the Weimar Republic registered more than 150 cases of the desecration of synagogues and Jewish cemeteries.[149] Physical violence against Jews also increased as a consequence primarily of the growth of paramilitary organizations such as the *Sturmabteilung* of the NSDAP. Yet even the SA, whose thugs struck terror among Jews, did not, as a rule, indiscriminately murder them. In fact, the use of lethal weapons against Jews came to be a taboo in SA circles – a remarkable fact when placed against the lethal viciousness of SA street violence directed against Communists in the last years of the republic.[150]

The Third Reich changed this situation – but not immediately and not in obvious ways. Historians have hitherto focused on the barrage of anti-Semitic legislation aimed at marginalizing and expelling the Jews of Germany. Yet there is now a growing appreciation for the importance of spontaneous, aggressive acts of terror manifested in specific violent attacks against Jews and communal-based, pogrom-like acts of violence. Partly, this greater sensitivity to active anti-Semitism from below stems from a historiographical turn interested in the criminal side of everyday life, partly it stems from the discovery in the Moscow *Sonderarchiv*

---

[148] David Clay Large, "'Out with the Ostjuden': The Scheunenviertel Riots in Berlin, November 1923," in Hoffmann et al., eds., *Exclusionary Violence*, 96.
[149] Walter, *Antisemitische Kriminalität*, 164.
[150] Ibid., 109.

of crucial documents, assumed lost, of the *Central Verein deutscher Staatsbürger jüdischen Glaubens*. These documents include the provincial reports of the CV, and from them it becomes clear that especially in the countryside and in small towns the willingness to engage in physical violence was higher than previously supposed. Some of this violence involved the SA demonstrating publicly its anti-Semitic convictions.[151] In one case, Gunzenhausen in Franconia in March 1934, an anti-Semitic riot ended in murder. We also know (mainly from memoirs) that Jews from small towns and from the countryside had more to fear from direct violence, and this direct violence is surely one reason for the accelerated dissolution of Jewish communities in rural Germany.[152] With this violence in mind, the historian Michael Wildt has even argued that by the summer of 1938, there was "pent up energy . . . for a pogrom . . . awaiting a command to be unleashed."[153]

The evidence for Wildt's hypothesis remains too slim and regionally bounded to generalize. The preponderance of evidence still points to a German population that rejected the pogrom, if more because of its form than of its intention. Yet the German population couched its objections so as not to confront the regime; and for the first time since the Middle Ages, Germany witnessed a pogrom that crossed the threshold, culminating in the killing of nearly 100 Jews, with countless more injured.[154] There were, in addition, a number of places in which whole towns participated, and in which Christians forced their Jewish neighbors to undergo humiliating denigration rituals. This was especially the case in smaller cities and towns, where, to cite Wolfgang Benz, "a clear break did not exist between activists who served as ringleaders – the functionaries of the NSDAP and their organizations – and bystanders."[155]

The ubiquitous degradations, humiliations, and physical assaults cut a caesura in German-Jewish relations. The November pogrom

---

[151] Benz, "The November Pogrom of 1938," 151.

[152] Noel Carey, "Anti-Semitism, Everyday Life, and the Devastation of Public Morals in Nazi Germany," *Central European History* 35.4 (2002), 565; Christhard Hoffmann, "Verfolgung und Alltagsleben der Landjuden im nationalsozialistischen Deutschland," in Richarz, ed., *Jüdisches Leben*, 375.

[153] Michael Wildt, "Violence against Jews in Germany 1933–1939," in David Bankier, ed., *Probing the Depths of German Antisemitism: German Society and the Persecution of the Jews, 1933–1941* (Jerusalem, 2000), 196.

[154] Most recently, and carefully, and with further literature, Peter Longerich, "*Davon haben wir nichts gewusst!*": Die Deutschen und die Judenverfolgung (Munich, 2006), 130.

[155] Benz, "The November Pogrom of 1938," 149, 151.

accelerated the flight of Jews from Germany and represented a preliminary highpoint in the history of a progressive devastation of public morals, tearing away at whatever bonds of solidarity may have existed between Christians and Jews as neighbors.[156] Regardless of their intentions, bystanders now participated in a ritual drama in which the humiliation of the other was the central point of the play. This is not just a matter of attitude, but of the change that occurs when people themselves participate, even as passive onlookers, in the brutality.

Is the November pogrom the end of the story? Has the history of anti-Semitic violence only brought us "toward but not to the Final Solution," as Jeffrey Herf has felicitously put it with respect to the history of anti-Semitism generally?[157] When the Germans invaded Poland in 1939, less than a year after *Kristallnacht*, it immediately transpired that volunteer detachments of the German minorities (*Volksdeutsche Selbstschutz*) massacred thousands of Jews and Poles in vigilante killings that bore at least a family resemblance to the worst pogrom murders of the Ukraine.[158] Meanwhile, a number of units of the German *Wehrmacht* engaged in what the author of the *Black Book of Polish Jewry* called "Blitzpogrome" – short, terrifying descents into Jewish communities involving plunder, rape, and murder.[159] And all of this transpired before, as Christopher Browning puts it, "the terror (in Poland) began to shift away from sporadic mass shootings of Jews and Poles to a more systematic 'liquidation' of particular categories of people."[160] Between "toward and to the Final Solution" there is indeed a chasm – but as concerns the history of anti-Semitic violence, the chasm is narrower than we often suppose.

[156] Michael Geyer, "Resistance as Ongoing Project: Visions of Order, Obligations to Strangers, and Struggles for Civil Society," in *Resistance against the Third Reich*, eds. Michael Geyer and John W. Boyer (Chicago, 1994), 334.

[157] Jeffrey Herf, *The Jewish Enemy: Nazi Propaganda during World War II and the Holocaust* (Cambridge, Mass., 2006), viii.

[158] Christian Jansen and Arno Weckbecker, *Der "Volksdeutsche Selbstschutz" in Polen 1939/40* (Munich, 1992), 8.

[159] Cited in Jochen Böhler, *Auftakt zum Vernichtungskrieg: Die Wehrmacht in Polen 1939* (Frankfurt am Main, 2006), 189.

[160] Christopher R. Browning, *The Origins of the Final Solution: The Evolution of Nazi Jewish Policy, September 1939–March 1942* (Lincoln, Neb. and Jerusalem, 2004), 31.

5

ELIMINATIONIST RACISM

In *Hitler's Willing Executioners: Ordinary Germans and the Holocaust*, Daniel J. Goldhagen averred:

By the end of the nineteenth century, the view that Jews posed extreme danger to Germany and that the source of their perniciousness was immutable, namely their race, and the consequential belief that the Jews had to be eliminated from Germany were extremely widespread in German society.[1]

As scores of historians familiar with late nineteenth-century German politics have argued, Goldhagen mistook political positions on the margin for positions at the center and willfully described as the mainstream a racial anti-Semitism ready to expel, if not kill, the Jews of Germany.[2] Demonstrably, this position was not the mainstream, though the matter is more complicated than a simple recounting of the dismal electoral fortunes of political anti-Semitism would suggest. As Massimo Zumbini has recently argued, the career of racial anti-Semitism in the Second Empire occurred in two stages. In the founding years of organized anti-Semitism, 1879–1881, the new anti-Semites modernized and radicalized anti-Semitism, rendering it political, racial, and increasingly tied to pseudoscientific thinking. Yet as their project proved a failure, the anti-Semites drifted toward the political periphery, where their anti-Semitism became radical, and their paranoia evident. Eliminationist anti-Semitism, to take Goldhagen's term, cannot be said to be representative of public opinion in Imperial Germany, but it can be found at

---

[1] Daniel J. Goldhagen, *Hitler's Willing Executioners: Ordinary Germans and the Holocaust* (New York, 1996), 72.
[2] For the first wave of responses, see *Ein Volk von Mördern?*, ed., Julius H. Schoeps, (Hamburg, 1996); for considered reflections on the debates, *The "Goldhagen Effect": History, Memory, Nazism – Facing the German Past*, ed. Geoff Eley (Ann Arbor, 2000).

the periphery – in the work of anti-Semites like Theodor Fritsch, whose *Handbook of the Jewish Question* became a bible of the extreme right and openly advocated deportation of East European Jews and revoking emancipation legislation. But as a matter of politics, this position hardly drew widespread support. Not the success but the abject political failure of the radical anti-Semites allowed them to cultivate extremist positions.[3]

But if "eliminationist" seems the wrong adjective for mainstream anti-Semitism in Imperial Germany, it is suggestive when coupled with what Imperial German writers called "lesser races," "natural races," or "primitive peoples." Here the elimination of peoples was possible to think and, in the colonial wars, that possibility nearly became a reality, with German parliamentarians, save for the Social Democrats and the Catholics, condoning the ruthless murder of Herero and Nama in Southwest Africa. In this case, as Isabel V. Hull has shown, an eliminationist discourse justified destruction rather than caused it.[4] Racist ideas cheapened a sense of the sanctity of human life and rendered increasingly brutal a colonial discourse that called into question the humanity of the colonized. But even the most radical nineteenth-century thinkers demurred before elimination, in the strong sense of the term, as genocide, "an act committed with intent to destroy, in whole or in part, a national, ethnic, racial or religious group, as such."[5] But if genocide remained impossible to think, forms of elimination below this threshold were not beyond the pale. One such possibility involved what we now call ethnic cleansing, a term that derives from a Serbian translation of "*Säuberung*" or "*Reinigung*," Nazi euphemisms for the "cleansing" of an area of "undesirable people."[6] The aim of ethnic cleansing is removal, not killing, though in one significant sense, as Norman

[3] Massimo Ferrari Zumbini, *Die Wurzeln des Bösen. Gründerjahre des Antisemitismus: Von der Bismarckzeit zu Hitler* (Frankfurt am Main, 2003). Zumbini's work is the first comprehensive synthesis of modern anti-Semitism in Germany that brings its social, cultural, and political aspects together. See also Peter Pulzer, *The Rise of Political Anti-Semitism in Germany*, rev. ed. (Cambridge, Mass., 1988), especially on the political dimension.

[4] Isabel V. Hull, *Absolute Destruction: Military Culture and the Practices of War in Imperial Germany* (Ithaca, 2005), 330.

[5] The definition of genocide adopted by the United Nations in 1948. Quoted and reflected upon in Robert Gellately and Ben Kiernan, Introduction to *The Specter of Genocide: Mass Murder in Historical Perspective*, eds. Gellately and Kiernan (Cambridge, 2003), 15.

[6] According to the *Oxford English Dictionary*, 2nd ed.

Naimark points out, "ethnic cleansing bleeds into genocide," as mass murder often occurs in the process of ethnic cleansing.[7]

If genocide remained inconceivable before World War I, forms of ethnic cleansing *avant la lettre* were thought, and this thinking suggests a continuity of German and European history. The continuity derives from the expulsion of Jews from late medieval and early modern cities and territories and the subsequent eradication of their traces; it also draws from the expulsion of Christian confessions in the early modern attempt to create religiously homogenous territories. Here the basic criteria of ethnic cleansing, namely removal from a concrete territory, was met. In the nineteenth century, however, lines of continuity were bent in new ways. At the beginning of the century, German intellectuals conceived of the expulsion of Jews and foreigners in national terms for the first time. Then, toward the century's end, modern racism suggested new rationales and possibilities for the elimination of peoples. In the latter period, experiments began – with human reservations, for example, and with concentration camps. There existed, to use Naimark's term, great areas of conceptual bleeding. Between expulsion (ethnic cleansing) and the physical annihilation of peoples (genocide), a wide band of possibilities emerged, including the erection of segregated societies and the degradation of peoples to a caste of indentured workers. These possibilities were conceived, moreover, in the context of public discussion in which racism assumed greater importance, with the physical annihilation of peoples a real possibility.

The following is an attempt to explore the history of fateful imbrications: modern anti-Semitism with racism, racism with elimination, and anti-Semitism with the kind of racism that imagined that peoples could be eliminated. As if braids stretched and then tied, these histories ran parallel before being twisted together. To understand how this happened, I consider three leading intellectuals: Heinrich von Treitschke, the doyen of Prussian-German nationalist historiography; Friedrich Ratzel, the Leipzig geographer who in the 1880s and 1890s popularized the idea of *Lebensraum*; and Paul Rohrbach, a colonial administrator turned publicist, whose influence the historian Friedrich

---

[7] Norman M. Naimark, *Fires of Hatred: Ethnic Cleansing in Twentieth-Century Europe* (Cambridge, Mass., 2001), 3–4.

Meinecke compared to Treitschke a generation earlier.[8] These intellectuals serve as a vantage point, a surveyor's tower, from which to limn wider discussions and to see how these discussions changed shape over time. Hannah Arendt famously defined the concentration and extermination camps as "laboratories in which the fundamental belief of totalitarianisms that everything is possible is being verified."[9] I ask in this chapter what was possible to think in the second half of the long nineteenth century, and what (still) lay outside the bounds of the conceivable.

I

The most popular historian of the Imperial period, the successor to Leopold von Ranke at the University of Berlin, Heinrich von Treitschke exercised a profound influence on the national imaginings of Germany's Protestant middle class. In his political essays, in his lectures (published as his *Politics*), and in his multi-volume *German History of the Nineteenth Century*, he developed an approach to history and politics characterized by a celebration of power over principle, by an uncritical veneration of Prussian values, and by an ahistorical projection of the national mission of the Prussian state into the distant past. To German historians, these facts, as well as his anti-Semitic writings, are common knowledge. Less familiar are Treitschke's reflections on the relationship of culture to power in his narratives of the waxing and waning of nations.

For Treitschke, the power of the state was mercury to measure the cultural level of the nation. Strong states reflected robust cultures, weak

---

[8] For Meinecke's comment on Rohrbach, see Friedrich Meinecke, *Werke*, vol. 2, *Politische Reden und Schriften*, ed. Georg Kotowski (Darmstadt, 1966), 62–63. On Ratzel, the best place to start is still Woodruff D. Smith, *Politics and the Sciences of Culture in Germany 1840–1920* (New York, 1991), 140–162. See also Andrew Zimmerman, *Anthropology and Antihumanism in Imperial Germany* (Chicago, 2001), and Jürgen Osterhammel, *Geschichtswissenschaft jenseits des Nationalstaats* (Göttingen, 2001), 151–169. On Rohrbach, see Rüdiger vom Bruch, *Weltpolitik als Kulturmission* (Paderborn, 1982), 73–76; and, for more detail, W. Mogk, *Paul Rohrbach und das "Größere Deutschland": Ethischer Imperialismus im Wilhelminischen Zeitalter* (Munich, 1972).

[9] Hannah Arendt, *The Origins of Totalitarianism*, rev. ed. (New York, 1973), 437. For reflections on imperial continuity in the sense here being described, see Dirk van Laak, *Über alles in der Welt: Deutscher Imperialismus im 19. und 20. Jahrhundert* (Munich, 2005), 182–3.

states withered ones. It followed that if a national culture could not succeed in creating a national state, then it could not claim a timeless right to existence. A general axiom of historical development, this insight also offered a specific explanation for Prussia's attempt to annihilate Polish culture. "A people not capable of creating and maintaining an external order in the form of a state for its cultural life deserves to perish as a nation," he told his students at the University of Berlin.[10] If this constituted the general principle, the fate of the Poles – to be Germanized and Russianized – provided a case in point. "Never have a people more justifiably been annihilated than the Poles," he explained.[11] Partly a fact of power, their annihilation resulted in equal measure from their own desert, for "over the centuries the modest virtues of citizenry died away among this accursed people."[12]

Treitschke believed the annihilation of their culture to be an act of progress and humanity. "What Prussia means for the civilization of humanity," he confided to his wife Emma in 1871, "one only begins to understand fully here in the east."[13] When he wrote this letter, he had just crossed the border from Upper Silesia into Austrian Galicia; the border crossing was like "a theater effect," and "the great difference" taught him to thank the Lord for "the undeserved fortune of being born a German."[14] Krakow proved especially unsettling. The German population had markedly declined, the Polish population remained desolate, and the only real life seemed to pulse in the Jewish quarter of Kazimierz. "Full of deceit," "wheeling and dealing, bantering and . . . screaming," the Jewish quarter seemed to Treitschke a "Bruegel's hell, only that no paintbrush could render the disgusting stink that hovers over this band (of Jews) like a cloud."[15] Jews as an affront to the senses – this image would stay with Treitschke throughout the next decades, and it informed

---

[10] Heinrich von Treitschke, *Politik: Vorlesungen gehalten an der Universität zu Berlin*, ed. Max Cornicelius, 2 vols. (Leipzig, 1897), vol. 1, 63. In this case, he refers to the Jews.

[11] Ibid., 22. On Treitschke's lecture style, see Hermann Bahr, *Selbstbildnis* (Berlin, 1923), 180–81.

[12] Heinrich von Treitschke, *Deutsche Geschichte im Neunzehnten Jahrhundert*, 5 vols., 5th ed. (Leipzig, 1907), vol. 4, 58.

[13] Heinrich von Treitschke, *Briefe*, by Max Cornicelius, 3 vols. (Leipzig, 1920), vol. 3, part 1, 334.

[14] Ibid.

[15] Ibid., 335.

his understanding of the east as a vast alien place to be subdued or held at bay by the strong arm of the Prussian state.[16]

The state was for Treitschke a civilizing power, its mission in the east its manifest destiny. "Many precious benefits of freedom are given to peoples only through state coercion," he maintained.[17] Liberation from the backward ways of local life constituted one such precious benefit. Freedom from clerical coercion and ignorance comprised another. "The German State forces parents to have their children educated," Treitschke declared, "it does not give them the right to their Catholic stupidity."[18] Similarly, by raising the cultural level of workers, the state could eradicate "the crudity and self-indulgence, envy and cupidity that flourished among the working classes."[19] The civilizing state thus created a homogenous and modern nation, not the reverse.

The state, not nation and still less race, was Treitschke's starting point. Yet precisely at the height of Treitschke's career in the 1870s a European discourse about race based on biological assumptions gained ground. Published in 1854, Count Gobineau's *Essay on the Inequality of Races* was the first book to make race the motor of history, as Marx had rendered class, and Hegel spirit. Yet Gobineau's *Essay* was not widely read in Germany until after the Franco-Prussian War, when its reception was spurred by the publication of Darwin's *Origins of Species* in 1859 and *The Descent of Man* in 1870.[20] Thereafter, a spate of publications popularized the idea that the rules of nature, defined by evolutionary struggle, governed politics as well. Darwin himself had kindled this nascent enthusiasm for applying his analysis of the natural world to the struggle of nations. "At some future period, not very distant as measured by centuries, the civilized races of man will almost certainly exterminate and replace throughout the world the savage races," he wrote in *The Descent of Man* in 1870.[21]

---

[16] On Treitschke's trip to the Memel, see Isaac Rülf, "Auch eine Kleinigkeit in Sachen Treitschke et Compe," in *Der Berliner Antisemitismusstreit, 1879–1881. Kommentierte Quellenedition*, ed. Karsten Krieger, 2 vols. (Munich, 2004) vol. 1, 416–8. Hereafter abbreviated as BAS.

[17] Treitschke, *Briefe*, vol. 3, 437.

[18] Ibid.

[19] Ibid.

[20] Ivan Hannaford, *Race: The History of an Idea in the West* (Baltimore, 1996), 272.

[21] Cited by Richard Weikart, *From Darwin to Hitler: Evolutionary Ethics, Eugenics and Racism in Germany* (New York, 2004), 186.

As racial thinking accelerated, Heinrich von Treitschke published his famous article, "Our Prospects," which appeared in the *Preussische Jahrbücher* in the fall of 1879. It is important to foreground this context because typically historians have perceived this article and the subsequent Anti-Semitism Debate as a crescendo to an ever more audible anti-Jewish sentiment associated with the economic crash of the founding years of the Empire. In fact, however, the article inaugurated its own explosion of writing about the Jewish question. One can see this by looking at the volume of anti-Semitic writing over a twenty-year span from 1870 to 1890. In the Bismarckian period, according to one scholar's counting, there were more than 400 pamphlets written on the "Jewish question," and of these over sixty percent were penned in the wake of Treitschke's article – between 1879 and 1883. Conversely, only thirty-eight pamphlets, or less than ten percent, had appeared before 1879.[22]

Treitschke's article stands at the beginning of a series of highly public debates centered on the Jewish question, which Treitschke defined in terms that brought the language of nation together with the vocabulary of race. The nation's demands to the Jews are simple, he declared: "they should become German, and should feel themselves plain and simply German." He did not ask them to give up their religion but warned against a coming together of the two cultures to produce a "German-Jewish mixed culture." Yet he also posited a deep division between Semitic and western essence and believed that "there would always be Jews who are nothing but German speaking Orientals" – "an alien element."[23] Here is the transitional moment: nationalism that insists on total assimilation, and nascent racist arguments that postulate the impossibility of assimilation. The bridge, significantly, is an oriental image, which historians (at least since Edward Said) have come to see as a discourse of knowledge engendering power over others.

The necessity of a conceptual bridge reminds us of the novelty of the concept of race in the 1870s when applied to Jews and the importance

---

[22] Uffa Jensen, *Gebildete Doppelgänger: Bürgerliche Juden und Protestanten im 19. Jahrhundert* (Göttingen, 2005), 197–268. On Treitschke's public engagement, see Ulrich Wyrwa, "Heinrich von Treitschke: Geschichtsschreibung und öffentliche Meinung im Deutschland des 19. Jahrhunderts," *Zeitschrift für Geschichtswissenschaft*, 51.9 (2003), 781–792.

[23] Treitschke, "Unsere Aussichten," in BAS, 15.

of the "east" to it. In "Our Prospects," the article that initiated the Anti-Semitism Debate, Treitschke started with a long consideration of the eastern question in the wake of the Congress of Berlin. He warned his readers about "the expansionary power of the Slavs," and the "blind fury of Pan-Slavists"; he noted that east and west had come more closely together in the age of the railroad; he saw inevitable conflict as the Ottoman Empire crumbled around the edges; and he wondered about the sagacity of the Habsburg occupation of Bosnia. Threatened from the east, Germany and Europe were also threatened from the inside: from the deleterious results of the crash of 1873, which brought to Germany a temporary collapse of the economy but a more lasting destruction of ideals; from the forces of unbelief, which wormed away at public morals; and from a "general regression of the masses," which the "spread of the secret arts of reading and writing" accelerated. His, then, was also a class anxiety, and Treitschke first mentioned the new anti-Semitic movements in the context of his dismay at this "noisy activity." But then he considered that "the instincts of the masses" were not groundless and that "year after year a hoard of ambitious young men selling pants [pushed] across our eastern boarders from the inexhaustible Polish cradle, whose children and grandchildren [were] someday to take over our stock exchange and newspapers." Many western Jews had in fact integrated into western nations, he wrote, but "we Germans must deal with Polish Jewish tribes."[24]

If racist, then hesitantly. Treitschke's image of Jews remained entangled in older, class-based fears of the east: its population surplus, its poverty, its alleged ruthlessness and rapaciousness. Emancipation was the process whereby Jews left a segregated eastern world and began their "entry" into German life – a chapter, as he wrote Friedrich von Meech, "that has never been honestly told to us."[25] It is indicative that Treitschke came to the idea of writing his anti-Semitic addendum to "Our Prospects" while composing the final chapters of the second volume of his *German History in the Nineteenth Century*, a volume that ends in the year 1819 – with the Carlsbad Decrees, the ebbing of the German national movement, and Jewish emancipation. Treitschke,

---

[24] Ibid., 11.
[25] Treitschke to Friedrich von Meech, (4/6/1879), in Treitschke, *Briefe*, vol. 3, part 2, 497.

who had supported Jewish emancipation, now criticized Jews for their materialism and economic speculation, which according to Treitschke undermined the idealism of the national idea.[26] In his own mind, he was hardly thinking race. When accused of being "a defender of racial hatred and intolerance," he responded with incredulity. And when the "Berlin Notables" in their famous "Manifesto against Anti-Semitism" of November 1880 charged him with "shaking the legacy of Lessing," Treitschke reacted with indignation.[27]

The discursive shift from nation to race started tentatively with Treitschke, but it took full swing in the course of the subsequent debate and in the wake of anti-Semitic practice. Here the intellectual context is important. From the start, Imperial German polemicists assumed that Treitschke meant race. Even Hermann Cohen, the great Kant scholar and Treitschke's most gentle Jewish critic, believed the idea of race to be the heart of the matter. Clearly, Treitschke did not have a racial idea in the pseudoscience sense of the social Darwinists, but he addressed Jews in national terms that shaded racial expressions. He thus sanctioned a new discursive practice, which had been circulating since the advent of the new anti-Semitism, especially from the pen of Wilhelm Marr and the orations of the court preacher Adolf Stoecker. Other pundits followed, with Catholics commixing the jargon of nation with the jargon of race, and radical anti-Semites, like Heinrich Nordmann, putting forward a racial vision that presaged Nazi formulations. Nordmann, for example, calculated the racial deterioration that allegedly happened when Christians and Jews intermarried, comparing the subsequent "mixed products" to the decline that supposedly occurs when unlike animals breed.[28] He also proposed a series of measures, which were to apply to Jews into "the third mixed generation." These measures included disenfranchisement, taking back emancipation, putting a stop to Jewish

---

[26] Ulrich Langer, *Heinrich von Treitschke* (Düsseldorf, 1998), 330. On this problem generally, see Fritz Stern's masterful, *Gold and Iron: Bismarck, Bleichröder, and the Building of the German Empire* (New York, 1977), 512. On the reception of Treitschke's *German History* among German liberals, Andreas Biefang, "Der Streit um Treitschkes 'Deutsche Geschichte' 1882/83: Zur Spaltung des Nationalliberalismus und der Etablierung eines national-konservativen Geschichtsbildes," *Historische Zeitschrift*, 262.2 (1996), 391–422.

[27] BAS, vol. 2, 551–554; Heinrich von Treitschke to Johann Gustav Droysen, (11/15/1880), in BAS, vol. 2, 576–7.

[28] Heinrich Nordmann, "Professoren über Israel," in BAS, 379.

immigration, the expropriation of Jewish property, and the dispersal of Jews throughout the country so that they are everywhere in the extreme minority.[29]

Nordmann was not the only anti-Semite whose thinking in 1880 augured the language of the Nuremberg Laws in 1935. In 1881, Eugen Dühring, an obscure thinker rendered famous by the vehemence of Friedrich Engels's combative pen, wrote a pamphlet entitled *The Jewish Question as a Question of Racial Harm* (*Die Judenfrage als Frage der Racenschädlichkeit*). In this work, Dühring put forward many of the proposals favored by Nordmann, including expulsion and expropriation. He modeled his proposals on *Kulturkampf* legislation, in particular the May Laws, though he envisioned something of greater finality. If the state could expel religious minorities and expropriate their property, as Bismarck had done with the Jesuits, it could do the same with Jews, especially if their alleged racial status made them a state within a state. The modeling reminds us of the complexity of the Imperial German context, and that German-Jewish history did not happen in isolation from other histories. Dühring opined, however, that "the rule of Christian priests is the smaller curse when compared to the racial domination of the Jews."[30] Like Treitschke, Dühring wrapped his turn to race in Orientalism. He likened the presence of Jews to "a material invasion and a spiritual infection, similar to an epidemic originating from Asia."[31] Moreover, Dühring targeted not some Jews in Germany, but all Jews, and argued not that Jews should become Germans, but that they should be expelled. Dühring was also the first thinker to consider reservations, even if he ultimately rejected the idea, since the Jews were nomads and a reservation, "an interned Jewish state," would mean the "Jewish eradication of the Jews."[32]

---

[29] Ibid., 384–5.

[30] The full title of Dühring's infamous work is: *Die Judenfrage als Frage der Racenschädlichkeit für Existenz, Sitte, und Cultur der Völker*. Cited in Zumbini, *Die Wurzeln des Bösen*, 177. On Dühring, see also Paul Michael Rose, "'Extermination/Ausrottung': Meanings, Ambiguities and Intentions in German Antisemitism and the Holocaust," in *Remembering for the Future: The Holocaust in the Age of Genocide*, eds. Yehuda Bauer et al. (New York, 2001), 734–5. Rose astutely notes that Dühring's text became more brutal over time, emphasizing with increasing vigor the imperative of violent extermination.

[31] Zumbini, *Die Wurzeln des Bösen*, 179.

[32] Ibid.

Then there is the case of Paul de Lagarde, an "oriental" scholar of immense range and sophistication, but also a sharp critic of Bismarck's Germany, which he thought marked by materialism and mendacity. Like Treitschke, Lagarde thought in national categories, but whereas Treitschke remained tied to the prose of *Realpolitik*, Lagarde took flight in the poetry of a higher vision. The vision was of a Europe of homogenous national states, a utopia of clean spaces shorn not only of ethnic minorities but also of Jews. He advocated a plan to deport all Austrian and Polish Jews to Palestine because, as he reasoned, Jews were incompatible with Germans, and the Germans faced the daunting challenge of fundamentally reordering the space of central Europe. Theoretically, German Jews could remain, but only if they fully assimilated in the sense Treitschke had advocated. Where Treitschke put forward hesitant proposals, Lagarde thought nationalist positions to their logical end. He put the possibility of deportation on the table and adopted increasingly racial language. He compared Jews to bacteria and averred that bacteria "is as quickly and completely eradicated (*vernichtet*) as possible."[33] He wrote these words in 1882. For the first time in the nineteenth century, the word "*vernichtet*" is applied to Jews in a physical sense, previous uses of the term having a cultural connotation.[34]

The new, more brutal language seemed confined to the margin, but it was not without wider consequence. In the summer of 1880, an anti-Semitic petition circulated, demanding limits on the immigration of foreign Jews, the exclusion of Jews from positions of public authority, a restoration of the Christian character of public schools, and a statistical accounting of the Jewish population. By April 1881, its anti-Semitic sponsors had gathered more than 250,000 signatures (among them nearly half of the 3,600 students then in Berlin, and one in four students throughout the Empire). Many of the students who signed the petition believed that Treitschke had sanctioned it, and he hardly contradicted their impressions. In the 1880s, every fourth student at the University of Berlin heard Treitschke's lectures, and many emerged

[33] Cited in ibid., 358.
[34] For a different view, Rose, "Extermination/Ausrottung," 731. The one possible exception is Hartwig von Hundt–Radowsky, *Judenspiegel: Ein Schand – und Sittengemälde alter und neuer Zeit* (Würzburg, 1819), where these terms come paired with genuine proposals for expulsion.

deeply influenced. They included the colonial publicist, Paul Rohrbach; the future leader of the Pan-German League, Heinrich Class; and the militaristic theorist of future war, Friedrich von Bernhardi. Born in the late 1860s, they saw the aspirations of 1848 as the pipe dreams of a previous generation. Quick to embrace the new, they took easily to racial theories wrapped in the scientific language of Darwin. And most students were anti-Semitic. Even Ludwig Quidde, who would later emerge as one of the Empire's most caustic critics and an engaged pacifist, conceded the "understandable antipathy of the people" and believed that the "racial division" (*Racengegensatz*) that "indisputably exists between us and our fellow Jewish citizens" is at its core "a national question."[35]

Ever suspicious of popular agitation, Bismarck silently passed over the anti-Semitic petition. But other acts soon followed. On the eastern edge of Pomerania, in the provincial town of Neustettin, violence erupted in July 1881. Astutely analyzed by the historian Christhard Hoffmann, the violence followed the burning down of the local synagogue in the previous February and the subsequent accusation that it was the Jews who set their own temple aflame. Among the greatest outbursts of popular revolt in Imperial Germany, the violence of Neustettin constituted the first large-scale popular attack on Jews since the Revolution of 1848. Hundreds of townspeople ambled through the streets chanting "hep hep" and "out with the Jews," demolishing the windows of about thirty Jewish houses and storefronts.[36] From Neustettin, the riots spread one after the next throughout the region, with the most frightening spectacle in the town of Schivelbein, where an ominous crowd of 600 rioters charged through the streets, some with crowbars and axes in hand.

It would be wrong to make Treitschke directly responsible for the actions of others, but the path from thought to deed, speech to act, writing to riot, was short and swift. The riots did not break out spontaneously, but were ignited by the agitation of one of the most vitriolic anti-Semites of the day, Ernst Henrici, a schoolteacher from Berlin who

[35] Ibid., 834.
[36] *Jüdische Presse* 12.31 (8/4/1881):(supplement). *Allgemeine Zeitung des Judentums* 45.31 (8/2/1881), 509. For a full description, see Christhard Hoffmann, "Political Culture and Violence against Minorities" in *Exclusionary Violence: Antisemitic Riots in Modern German History*, eds. Werner Bergmann, Christhard Hoffmann, and Helmut Walser Smith (Ann Arbor, 2002), 67–92.

unabashedly propagated an anti-Semitism of race. Jews could never become really German, he believed, because the stain of blood stayed with people forever. When he first came to Neustettin in February 1881, he demanded the expulsion of all Jews from German soil and called upon Germans "to beat the Jews to death." Five days after his visit, the synagogue went up in flames with the townspeople watching, "laughing faces in the crowd."[37] When Henrici returned in late June, the people hailed him and decorated his carriage with flowers and wreaths.

Neustettin suggested the volatility that occurred when the novel concept of race was soldered together with the perfidious aspects of modern politics, "politics in a new key" to use Carl Schorske's felicitous phrase.[38] This was the politics that emerged from the collapse of liberalism in the 1870s, and it is no accident that Henrici had initially attempted to fuse left-liberal politics with anti-Semitic rhetoric. New was also the style: the bombast, the ceaseless self-aggrandizement, the fast travel from town to town (made possible by the railway and the bicycle), and the reliance on a steady stream of propaganda in the form of cheap newspapers and penny pamphlets. And new was the insistence that one was not merely speaking for the people, but that one belonged to the people and spoke from the gut.[39] All of this changed the dynamics of anti-Semitism. For the first time in German history, the passions behind anti-Semitic riots had been consciously stoked by men who claimed politics as their profession.

These men brought the language of race to the broader strata. Like other anti-Semitic riots, Neustettin was essentially backward-looking. The smashing of windows, the beating of houses with sticks, the threatening poses, and the setting fire to the synagogue essentially exhausted the symbolic expression that inhered in the drama of anti-Semitic violence. Rarely, at least in the German Empire, did this violence spill over into physical harm and murder. But nor was it senseless. Instead, the violence reenacted the drama of Jewish expulsions and, in this sense, participated in an enduring ritual of Christian-Jewish history. Yet the

---

[37] *Jüdische Presse*, 12.3 (2/21/1881), 79.

[38] The term is from Carl E. Schorske, *Fin-de-Siècle Vienna* (New York, 1981), 116–180. For a sustained, multi-layered analysis of the riots in Neustettin, see Hoffmann, "Political Culture and Violence against Minorities."

[39] On the style of imperial politics, Margaret L. Anderson, *Practicing Democracy. Elections and Political Culture in Imperial Germany* (Princeton, 2000).

purveyors of politics in a new key introduced a new language justifying the practice of persecution. Race cannot be said to have motivated the riots, or even to have expressed something of the meaning of collective violence, but once the riots had taken place, the language of race – which answered the question as to why the Jews were always persecuted – insinuated itself more easily into exculpatory rhetoric.[40]

But while the language of race troubled many of Treitschke's Jewish critics, it was the connection between word and deed that distressed Treitschke's non-Jewish, liberal interlocutors. This can be seen by analyzing the chronology and provenance of criticism lodged against the Berlin historian.

After Treitschke's first salvo in the Anti-Semitism Debate, "Our Prospects," only one liberal newspaper, the venerable *Vossische Zeitung*, printed a counter from the pen of a non-Jewish publicist, a Protestant pastor who had converted from Judaism in 1855 and now worked in the Protestant mission to convert Jews. From November 1879 to February 1880, Treitschke's critics were exclusively Jewish. Most prominent among them were the historians Heinrich Graetz and Harry Breßlau, the psychologist of nations Moritz Lazarus, the newspaper editors Ludwig Philippson and Seligmann Meyer, the politician Ludwig Bamberger, and the young philosopher Hermann Cohen. Non-Jewish Germans either approved of Treitschke (the case with conservatives and Catholics and not a few liberals) or fell silent. Within the Berlin community of notables, even those who felt dismay only expressed their disappointment through social distancing. As the historian Uffa Jensen has shown, there were not one but two anti-Semitism debates between 1879 and 1881, and only in the second do we hear critical voices from the liberal sphere, which were both non-Jewish and avowedly public. Moreover, the turn came not because of Treitschke's words, but the effects they produced. Not until the late summer of 1880 did the Berlin Notables (which included Theodor Mommsen, Johann Gustav Droysen, and the Lord Mayor, Max Forckenbeck) decry the "racial hatred and medieval fanaticism that has been called into existence and directed at our fellow Jewish citizens."[41] By then, the anti-Semitic petition had already circulated, and

[40] Jan Philipp Reemtsma, "Die Falle des Antisemitismus," in *Das Eigene und das Fremde*, ed. Ulrich Bielefeld (Hamburg, 1991), 269–282.
[41] "Manifest der Berliner Notabeln gegen den Antisemitismus von 12.11.1880," in BAS, 552.

the students at the University of Berlin had already begun to organize themselves in anti-Semitic groups.

In the second phase of the Anti-Semitism Debate, starting in the summer of 1880, Theodor Mommsen made his misgivings publicly known. Alarmed by the threatening "calamity" of a "civil war of the majority against a minority," and by the stir of politics in a new key, Mommsen insisted that the young nation-state must remain unified. "The sentiment of great commonality made the nation, and this would disappear if the various tribes (*Stämme*) should begin to feel estranged from each other," he wrote.[42] Mommsen saw Jews as both a religious group, whose rights were to be protected, and as a tribe, like the Saxons or the Pomeranians. "What does it mean," he rhetorically asked of Treitschke, "that they [the Jews] should become German?" And answered: "They already are so, as much as he and I." But then he conceded that while it is inadmissible to make all Jews responsible for the mistakes of individuals, "part of the blame still lies with the Jews." Christianity, he reasoned, is the fundamental mortar of "international civilization" and "to remain outside it and exist within the nation is possible, but difficult and full of danger."[43] Just as the Hanoverians, the Hessians, and the Holsteiners are asked to shed their particularism, so the Jews must rid themselves, "as much as they can without acting against their conscience," of their own particularities (*Sonderart*).[44]

Then and now, commentators have pointed out that while Treitschke wanted Jews to become Germans, Mommsen abjured them to become Christians. Yet while this may follow from Mommsen's critique, it is not a position he publicly held. Instead, the debate between the two became more acrimonious, with Mommsen denouncing Treitschke's demagogy and questioning his professional behavior. Stung by Mommsen's opprobrium, Treitschke compensated with still more radical positions. In the *Preussische Jahrbücher*, he now talked about the possibility of revoking Jewish emancipation.[45]

---

[42] Theodor Mommsen, "Auch ein Wort über unser Judenthum," BAS, 698, 700. On this aspect of the conflict, see Christhard Hoffmann, "Die Verteidigung der liberalen Nation: Mommsen gegen Treitschke im 'Berliner Antisemitismusstreit' 1879/1880," in *Theodor Mommsen: Wissenschaft und Politik im 19. Jahrhundert*, ed. Alexander Demandt (Berlin, 2005), 62–88.

[43] Mommsen, "Auch ein Wort über unser Judenthum," BAS, 708–9.

[44] Ibid., 709.

[45] Ibid., 715.

The thought of revocation, Treitschke came to realize, was not *salonfähig*, still less any kind of eliminationist anti-Semitism. Even modern racism remained largely absent in Treitschke's work. He addressed race in his *Politics*, the posthumously published transcription of his popular lectures, a composite of student notes, but he only gave it fleeting attention. He divided the world into four main races, the yellow, red, black, and white, and the last into Aryan and Semitic. The divisions, in which each race corresponded to a cliché (yellow, despotic; red, decaying; black, serving; white, culture-creating) suggests that Treitschke had assimilated broader concepts of race into his thinking about Germans and Jews.[46] Tellingly, however, he considers Jews, as opposed to Semites, in his subsequent discussion of nationality. He calls the Jews a nomadic people and carefully points out that "part of European Jewry has succeeded in nationalizing itself into the nations in which they live, and have become good Germans, French, and English," with Disraeli and Mendelssohn as luminous examples. Yet he also believes that "in Berlin and especially further to the east there are many Jews, who despite language have remained inwardly unalloyed Orientals."[47]

Orientalism, as we have seen, was the bridge Treitschke laid down to race, which others then crossed. As a result of Treitschke's words, and the discussion and the actions that followed, race became a more acceptable vocabulary for discussing "the Jewish question," which many people now supposed existed. And within this racialized discourse, there were some positions, like that of Nordmann, Dühring, and Henrici, for which the term "eliminationist" is apt – not in the strong sense of killing, but in the weaker if still significant sense of expropriation and expulsion, early forms of ethnic cleansing. But as pertaining to German citizens of the Jewish faith (as opposed to foreign-born Jews), these positions remained on the margin.

II

A generation later, in the shadow of the great transatlantic migrations and the European and American occupation of more than four-fifths of the globe, the "eliminationist" element of racism became more central,

---

[46] Treitschke, *Politik*, I, 273–275.
[47] Ibid., 276.

especially for men who had read Treitschke's histories, consumed his pamphlets, and heard his lectures. In the course of the 1880s, the world had changed significantly. Markers of this change include the shift from informal to formal imperialism and from indirect to direct colonial rule in Africa. More conservative governments came to power – in France following the Boulanger Affair, in England with Lord Salisbury's aggressively imperialist platform and opposition to Irish home rule, in Russia following the assassination of the liberal Czar Alexander II and the repressive turn to a policy of "orthodoxy, autocracy, and nationality." Ushered in by a transatlantic downturn in economic fortunes in the late seventies, the turn had significant consequence for both race and anti-Semitism. In the southern part of the United States, the advent of Jim Crow laws cemented color lines with the rule of specious law, allowing a segregation society to arise from the ashes of the Civil War like a malevolent phoenix. Based on an ideology of white supremacy and on the political and social disenfranchisement of African-Americans, its force also rested on terror, especially in the form of lynch mobs. In the Russian Empire, a similar kind of terror visited the Jews. The first pogrom fell in 1881 in the Ukrainian city of Elisavetgrad, as mobs attacked the Jews during Holy Week. Fueled by demagogues in the cities, one after another riot thereafter ignited throughout the Pale of Settlement so that by the end of 1881 there had been an estimated 259 pogroms, leaving thousands of Jews homeless, roughly forty Jews killed and hundreds injured.

The violence in the Russian Empire and in the American South initiated immense movements of peoples. Between 1881 and 1914, roughly 2.5 million Jews left the Russia Empire for the United States; and by the turn of the century, the slow stream of migration of African-Americans in the South to the cities of the north would become a torrent. The 1880s also witnessed mass waves of European migration, especially from northern and central Europe. In the last two decades of the nineteenth century, only the dimensions of Irish emigration rivaled the immensity of the German, which swelled into a last great wave in the early 1880s, and continued, only slightly abated, until 1893.[48] If still insufficiently

---

[48] Walter Nugent, *Crossings: The Great Transatlantic Migrations, 1870–1914* (Bloomington, Ind., 1992). On the topic of German labor migration, see the reflections in Sebastian Conrad, *Globalisierung und Nation im Deutschen Kaiserreich* (Munich, 2006), 233–235.

appreciated by scholars, the exodus was the largest ever from German soil.[49] Young men and women, many of whom had never experienced so much as a whiff of economic independence, boarded ships destined for the United States, where the possibility of a five-acre homestead on the great plains of Kansas beckoned them. Moreover, significant migrations continued within Germany well into the new century: from the eastern territories of Prussia to its western steel mills and smelting factories and to the dark shafts of the coal mines of the Ruhr. As is still true of the poor places of the earth, migration remained the bitter tribute paid by the poor to their poverty.

Segregated societies and hardened color lines; the clash of civilizations as Europe implemented ever more brutal colonial regimes; ethnic, racial, and religious violence; and the mass movements of peoples across vast waters and territories – all of this permeated the work and thought of Friedrich Ratzel. Along with the English statistician E. G. Ravenstein, Ratzel counted as the leading theorist of human movement in his day, and with the historian Karl Lamprecht and the ethnopsychologist Wilhelm Wundt, he was a key figure in the "*Laboratorium Leipzig*," an experiment in early cultural studies.[50] Ratzel received his *Habilitation* in 1876 with an examination of Chinese migration to the United States; thereafter, he turned his attention to the "natural peoples" who inhabited the vast colonial empires of Europe. In the 1880s and 1890s, first at the Polytechnical University of Munich, then at the University of Leipzig, Ratzel composed three major works documenting the ways in which human migrations and the natural environment shaped the development of cultures and civilizations. These works comprised *Anthropogeography*, published in 1882; *Ethnology (Völkerkunde)*, which came out in two volumes in 1894 and 1895; and *Political Geography*, which appeared in 1903.

In all three works, Ratzel attempted to show that the continuous movement of peoples constituted the fundamental condition of humanity. Expansion, not stasis, defined human history. The necessity of expansion derived, he argued, from the continual search, endemic to

---

[49] Klaus J. Bade, *Europa in Bewegung: Migration vom späten 18. Jahrhundert bis zur Gegenwart* (Munich, 2000).
[50] The best guide is Roger Chickering, *Karl Lamprecht: A German Academic Life* (Atlantic Highlands, N.J., 1993).

peoples of all cultural levels, for *Lebensraum*.⁵¹ The consequences of this natural law were twofold. First, as he put it in his *Anthropogeography*, "the tendency of history is to create ever larger empires, for with the development of culture the possibility of dominating space grows."⁵² Second, as he explained in a scholarly article published in 1880, history, the movement of peoples, meant that "humanity would become ever more homogenous, for mixture is inseparable from movement."⁵³

Ratzel's vision of mighty tribes, nations, and empires dominating and absorbing less powerful peoples seems at first glance to confirm squarely the observation of Claude Levi-Strauss, now rather self-evident, that early anthropology unabashedly served as the ideological "handmaiden of colonialism."⁵⁴ Ratzel was, in fact, the chairman of the Leipzig branch of the German Colonial Society.⁵⁵ Yet closer analysis renders the case, not contrary, but more complex. For Ratzel's historical narrative, more than Treitschke's, was ultimately inclusive, if also predicated on assimilationist assumptions. He considered "the introduction of the so-called lower races into the circle of the higher civilizations ... to be the greatest achievement of humanity in our century" and believed that the historiographical inclusion of peoples who had not hitherto been regarded as possessing a history constituted a juster notion.⁵⁶ Conversely, he argued against racist views that African nations could never achieve cultural distinction, as well as against a strictly evolutionist position that perceived the "lower" races of humankind as a mere transition from beast to man. Rather, as he put it in his *Ethnology*, "culture alone

---

⁵¹ For a summary of Ratzel's positions, see Woodruff Smith, *Politics and the Sciences of Culture*, 140–161. For Ratzel's larger context, see Conrad, *Globalisierung und Nation*, 60–61.

⁵² Friedrich Ratzel, *Anthropogeographie* (Stuttgart, 1891), 180.

⁵³ Cited by Ratzel in ibid., 438.

⁵⁴ Levi-Strauss as cited by Edward Said, *Culture and Imperialism* (New York, 1993), 152.

⁵⁵ Kevin Repp, *Reformers, Critics, and the Paths of German Modernity: Anti-Politics and the Search for Alternatives, 1890–1914* (Cambridge, Mass., 2000), 246.

⁵⁶ Friedrich Ratzel, *Völkerkunde*, vol. 1 (Leipzig, 1885), 9; Ratzel, *Anthropogeographie*, 347. Unless otherwise noted, all citations from Ratzel's *Völkerkunde* are from the first edition. In some cases, I have quoted from the revised second edition published in 1894–95. The second edition was translated into English and appeared as Friedrich Ratzel, *The History of Mankind*, tr. A.J. Butler, 3 vols. (London, 1896). In the case of citations from the second edition, I have used Butler's translation.

can draw a boundary between us and the natural races . . . natural races are nations poor in culture."[57]

The progress of nations turned, then, on cultural development. But Ratzel did not imagine this development as linear or peaceful. Rather, it resulted from contact and conflict between unequal cultures. Power and coercion therefore determined its outcome, the final consequence of which could well include the annihilation of peoples. "Through the clash of unequal cultures," he wrote in his *Anthropo-geography*, "whole countries have been depopulated, whole peoples destroyed."[58] The European invasion of the Americas and Australia served as a case in point. "The majority of the tribes who confronted the discoverers in the new worlds have disappeared," he pointed out.[59] But the collision, as well as the destruction it wrought, ultimately redounded to the benefit of cultural progress. As Ratzel put it, frankly, pithily, and brutally, "thousands of natives less, hundreds of thousands of square kilometers of free land more for the whites. More space for culture, more people who contribute to culture, more people who enjoy its blessings."[60] Contact did not necessarily entail annihilation, though it often did. As well, it brought the "natural peoples" into "the realm of history," a painful process, typically marked by the tendency of "the natural peoples to rapidly decline."[61] The reason for the almost universal decline was not however "the barbarity of the whites," but the lure of culturally superior institutions, which undermined native tradition, dissolved centuries-old tribal ties, and leveled the social edifice.[62]

A kaleidoscope of cultural assumptions colored Ratzel's vision. He perceived declining peoples as plagued by a series of unnatural vices, "from infanticide to abortion, polygamy and cannibalism."[63] Declining peoples, he supposed, more readily engaged in sexual license than vigorous, expanding peoples, and they more readily gravitated toward

---

[57] Ratzel, *Völkerkunde*, 10.

[58] Ratzel, *Anthropogeographie*, 358–359.

[59] Friedrich Ratzel, "Einige Aufgaben einer politischen Ethnologie," *Zeitschrift für Sozialwissenschaft*, 3.1 (1900): 1–19. Here cited in Ratzel, *Kleine Schriften*, ed. Hans Helmolt (München, 1906), vol. 2, 413.

[60] Ratzel, *Anthropogeographie*, 358–9.

[61] Ibid., 349–50.

[62] Ibid., 395.

[63] Ibid.

communistic attitudes toward private property.[64] Yet high cultures universally displayed a homogenizing dynamic, and low cultures or lesser races survived by subordination and integration. "A glance at the present day," he wrote in his *History of Humanity*, "is enough to show that Mulattos, Mestizos, Negro and Arab half-breeds stand in America and in Africa at the head of Indians and Negroes. The mixture once begun continues to progress, and each fresh infusion of higher blood tends to reduce the interval of leveling up."[65] Similarly, he argued that the Iroquois, though they will be exterminated as a race, will survive, in part, through the mixture of their blood with the white race.[66] In the last analysis, therefore, the outcome of the clash of races and cultures depended on the ability of the superior race, the dominant culture, to assimilate inferior races, weaker cultures. And this law he considered to be as true of the United States, dominated in his mind by Anglo-Celtic culture, as of neighboring Austria, where Germans predominated over Slavic peoples.[67]

In Ratzel's ethnography, racist assumptions pushed through the seams of a cultural theory that contained an unabashed teleology. "We speak of cultural stages," he wrote, and "we apply to the various civilizations on earth a certain standard which we have ourselves attained. Civilization means our civilization."[68] Yet precisely his cultural ethnocentrism allowed him to construct an inclusive narrative of world history, driven by the movements of peoples, the "unconscious ultimate aim" of which is the "fusion of mankind."[69] This fusion will be obtained by what he called "the victorious spread of the white race over the earth," or, as he qualified it, "the European branch of the white race."[70] The end of history, he believed, would make peoples coeval – but the price was assimilation, absorption, and ultimately annihilation.

---

[64] Friedrich Ratzel, *Völkerkunde*, 2 vols. (Leipzig, 1895), *The History of Mankind*, 117–118.

[65] Ratzel, *Völkerkunde*, 12.

[66] Ratzel, *Anthropogeographie*, 353.

[67] Friedrich Ratzel, "Nationalität und Rassen," *Türmer–Jahrbuch* (1903), 43–47. Here cited in Ratzel, *Kleine Schriften*, vol. 2, 485.

[68] Ratzel, *Völkerkunde*, 23.

[69] See also Friedrich Ratzel, "Einige Aufgaben einer politischen Ethnologie," *Zeitschrift fuer Sozialwissenschaft*, 3.1 (1900), 1–19. Here in *Kleine Schriften*, 403, where he refers to this fusion as a task bequeathed by revelation.

[70] Friedrich Ratzel, *Politische Geographie*, 3rd ed. (Munich and Berlin, 1925), 107.

Ratzel's narration of the clash of cultures fit into a long history of extinction discourse. European and trans-Atlantic in bearing, this discourse, as Patrick Brantlinger has argued, often took "the form of proleptic elegy," which Brantlinger defines as "sentimentally or mournfully expressing, even in its most humane versions, the confidence of a self-fulfilling prophecy, according to which new, white colonies and nations arise as savagery recedes."[71] This discourse was proleptic because it assigned to primitive peoples a time anterior to the present and elegiac because it lamented their passing. Comforting white colonizers by emphasizing the inevitability of extinction, proleptic elegy also justified white rule by showing that extinction served the higher end of humanity. In the nineteenth century, proponents of proleptic elegy ranged from Thomas Malthus to Charles Lyell to Thomas Henry Huxley to Charles Darwin, with Darwin setting the discourse in the stronger cement of scientific observation. But while Darwin saw the differences between the races of man as resulting from history and environment, Thomas Huxley divided races into eleven kinds, supposing an unbridgeable gulf between the highest and the lowest, and insisting on the utility of Darwin's insights for the administration of colonial rule. Set against European standards, then, Ratzel counts as a representative of a more humane vision. Within Germany, too, he insisted on less radical positions. Ratzel criticized contemporary anthropologists, like Adolf Bastian and Felix von Luschan, for their unbending interpretation that the "natural peoples" represented a fossilized *Urstand* of humanity. He also upbraided contemporary historians for their casual assumptions that non-literate peoples are incapable of culture, and thus outside the legitimate purview of history. Like his colleague Karl Lamprecht, Ratzel argued for a more inclusive understanding of historical research, one that considered the non-European world more seriously.[72]

Ratzel's relative position to others suggests something of the markers of mainstream thought. As Treitschke's reluctance to embrace a fully

---

[71] Patrick Brantlinger, *Dark Vanishings: Discourse on the Extinction of the Primitive Races, 1800–1930* (Ithaca, 2003), 3.

[72] Friedrich Ratzel, "Geschichte, Völkerkunde und historische Perspektive," *Historische Zeitschrift*, 93 (1904), 1–46. For the context, especially in anthropology, see Andrew Zimmerman, *Anthropology and Antihumanism in Imperial Germany* (Chicago, 2001), 203–206. On Bastian, H. Glenn Penny, *Objects of Culture: Ethnology and Ethnographic Museums in Imperial Germany* (Chapel Hill, 2002). 18–29.

articulated racist position tells us about the difficulties of alloying anti-Semitism with racism in Bismarckian Germany, Ratzel's place in the colonial discussions of the turn of the century suggests the dispersion of modern racism in social Darwinist guise. On the left and on the right, in Germany and in Europe, more and more people believed that humanity progressed by dint of constant struggle, in which weak peoples go to the wall.[73] This assumption also animated the eugenics movement, which in the 1890s gained notoriety. In *Inquiries into Human Faculty*, published in 1883, Francis Galton first referred to "eugenic questions" in conjunction with "various topics, more or less connected with the cultivation of race."[74] Nowhere was this connection to racial science stronger than in Germany, where in 1895 Alfred Ploetz introduced the term "racial hygiene" as a synonym for eugenics in his influential work, *The Fitness of Our Race and the Protection of the Weak*. Ploetz saw the dilemma of the social Darwinists as a conflict between the instinct to protect the defenseless and the deleterious effect that this necessarily had on the long-term fitness of the race. Medical care, he argued, means medical care for the weak, and while humane for the individual, it also effects a degeneration of the race. His solution, presented as a thought experiment, was to allow only fit babies to be born; those deemed unfit would be given a dose of morphine; at puberty another selection would take place, and those deemed unfit would not be allowed to marry. Otherwise, competition from equal starting points would govern society, thus ensuring that the fittest, and not merely the nobly born, would come out on top. Those who could not keep up would starve. Frightened by his own thought experiment, Ploetz suggested a more humane alternative in that only healthy people should be encouraged to procreate.[75] No weaklings, he reasoned, no extermination.

---

[73] Repp, *Reformers, Critics, and the Paths of German Modernity*. See also Richard J. Evans, "In Search of Social Darwinism: The History and Historiography of a Concept," in *Medicine and Modernity: Public Health and Medical Care in Nineteenth- and Twentieth-Century Germany*, eds. Manfred Berg and Geoffrey Cocks (New York, 1997), 55–80. Weikart, *From Darwin to Hitler*, 196; and on the coming together of colonialism, social-Darwinist thinking and eugenics more generally, Pascal Grosse, *Kolonialismus, Eugenik und bürgerliche Gesellschaft in Deutschland 1850–1918* (Frankfurt am Main, 2000).

[74] Francis Galton, *Inquiries into Human Faculty and its Development* (London, 1883), 17.

[75] See Alfred Kelly, *The Descent of Darwin: The Popularization of Darwinism in Germany* (Chapel Hill, 1981), 106.

If eugenics only attracted a small, elite following, it would be hard to overstate the general influence of social Darwinism.[76] The two best-selling books of nonfiction at the fin de siècle propagated social Darwinist themes: Ernst Haeckel's *World Riddle*, 1899, and Wilhelm Bölsche's *The Love Life of Animals*, 1899–1900; and when in 1899 the readers of the *Berliner Illustrierte Zeitung* were asked to name the most important thinkers of the nineteenth century, they listed Helmuth von Moltke first, followed by Kant and Darwin.[77] Structural transformations within Germany reinforced this general receptivity to Darwin. If in 1871 roughly five percent of the population lived in urban centers (with a population of over 20,000), by 1910 this number had increased to more than twenty percent. Marred by working-class slums and abject poverty, urban centers brought forth worrying demographic indicators, including higher rates of infant mortality. Some saw these indicators as a marker of racial degeneracy, exacerbated rather than ameliorated by industrial society. As industry drew workers from the land, workers as a class swelled in numbers, and the power of their political expression in social democracy grew apace. Moreover, as propagators of racial hygiene argued, the working class reproduced at higher rates than the middle class, causing the unfit to grow faster than the fit and the race to degenerate.

New ways of seeing criminality further distended this image. The translation of Cesare Lombroso's *L'uomo delinquente* (1876) into German between 1887 and 1890 inaugurated what the historian Richard Wetzell has called a "drastic shift in emphasis from social to medical-biological explanations of crime."[78] Lombroso defined "criminal man" as born not made, and as identifiable by small skull type, taller body, obliviousness to pain, and by a host of identifying marks. These marks, he believed, revealed an atavistic throwback to an earlier era, as

---

[76] On the relative importance of these movements, Edward Ross Dickinson, "Biopolitics, Fascism, Democracy: Some Reflections on Our Discourse About 'Modernity,'" *Central European History*, 37,1 (2004), 1–48.

[77] Nor was the interest in Darwin confined to the middle classes. "*Darwinia*" made up four among the ten most requested titles in German Workers Libraries in 1898. Repp, *Reformers*, 50. On this whole complex of popular science, centering on the Darwinian revolution, see the remarkable work by Andreas Daum, *Wissenschaftspopularisierung im 19. Jahrhundert: Bürgerliche Kultur, naturwissenschaftliche Bildung und die deutsche Öffentlichkeit*, 2nd ed. (Oldenburg, 2002).

[78] Richard F. Wetzell, *Inventing the Criminal: A History of German Criminology, 1880–1945* (Chapel Hill, 2000), 15. What follows is largely based on Wetzell's groundbreaking work.

the criminal "reproduces in his person the ferocious instincts of primitive humanity and the inferior animals." If not all German criminologists followed Lombroso's insistence on the physical attributes of criminals, they largely accepted his notion that criminal traits were hereditary. And those who did not, like the prominent criminal psychiatrist Gustav Aschaffenberg, nevertheless believed that racial degeneracy was linked to crime, and that a disproportionate number of criminals evinced signs of mental inferiority.[79] What followed was the necessity of protecting society from people deemed mentally deficient and the imperative to stop the growth of criminality in its biological tracks. Concretely, this meant surveillance, internment, and sterilization. In Germany's legal journals and daily newspapers, lay and professional criminologists put forth proposals ranging from medical examinations in schools to cull out the mentally deficient, to preventive incarceration in order to keep the mentally deficient from committing crimes, to male vasectomies for habitual criminals, as well as for people of "pronounced criminal natures" and the "mentally deficient" regardless of their criminal record. This last policy recommendation, sterilization, was first made in the German context by Paul Näcke in 1899. As Wetzell points out, it preceded both the organizational consolidation of the German eugenics movement (Ploetz did not establish the *Deutsche Gesellschaft für Rassenhygiene* until 1905), and the scientific acceptance of the Mendelian view of physical traits as inherited.[80] Within the intellectual coordinates of the eugenics movement, Mendel's insight, augmented by August Weismann's experiments, implied that the inherited traits of criminals, impoverished peoples, and the mentally ill could only be halted by arresting procreation. As the elimination of natural peoples enabled the spread of white culture across the earth, the elimination of "inferior people" fortified the white race, rendering it strong and lithe.

In a now classic essay, entitled "The Genesis of the 'Final Solution' from the Spirit of Science," first published in 1981, the historian Detlev Peukert identified the practical dilemmas of progressive social reform and the theoretical positions staked out by the turn of the century human sciences as the starting point of a "fatally racist dynamic."[81] Fatally new,

---

[79] Ibid., 69.
[80] Ibid., 101–103.
[81] Detlev Peukert, *Max Webers Diagnose der Moderne* (Göttingen, 1989), 104.

according to Peukert, was the qualitative division of humanity according to worthy (*wert*) and worthless (*unwert*) coupled with a view that not man is the measure, still less individual men and women, but the body of the nation or the race (*Volkskörper*). When the parsing away of unworthy life serves the race, death is the subject of public negotiation, and life no longer sacrosanct. Peukert set his interpretation against "the traditional history of Jew hatred and persecution" and argued that while there can be no monocausal explanation for Auschwitz, it is still necessary to consider the "red thread that allows us to reconstruct the genesis of the historically singular decision for the industrial extermination of abstractly defined categories of victims."[82]

Piercing, illuminating, and influential, Peukert's "genesis" is however synchronically and diachronically narrow: synchronically because it emphasizes the German context of movements (in eugenics and criminology, for example) that were genuinely transnational and wrenches these movements out of wider contexts implicated in colonialism and projects of white supremacy; and diachronically because it considers neither older discourses of extermination nor their targeting of concretely defined victims. Moreover, to consider the history of anti-Semitism as incidental to the problem of Auschwitz seems disingenuous, and not merely because, as Peukert conceded, Jews constituted the numerically largest group of victims. Rather, anti-Semitism has long been precise mercury measuring the rise and demise of humane attitudes toward others. Turn of the century human sciences were, on the other hand, hardly all of the same die.[83] Ratzel, for example, distrusted biological determinism and abhorred the metaphors of disease that accompanied the new language of race. And he criticized those writings, like Houston Stewart Chamberlain's *Foundations of the Nineteenth Century* (1899) that rendered the past hundred years as a century of race, as against Leopold von Ranke's depiction of it as a century of nations. Instead, Ratzel retained an old-fashioned view that environment determined the possibilities of peoples and that a basic unity underlay the races of man. But Peukert was no doubt right when he argued that the way forward traversed a different route.

---

[82] Ibid.
[83] Houston Stewart Chamberlain, *Die Grundlagen des neunzehnten Jahrhunderts* (Munich, 1899), 7, 23.

III

In the imperial sphere, the prophet of new politics was Paul Rohrbach. Born in 1869 in a Baltic German enclave in what is now Latvia, he was educated at the University of Dorpat in Estonia, where the pressures of Russification soon forced him to pursue higher studies at the University of Berlin. In Berlin, he attended Treitschke's lectures and hoped, as he put it in a letter to the aging but still vigorous professor of history, "to one day become a man like Heinrich von Treitschke."[84] But for all his admiration for Treitschke, Rohrbach worked more closely with Hans Delbrück, who would emerge as a genuinely acute chronicler of military history, and he wrote his dissertation with Adolf von Harnack, perhaps the greatest representative of liberal mediation theology in Germany. When Rohrbach could not find a way to pursue a *Habilitation* in the Russian Empire, he returned to Germany permanently, becoming a Prussian citizen in 1894. He then studied Protestant theology in Berlin and Strasbourg and drifted ever more toward liberal positions. As his theological liberalism hindered his academic career, he drifted into the world of religious and political publishing, writing for liberal newspapers such as the *Frankfurter Zeitung* and journals such as the *Preussische Jahrbücher* and *Die Hilfe*. In his first major statement, published in 1900 and entitled *The Greater Germany*, he admonished his fellow Protestants to take up the challenge of world policy. Germany's increasing population raised the specter of a country unable to feed itself with its own stores, thus making it dependent on the goodwill of other nations, especially Russia and the United States. Rohrbach urged his countrymen to turn their imperial attention eastward and to infuse Germany's imperial ambitions with a serum of Christian values. Not sheer power and domination, but moral leadership and the export of German knowhow should guide policy.[85] Informed by extensive travel to the Ottoman Empire and Persia, his policy prescriptions harbored a mixture of ambition and utopia, as when he imagined that German irrigation engineers would return the land between the Tigris and Euphrates to a verdant paradise. Then, in 1903, the Colonial Office appointed Rohrbach settlement commissioner in Southwest Africa, and in this capacity,

---

[84] Cited in Mogk, *Paul Rohrbach*, 27.
[85] Ibid., 76–80.

he analyzed the economic aspects of Germany's African colonies, the geopolitical issues of sub-Saharan Africa, and the relations between white German settlers and indigenous peoples.[86] Widely considered an astute commentator, he also revealed what he understood as the just outcome of cultural collision between "civilized" and "natural" peoples.

In Southwest Africa, that collision was unequal and would remain so. For in Rohrbach's mind African peoples (unlike the Turks or Chinese or Indians) were "*kulturunfähig*," incapable of cultural achievement. They could mimic European ways, but they "lacked the capacity to be educated to moral independence (*sittlicher Selbständigkeit*)."[87] *Bildung*, for the liberal tradition the elixir that transformed nations and classes, could not radically change this situation. Rohrbach therefore insisted on its narrow circumscription: *Bildung* meant teaching Africans to work. "The education of the African race to a higher level of development . . . is in the first instance synonymous with the education of the Blacks to work," he wrote in *The Colony*, a book published in 1907 as part of the famous series of progressive monographs entitled *The Society* (*Die Gesellschaft*), edited by Martin Buber.[88] This education redounded to the benefit both of the Europeans and the Africans: to the former because by "developing the raw and underdeveloped workforce, which lies latent in the native peoples of Africa we . . . increase our material and moral goods . . ."; to the latter because the education to work improves them morally and raises their material standard of living.[89] This "service to them," in turn, justifies the "moral right of domination."[90] That domination was to be permanent. Nowhere in Rohrbach's writings does one encounter the idea that education may, in time, lead to equality.

Instead, Rohrbach denied the possibility of Africans being equal in theory and recommended concrete measures to prevent it in practice. He warned repeatedly against "a pedagogical system" that attempts to "raise" Africans to a higher cultural level by schooling. In fact, he

---

[86] See especially, Paul Rohrbach, *Deutschland unter den Weltvölkern* (Berlin, 1903); Paul Rohrbach, *Deutsche Kolonialwirtschaft*, vol. 1, *Südwest-Afrika* (Berlin, 1907); Paul Rohrbach, *Aus Südwestafrikas schweren Tagen* (Berlin, 1909); Paul Rohrbach, *Die Kolonie* (Frankfurt am Main, 1907).

[87] Rohrbach, *Die Kolonie*, 68–9.

[88] Ibid., 70.

[89] Ibid., 98. On conceptions of labor in the African colonies, Conrad, *Globalisierung und Nation*, 74–123.

[90] Ibid.

considered mission and public schools to be a great threat to the European domination of Africa. "Nothing is more preposterous," he wrote in *The Colony*, "than indiscriminately giving the natives of Africa access to any one of the European cultures and written languages."[91] Rohrbach's insistence on denying access derived partly from the specter of "Ethiopianism" (referring to the successful Ethiopian wars against Italy, culminating in the Italian defeat at Adowa in 1896). Not without reason, Rohrbach feared that common language links among linguistically separate African nations would create the preconditions for militarily coordinated acts of resistance against European colonizers.[92] But his resistance to making written European language accessible also stemmed from a chain of cultural assumptions, central to the European intellectual tradition, which linked writing to culture to humanity. Henry Louis Gates Jr. has eloquently elucidated the logic of this chain: "Without writing, no repeatable sign of the workings of reason, of mind, could exist. Without memory or mind, no history could exist. Without history, no humanity."[93] Rohrbach, who denied writing to the indigenous nations of sub-Saharan Africa, could not, also, conceive of their culture or admit of their history, which, in the framework of his own assumptions, meant a still more fundamental (and for Rohrbach unanswered) question as to their humanity.

Here one must consider the confluence of cultural assumptions with a position that must be seen for what it is: unalloyed racism. Treitschke, in his reflections on Slavic peoples, posited the just subjugation of the Poles because he considered them unfit to make a state. For him, culture and power were intimately tied, but power determined the fate of cultures and, consequently, of peoples and races. To be sure, Treitschke also harbored racist assumptions, especially with respect to Jews; but when reprimanded by his peers, he hesitated to push these assumptions further, and race never became central to his larger thinking on power and politics. For Friedrich Ratzel, cultural collision – destructive, violent – contributed, however imperfectly, to the advance of culture. Racist assumptions also pushed their way into his ethnography, but a theoretically racist stance is not to be found in his work. The most progressive of the

---

91 Ibid., 99–100. See also Rohrbach, *Kolonialwirtschaft*, vol. 1, vii.
92 Ibid.
93 Henry Louis Gates Jr., "Writing 'Race' and the Difference it Makes," in Gates Jr., ed., *"Race," Writing and Difference* (Chicago, 1986), 11.

three thinkers, Rohrbach was different; he articulated explicitly racist positions, and these positions shaped the way he narrated the clash of unequal cultures and the subsequent elimination of peoples.

Racism, to cite George Fredrickson's succinct if partial definition, assumes that differences between peoples "are due mainly to immutable genetic factors and not to environmental or historical circumstances."[94] This clarifies an important part of Rohrbach's vision. For Rohrbach was indeed concerned with genetic issues, especially with respect to mixed marriages and the resultant "creolization" of peoples. In his writings, he supported judicial sanctions against mixed marriages – even though this "process of purification and differentiation will mean hardship for certain individuals" – and based his argument on the necessity of maintaining a strict, hierarchically ordered, color line.[95] Moreover, a rhetorical appeal to images of class and gender, signifying power and dominance, studded his arguments. In his major work, *Colonial Economy*, published in 1907, he wrote of "an emerging bastard race" in which "half-whites" live with "colored concubines" and "in a surprisingly short time each and every sense for morality, culture, social order and national worth gets lost."[96] In Rohrbach's descriptions, white men are declassed by the lure of women whose race and status are reduced to a signifier of illicit sexuality ("colored concubines") and whose offspring are forever polluted as "dirty bastard children."[97] And the pollution, to borrow from Mary Douglas, symbolizes both transgression into the forbidden and descent into the immoral.[98] That descent was, moreover, irreversible; it followed the logic of caste rather than class.

Rohrbach clung tenaciously to the idea that while class differences are fluid, racial barriers, like boundaries of caste, are, and should be, impermeable. In this regard, he set himself off from Ratzel, for the latter could imagine a time – however far off in the distant future – when the homogenizing sweep of modernity leveled differences between peoples. Rohrbach could only imagine this for some, but not for all peoples. The analytical distinction between class and caste is, in this context, of

---

[94] George M. Fredrickson, *White Supremacy: A Comparative Study in American and South African History* (New York, 1981), xii.

[95] Rohrbach, *Die Kolonie*, 40.

[96] Rohrbach, *Kolonialwirtschaft*, vol. 1, 393.

[97] Ibid., 63.

[98] See Mary Douglas, *Purity and Danger: An Analysis of the Concepts of Pollution and Taboo* (New York, 1966).

considerable importance. Class societies may be inhumane, but they do not presuppose the literal inhumanity of those on the bottom. But this is precisely the case with Rohrbach, who wondered aloud about whether he was not, in fact, looking at "two kinds of humanity," and who posited "a special morality for the tropical dominions and protectorates of the white race."[99] This morality encouraged severity; it justified brutality and claimed to civilize through violence. And if this morality did not advocate the annihilation of peoples, as Rohrbach's did not, it justified killing.

IV

An annihilation, not merely cultural but physical, had indeed taken place. In the course of the Herero Uprising of 1904, General von Trotha, the commander of the colonial troops in Southwest Africa, pursued his opponents into the Omaheke desert, which, when sealed off, spelled death by starvation and thirst for the majority of the Herero, including women, children, and old people. Many of the civilians who did not die in the desert were simply shot, often in the back as they were running away, or as they were trying to surrender.[100] "Within the German borders, every Herero, whether armed or unarmed, with or without cattle, will be shot to death," von Trotha insisted in his infamous "extermination order," "I will no longer receive women or children but will drive them back to their people or have them shot at."[101]

The order justified racial violence rather than causing it. In fact, von Trotha did not issue the order until a full month after the massacre had occurred. The cause of the massacre, as Isabel V. Hull has argued, is to be found in the frustrations of a German military committed to the complete destruction of the enemy on the one hand, and the racist image that von Trotha held of the Africans as sub-human on the other. Hull emphasizes the former over the latter in explaining "the mass death of noncombatants." "That result was compatible with von Trotha's racist views," she writes, "but it actually evolved from standard military doctrines and practices."[102] These were the practices of an institution that

99 Rohrbach, *Die Kolonie*, 30–31, 58.
100 Hull, *Absolute Destruction*, 45–51.
101 Cited in ibid., 56.
102 Ibid., 53.

enjoyed the shield of constitutional immunity – an army, as Chief of the Military Cabinet Hahnke put it in 1895, "into which no one dare peer with critical eyes."[103] But the army also enjoyed social admiration, especially after its swift victory over France in 1870. This admiration rendered the German Army both cocksure and unable to entertain anything but total victory, especially against indigenous warriors in sub-Saharan Africa. Von Trotha had actually botched the battle of Waterberg by leaving open the escape route into the desert, and precisely that moment of failure encouraged the escalation into mass murder – the shift, as Rohrbach put it, from destroying the resistance of the enemy to destroying physically the whole tribe. But it still seems unthinkable without von Trotha's fundamental attitudes toward the Herero. "Against non-humans [*Unmenschen*] one cannot conduct war 'humanely,'" he allegedly said nine days before the battle. Moreover, since serving as lieutenant colonel and then deputy governor in German East Africa, von Trotha had learned, as he later claimed, the tactics of "racial war," which included burning down villages, starving out local populations, summary executions, and other forms of "terrorism," as von Trotha called it.[104] It would be too much to argue that when von Trotha arrived in German Southwest Africa, he was already "pregnant with murder," or that he had from the start a clear "aim of annihilating the Herero." But that he was more bloody-minded than his predecessor, Governor Theodor Leutwein, Rohrbach understood from the start. Paired with a racial ideology that questioned whether the Herero belonged to the family of man, this bloody-mindedness allowed him to slide more easily from war to mass murder. He ordered his troops to shoot the Herero rather than taking prisoners and pronounced the necessity of a different kind of warfare, one ending in the destruction of the enemy. As a military commander, he created an atmosphere that permitted and even encouraged gratuitous violence. His troops – inexperienced recent reinforcements, nerves frayed, and plagued by hunger and thirst – no doubt assumed that von Trotha at least approved, more likely ordered, the massacres of unarmed men, women, and children.[105]

[103] Cited by Gordon Craig, *The Politics of the Prussian Army, 1640–1945* (Oxford, 1955), 247.
[104] Hull, *Absolute Destruction*, 25–27.
[105] Ibid., 51.

The transition from military massacre to genocide also became evident in the condition of what contemporaries already called concentration camps. First set up by the Spanish in Cuba in 1896, they became infamous during the Second Boer War, when Lord Kitchner concentrated non-combatants in South Africa, at first benignly, then with increasing severity. In the more than thirty camps spread throughout South Africa, some 28,000 Boers had mortally languished by the end of the war, a death rate of roughly twenty percent. Roughly 14,000 black men, women, and children also died, at a rate of about twelve percent.[106] Most had been struck down by disease, especially dysentery, which in turn had been caused by criminal neglect, malnutrition, and unsanitary conditions. The German concentration camps in Southwest Africa were not different in kind from those the British had set up, but the Germans administered the camps with greater severity and with still less concern for whether inmates lived or died. As a result of this callousness, death rates ranged higher. According to one calculation, the total death rate for the Nama at the concentration camp on Shark Island was over 100 percent, which means that every year the original prison population died, and already within the year a significant proportion of new prisoners perished as well. In 1906, the situation was especially horrendous, with Shark Island registering an annual death rate of 227 percent for the Nama, eighty-six percent for the Herero; and other camps, such as Windhoek, showing mortality rates as high as sixty-one percent. It is true that the "concentration camps" of Southwest Africa were built with different purposes in mind than the concentration camps of the Third Reich. But the camps in Africa were significantly more deadly than the concentration camps of the first nine years of Nazi rule; it is not until the Second World War and the setting up of extermination camps that an altogether different universe of killing dawned. If continuity suggests itself, it is instead with the lack of regard for human life with which the German Army incarcerated and killed Russian POWs. But at Windhoek, Shark Island, Okahandja, Swopkopmund, Germans incarcerated and killed civilians as well.

The total number who died in Southwest Africa is difficult to discern. By 1911, there were 13,858 Nama still alive and 19,962 Herero. This means that the Nama lost roughly half its people, the Herero closer to

---

[106] Ibid., 151–2.

two-thirds. German losses included 676 killed in battle, 76 missing, and 689 who perished from disease.[107] At the same time, a less genocidal, but for that more destructive war raged in German East Africa. Here there was not one decisive battle, which in failure led to a relentless, genocidal pursuit; nor did concentration camps decimate the remaining population; and an annihilation order was not issued. Yet the policy of scorched earth, forced starvation, summary executions, and plunder led to the deaths of at least 100,000 Africans in the course of the Maji Maji War, which raged between 1905 and 1907.[108] Altogether, then, the German Army shot down, starved, thirsted, and otherwise killed, on a conservative estimate, 200,000 African men, women, and children between 1904 and 1907.

The civilian reaction to the killing ranged from unqualified assent to harsh criticism. In a series of Reichstag debates that began in March 1904, these positions were hammered out, with conservatives and national liberals arguing now for qualified eradication, now for clearly visible forms of white supremacy; and liberals on the left considering how economic imperatives could be paired with universal maxims of humanity (to which the massacre was an affront).[109] Ernst Müller

---

[107] Ibid., 88. The figures have been contested, though not with sufficient evidence. For the argument that genocide did not occur, see Gunther Spraul, "Der 'Völkermord' an den Herero," in *Geschichte in Wissenschaft und Unterricht,* 12 (1988), 713–740. For a corrective to Spraul, see the careful work of Henry Harpending and Renee Pennington, who assume that there were roughly 7,000 refugees from the German attempt at genocide in 1904. See Henry Harpending and Renee Pennington, "Herero Demographic History," in *Minority Populations: Genetics, Demography and Health* (London, 1992), 68–82; and, for more detail, Renee Pennington and Henry Harpending, *The Structure of an Africanist Pastoral Community* (Oxford, 1993).

[108] See now *Der Maji-Maji-Krieg in Deutsch-Ostafrika, 1905–1907,* eds. Felicitas Becker and Jigal Beez (Berlin, 2005). Ludwig Wimmelbücker, "Verbrannte Erde: Zu den Bevölkerungsverlusten als Folge des Maji-Maji-Krieges," in ibid., 92, suggests total losses at 180,000. On the continuity of genocide as part of colonial practice, see the controversial but revealing work of Jürgen Zimmerer, *Deutsche Herrschaft über Afrikaner. Staatlicher Machtanspruch und Wirklichkeit im kolonialen Namibia* (Münster, 2002). See also *Völkermord in Deutsch-Südwestafrika. Der Kolonialkrieg (1904–1908) in Namibia und seine Folgen,* eds. Jürgen Zimmerer and Joachim Zeller (Berlin, 2003).

[109] On these debates, Helmut Walser Smith, "The Talk of Genocide, the Rhetoric of Miscegenation: Notes on Debates in the German Reichstag concerning Southwest Africa, 1904–1914," in *The Imperialist Imagination: German Colonialism and its Legacy,* eds. Sara Friedrichsmeyer, Sara Lennox, and Susanne Zantop (Ann Arbor, 1998), 107–124. See, now, however, the more thorough treatments in Lora Wildenthal, *German Women for Empire, 1884–1945* (Durham, 2001), 131–171, and Birthe Kundrus, *Moderne Imperialisten: Das Kaiserreich im Spiegel seiner Kolonien* (Vienna, 2003), 219–280.

Meiningen, a left liberal, proposed as a humane solution reservations, "much as we have reservations for wild animals, much as we have Indian reservations in North America."[110] Only the Catholic Center Party and the Social Democrats generated criticism based on the language of rights – in the Catholic case with special force in areas of immediate concern (the sanctity of mixed marriages against those who wanted the state to annul them), and in the Socialist case with respect to the violence itself, which August Bebel thought "not only barbaric, but bestial."[111] In the Reichstag debate concerning genocide, not even the bloody-minded conservatives on the right argued that the Germans ought to exterminate the Nama and Herero. Yet most parliamentarians, excluding the Socialists and with some qualifications the Catholic Center deputies, defended the killing that had occurred. They argued that violence was already inherent in the lands and peoples they annexed and that it was not a matter of accepting or rejecting violence but seeing that the new violence in question served German interests or the larger requirements of progress. They also believed that violence inhered in the logic of a situation, that it tended to its own suspension, and that it was necessary to understand the totality to which it belonged.

The elimination of peoples, not as a policy prescription but as the acceptance of a policy fact, thus became inextricably paired with racial thinking, and racial thinking came to inform politics across the political spectrum, halting only hesitantly at the Socialist and Catholic milieus. Not, then, that "on or about December 1910, human character had changed," as Virginia Woolf famously wrote in 1924, but that who counted as fully human had become restricted and the reach of humanity less generous.

V

Two works allow us to trace the deeper logic of eliminationist racism in Wilhelmine Germany on the eve of the war. Each work was remarkably successful; each eschewed a narrow position, whether anti-Semitism or colonial; and each started from a nationalist position, and from there

---

[110] Cited in Smith, "Talk of Genocide," 114–5.
[111] Cited in ibid., 111.

integrated eliminationist racism into a coherent national program. The first was from the left, the second from the right.

The first book, written with the official sanction of the foreign office, is Paul Rohrbach's *The German Idea in the World* (*Der Deutsche Gedanke in der Welt*).[112] Between 1912, when it was published, and 1914, when war broke out, 75,000 copies of the book were sold.[113] Its English translator, an instructor at Harvard, claimed that "this book probably inspired more Germans than any other book published since 1871."[114] As World War I came in between, it is impossible to gauge what the long-term resonance of Rohrbach's book might have been in more peaceful times. A renewed call for an "ethical imperialism," the book owed its considerable popularity on the eve of the war to its patient insistence that the German mission abroad was not just a matter of power and dominance, but also, and more importantly, of culture and humanity. "We start very consciously," Rohrbach wrote in the introduction, "with the conviction that we have been placed in the arena of the world in order to work out moral perfection, not only for ourselves, but for all mankind."[115]

Rohrbach's appeal to humanity was more than mere cant. Rather, as we have seen, he emphasized the confluence of culture and humanity in the imperialist mission. Power, a force that transfixed previous generations of German nationalists, did not hold the same fascination for him; culture, more than power, determined the ultimate influence of nations. "The world is there for the purpose of being the sphere of expansion not only for one's ships and goods," he argued, "but also for one's national idea."[116] Consequently, the colonial race determined which country would rule the globe as well as which national culture, which national idea, would shape humanity.

But in the struggle of nations, Germany, an incomplete nation, projected an incomplete national idea. Though politically unified for nearly half a century, Germany continued to suffer from divisions of caste,

---

[112] Rüdiger vom Bruch, *Weltpolitik als Kulturmission: Auswärtige Kulturpolitik und Bildungsbürgertum in Deutschland am Vorabend des Ersten Weltkrieges* (Paderborn, 1982), 15.

[113] Ibid., 73.

[114] Paul Rohrbach, *German World Policies* (*Der Deutsche Gedanke in der Welt*) tr. Edmund von Mach (New York, 1915), viii.

[115] Paul Rohrbach, *Der Deutsche Gedanke in der Welt* (Düsseldorf and Leipzig, 1912), 6.

[116] Ibid., 56.

class, and confession. Unduly divisive politics further debilitated the German nation, crippling the German idea. Yet Rohrbach did not merely repeat the standard shibboleths of his age. His call for unity did not entail a ritual denunciation of the Socialists or the equally common denigration of the Catholics. Rather, Rohrbach insisted on genuine national unity and authentic harmony as the precondition of successful world politics. Significantly, *The German Idea in the World* was bereft of anti-Semitism.

The real violence that inhered in his thought happened elsewhere – in the colonies, where the German idea commixed with the annihilation of primitive nations. Of German civilians, he had been among the best informed about the genocide of the Herero and Nama, and he had criticized von Trotha for the massacres. Yet his reasoning is instructive. The rebellion in the German colony of Southwest Africa, Rohrbach argued, derived from the lenient policies of governor Leutwein, who failed to show the natives that "the greater power is with us and that they are unconditionally the weaker ones."[117] Rather than attempt to annihilate the two nations, he believed, it would have been economically wiser and politically more astute to expropriate the land and cattle of the indigenous peoples and degrade them to the status of indentured servants – "in the manner of the so-called Kaffirs with the Boers."[118] Instead, von Trotha delayed the peace necessary for the economic exploitation of the colony and raised exponentially the costs associated with the prosecution of the war. Rohrbach's criticism of von Trotha rested, then, on arguments of expediency. But as concerned "the perspective of humanity," Rohrbach sided with von Trotha. "One must admit," Rohrbach wrote, "that in certain conditions, in order to secure the peaceful settlement of the whites in the face of a rapacious native tribe incapable of culture, it can be necessary to actually destroy them." So that his readers understood what was at issue, he defined this destruction as "not only in the self evident military sense, that is the destruction of resistance, but the real eradication of the tribe" (*wirkliche Austilgung des Stammes*).[119]

In 1912, in his *German Idea in the World*, Rohrbach did not revisit the near eradication of the Herero and Nama. In fact, he passed over it in silence. He nevertheless reiterated the theoretical basis for elimination.

---

[117] Rohrbach, *Koloniale Wirtschaft*, 339.
[118] Ibid., 354–5.
[119] Rohrbach, *Koloniale Wirtschaft*, 47. See also Helmut Bley, *Southwest Africa under German Rule, 1894–1914* (Evanston, Ill., 1971), 226.

"No false philanthropy or race-theory," he wrote, "can prove to reasonable people that the preservation of any tribe of Nomadic South African Kaffirs or their primitive cousins on the shores of Lakes Kiwi or Victoria is more important for the future of mankind than the expansion of the great European nations or the white races as a whole."[120] What impresses is the confluence of ideas of progress and modernity with the self-evident assumption that peoples of lower culture do not contribute to humanity. The "countless ages" in which "barbarians and primitive peoples" had eked out an existence from the fields and steppes of Africa represented "lives equally useless to the culture and social economy of the world."[121]

This was a modern view – the possibility of elimination is thought, justified, but not advocated. Within three years, Rohrbach would revisit the issue of elimination when the Turks began the systematic eradication of the Armenians. Rohrbach had traveled widely in Asia Minor, and in 1914 he had become a founding member of the German-Armenian Society. He believed the Armenians to be a people capable of culture and receptive to German ideas and institutions. Unlike his critique of von Trotha, which emphasized the impracticality of genocide for the economic expansion of white settlers, Rohrbach's critique of the Turkish attempt to annihilate the Armenians centered on fundamental considerations of morality.[122] Toward the Armenians, he felt a deep kinship, absent in his relation to black Africans, and this sense of kinship no doubt informed his principled position on the second genocide. Perhaps, too, Rohrbach's career illustrates Michael Ignatieff's more general observation that "[e]veryone's universalism ultimately anchors itself in a particular commitment to a specifically important group of people whose cause is close to one's heart or conviction."[123]

If Rohrbach's *The German Idea in the World* tells us about the status of eliminationist racism among the liberal left and center in Germany on the eve of World War I, then Heinrich Class's *If I Were the Kaiser* (*Wenn ich der Kaiser wär*), epitomized it for the mainstream of the German

---

[120] Rohrbach, *Der Deutsche Gedanke in der Welt*, 143.
[121] Ibid., 142.
[122] Hull, *Absolute Destruction*, 273, 331.
[123] Cited by Margaret Lavinia Anderson "'Down in Turkey, far away': Human Rights, the Armenian Massacres, and Orientalism in Wilhelmine Germany." *The Journal of Modern History*, 79 (March 2007), 109.

right.[124] Leader of the Pan-German League since 1908, Class can only be described as a conservative revolutionary. Already the title of his book signaled an affront to a calm and cautious dynastic nationalism – for here a commoner arrogated to himself the competence to know better than the Kaiser himself what the Kaiser should do. Few books so tersely stake out the threatening possibilities of twentieth-century politics. It starts with a concept of nation, but one that subordinates all other elements to it: there are no particularistic loyalties here, no querulous religious denominations. Unlike Treitschke, for whom the state gave shape and form to the nation, Class sees the nation, defined in terms of race, as the historical subject, and the state subordinate to it.[125] Some German conservatives, Class complains, still resist the idea of race, but this is a backward view, timid conservativism. Believing himself to be in the tradition of Bismarck, the "white revolutionary," Class takes leave of conservative ideas conventionally conceived and stakes out a "national revolutionary" position. He has, for example, abandoned Protestant antagonism against the Catholic Center Party, and while he loathes the Socialists, he distrusts big business because its captains place profit before the interests of the nation. He holds conservative views of women and cannot imagine any role for them save to keep their houses "holy and pure" and to draw "a sharp boundary between them and everything impure."[126] At the same time, though not inconsistently, he takes on eugenic prescriptions for keeping the race healthy, including sensible nutrition, outdoor activity, and efforts to eradicate alcoholism. He is ready to abandon equality before the law and substitute for it a legal system that takes into account "the service of the individual for the collectivity."[127] He likewise counsels adopting a new constitution that would reserve the vote for men of "education and property;" these men, "a nobility of merit next to a

---

[124] On Class, see Roger Chickering, *We Men Who Feel Most German* (Boston, 1984), 286–7; and Geoff Eley, *Reshaping the German Right: Radical Nationalism and Political Change after Bismarck* (New Haven, 1980), 320–21, and, for the radical nationalist milieu and its ideology, 147–205. On Class in the Weimar Republic and the Third Reich, see Rainer Hering, *Konstruierte Nation: Der Alldeutsche Verband 1890 bis 1939* (Hamburg, 2003), 355–365.

[125] For a terse summary of the difference between Class and Treitschke, see Stefan Breuer, *Grundpositionen der deutschen Rechten* (Tübingen, 1999), 40.

[126] Daniel Frymann (pseud. for Heinrich Class), *Wenn ich der Kaiser wär. Politische Wahrheiten und Notwendigkeiten* (Leipzig, 1912), 121.

[127] Ibid., 124.

nobility of birth," would then elect a Reichstag, which would appoint ministers, and even counselors, to the Kaiser. This system, Class reasons, will bring forth a new and better relationship between the Kaiser and the people and, far from remaining a distant monarch, the Kaiser will emerge as a genuine "*Führer.*"

With respect to question of race, and to the question of German power, his radicalism pushes through the seams in startling twentieth-century ways. He has sympathy for the efforts to colonize Africa, but he believes that "the right colonial policy lies in the east of the Empire," and that to spread Germans around the globe would only dissipate their strength. He urges instead for Germany to push the bounds of Empire at home, and this most likely means the pursuit of a ruthless Polish policy and the settlement of Germans in the eastern parts of the Empire. It also means expansion to the southeast, preferably in tandem with the Habsburg crown, which he counsels should put itself more firmly on a German national foundation. But Class also gives consideration to offensive war against either France or Russia, both cases in which victory would leave Germany with tracts of land filled with antagonistic foreigners. It is at this point that he raises the possibility that Germany should demand "depopulated land."

German authors had raised the specter before. In 1807, Fichte speculated about the possibility of expelling unassimilated Poles and Jews in his unpublished fragment, *The Republic of the Germans in the Twenty-Second Century*. It was perhaps the first time that a German intellectual conceived of expulsion in the context of the new nationalism. Then, in 1814, Heinrich Luden, a liberal professor of history at the University of Jena, and decisive influence on the students at Wartburg, considered "removing citizens belonging to foreign peoples beyond the natural borders of our state and in this way to purify it" – but thought deportation "terrible and inhumane."[128] A year later, Jacob Fries raised the possibility of the Spanish model of expulsion should the Jews of Germany fail to assimilate. The Wars of Liberation constituted the intellectual hothouse in which these ideas were first, if hesitatingly, spawned – principally from the left, as then defined. Thereafter, ethnic cleansing remained a

---

[128] Heinrich Luden, "Das Vaterland, oder Staat und Volk," *Nemesis: Zeitschrift für Politik und Geschichte*, 1 (1814), 324. On this remarkable essay, see Karl Schlögel, "Kosovo war überall," *Die Zeit*, 18/1999.

theoretical possibility within the tradition, but it was by no means central to it. During the Revolution of 1848, no one in the Frankfurt Parliament advanced expulsion as a legitimate solution to the ethnic geography of central and eastern Europe.[129] Instead, the delegates insisted that constitutional legality should structure national arrangements. Austrian liberals, who faced more complicated ethnic challenges, similarly relied on an open-ended and inclusive sense of German nationality – in 1848, and for three decades thereafter, as Pieter Judson has argued.[130] But the possibility of expulsion never disappeared entirely. In 1854, Paul de Lagarde revived the idea with respect to Jews, insisting on complete assimilation or expulsion. His ruminations remained marginal, however, and did not resonate widely until the late Wilhelmine period.[131] During the post-revolutionary period, nationality politics on the right remained too tied to the state, and too involved in questions of constitutionality, to entertain the idea of ethnic cleansing. To Ludwig August von Rochau, the progenitor of *Realpolitik*, the proposition would have seemed foreign. And Heinrich von Treitschke, for all his disparagements of Poles and Jews, maintained great faith in the civilizing capacity of the modern state. Not until Treitschke published "Our Prospects" in 1879 did expulsion resurface as an issue of public debate, but mainly, as we have seen, on the margins of politics and with respect to Jews. In the Austrian lands as well, the first decisive stirrings of radical German nationalism began in 1879, following the liberal fall from power, and even then it was not until circa 1900 that ethnic conceptions of nationhood had significant traction within the liberal milieu.[132] By this time, the idea of "an ambitious policy of evacuation" with respect to the eastern territories began to appear in isolated articles and pamphlets of the radical

---

[129] One exception, in a published work, is the radical democrat, Gustav Struve, who reflected on the possibility in the fourth volume of his *Grundzüge der Staatswissenschaft*, published in 1848 – but his proposal to iron out ethnic irregularities remained isolated, even in his own politics. On this proposal, see Brian Vick, *Defining Germany: The 1848 Frankfurt Parliamentarians and National Identity* (Cambridge, Mass., 2002), 45.

[130] Pieter M. Judson, *Exclusive Revolutionaries: Liberal Politics, Social Experience, and National Identity in the Austrian Empire, 1848–1914* (Ann Arbor, 1996), 269–70.

[131] Fritz Stern, *The Politics of Cultural Despair: A Study in the Rise of the Germanic Ideology* (Berkeley, 1961), 90–91. On Paul de Lagarde, there is now a definitive intellectual biography: Ulrich Sieg, *Deutschlands Prophet. Paul de Lagarde und die Ursprünge des modernen Antisemitismus* (Munich, 2007).

[132] Judson, *Exclusive Revolutionaries*, 260–261.

nationalist press in both Austria and Imperial Germany.[133] Yet writing in 1912, Heinrich Class still thought it a policy "alien to the sensibilities of the age," and considered "evacuation a policy measure of last resort."[134] Germans, he believed, "should not think about attacking a foreign country for the goal of evacuation, but we should get used to the idea of considering such a measure acceptable as an answer to a foreign attack."[135]

At the time that Class wrote, in 1912, the first full-scale expulsion had commenced in the margins of Europe, with the Macedonian expulsion of Muslim Turks during the Second Balkan War.[136] Class's reservations about "evacuating" whole territories remind us that we are at the threshold of the twentieth century, not at its epicenter. Even the Treaty of Adrianopel of 1913, arguably the first to regulate population transfers, limited the exchange of peoples between Turkey and Bulgaria to voluntary migration and to the border regions. It would be a further decade, and a world war, before the Treaty of Lausanne sanctioned, if largely *ex post facto*, the exchange of 1.35 million Greek nationals in Turkey for 430,000 Turks in Greece. Even then, the British foreign minister, Lord Curzon, head of the British delegation, thought the exchange "a thoroughly bad and vicious solution," for which "the world will pay a heavy penalty for a hundred years to come."[137]

When in 1912 Heinrich Class wrote *If I Were the Kaiser*, the term "unmixing populations" had yet to become a political concept, nor "ethnic cleansing" a household word. And far from being a reality, the "new order of ethnographic relations," which Hitler threatened on October 6, 1939, was only barely thinkable. But Class proved revolutionary in thinking it – in thinking, not of killing a people, but of eliminating them from the demarcated space of the German national state.

---

[133] Even within these milieus, ethnic cleansing remained an extreme view. See, for one example, Otto Tannenberg, *Gross Deutschland: Die Arbeit des 20. Jahrhunderts* (Leipzig, 1911).

[134] Class, *Wenn ich der Kaiser wär*, 140.

[135] Ibid., 141.

[136] On the significance of the margins for twentieth-century European history, see Dan Diner, *Das Jahrhundert verstehen: Eine universalhistorische Deutung* (Frankfurt am Main, 2000), 12, 199.

[137] Cited in Jennifer Jackson Preece, "Ethnic Cleansing as an Instrument of Nation-State Creation: Changing State Practices and Evolving Legal Norms," *Human Rights Quarterly*, 20.4 (1998), 817.

Elimination also permeated Class's position on Jews in the German Empire. For a start, Class insisted that "all foreign Jews, who do not yet have citizenship, be quickly and ruthlessly and to the last man expelled." But this could only be a start. Jewish citizens of Germany then had to be placed under special law. But who was Jewish? Religion was for Class an outward sign of the inner condition of "racial belonging." As Class thought in racial terms, he saw miscegenation as a central problem and believed it necessary not only to address future damage to Germans but also past harm. He therefore proposed a definition that bears uncanny resemblance to the definition hammered out in Nuremberg in 1935. "Jew in the sense of the requested special law is every person, who on 18 January 1871 belonged to the Jewish religious community, as well as all progeny of persons who were Jews at the time, even if only one parent was or is Jewish."[138] The definition was intended to cut through what for genuine racists was the Gordian knot of miscegenation. It also meant to dam in "Jewish influence." As part of the special laws, Class proposed that Jews be precluded from public office, service in the military, the right to vote, the legal profession, teaching at all levels, possessing land, directing public entertainment, and if newspapers employed Jewish journalists, they were to make this fact known. Finally, Class proposed that as "compensation for protection, which the Jews enjoy as national aliens" (*Volksfremde*), they were to pay twice the tax of Germans.[139] These measures presaged the persecution of Jews in the 1930s – in the literal sense of eliminating Jews from Germany or returning them to the precarious status of Jews thinly protected.

Espousing an eliminationist anti-Semitism that stopped just short of ultimate measures, Class's *If I Were the Kaiser* sold extremely well, and by the time war broke out, it was already in its fifth edition. The book is important not because it represents an extreme anti-Semitic position, but because its position had become mainstream within the German right – at the very least in the sense of becoming socially acceptable, and in a stronger sense of being, as Roger Chickering has pointed out, a "manifesto of the [Pan-German] League."[140] The book is also a bridge from the long nineteenth century to the short, violent twentieth. It takes

---

[138] Class, *Wenn ich der Kaiser wär*, 75.
[139] Ibid., 76.
[140] Chickering, *We Men Who Feel Most German*, 286.

up positions approached by Treitschke, furthered by colonial theorists, and implied in the work of a range of progressive social reformers, especially in eugenics and criminology. But Heinrich Class now brought together what had been largely separate: anti-Semitism, racism, and the elimination of peoples. For Class, elimination still meant elimination from the soil of Germany. But it was elimination nonetheless, with the thought of killing a deduction away – a deduction that separated the long nineteenth century from the violent twentieth.

CONCLUSION

Continuities in German History

"It is not the eighteenth but the nineteenth century that stands between Lessing and us."

> Hannah Arendt

What was lost in the nineteenth century, according to Hannah Arendt, was a form of human solidarity. In *Men in Dark Times*, Arendt has Lessing stand neither for reason nor for tolerance, but for compassion, and not for the egalitarian compassion of fraternity, but for the selective compassion of friendship. The political relevance of this point becomes evident when we consider what, for Arendt, was the antithesis of friendship, namely cruelty. When higher and more powerful ideas held sway – whether the inexorable progress of history, the natural egoism of nations, the necessity of creating a more perfect society, or even the imperative of logical non-contradiction – more limited commitments, requiring discrete acts of courage, diminished. Cruelty then became thinkable. More precisely, it became a reality in the nexus between thought and act. Arendt illustrates the argument with Germans and Jews in the Third Reich. The antithesis to Nazi policies, she insisted, was not to say "are we not both human beings?" but to say, to each other, "Germans and Jews, friends."[1] The first response constituted a cosmopolitan appeal to universals; it ignored what, in fact, had transpired by the time of the Nuremberg Laws. The second response demanded a

---

[1] Hannah Arendt, *Men in Dark Times* (New York, 1968), 23. The citation at the beginning of the chapter is from p. 8.

counter-assertion of ties to one's neighbor and a refusal to concede the Nazi state's severance of human solidarities.[2]

How should the historian study this severance? One possibility is to focus on the ruptures of the twentieth century; this approach has the benefit of being able to trace, within the lives of historical actors, the concrete events and processes of socialization that shaped the people whose decisions and acts directly brought about immense cruelty. Another is to follow Arendt's insight and to explore aspects of what made the nineteenth century the century that stood between Lessing and us. This has meant, for me, reaching back in an attempt to discern how history, circa 1800 to circa 1900, militated against solidarity with strangers, and I have seen nationalism, religious violence, and racism as at the center of this story. I have also argued that for understanding the timing, pace, and reasons for the "rejection of the possibility of human solidarity with strangers," the relationship of Germans and Jews proves extremely good to think.[3]

The history of Germans and Jews is an old history, and the adjective is deliberate. Much of the best historical thinking about the origins of "the final solution" emphasizes not old histories but modern ones. In "The Genesis of the 'Final Solution' from the Spirit of Science," Detlev Peukert, for example, discerned in the theoretical positions of human sciences, circa 1900, the starting point of a "fatally racist dynamic" centered on the separating out of worthy and unworthy life and the abnegation of the individual in favor of the communal ends of social reform.[4] In the wake of the *Historikerstreit* of the mid-eighties, he was among the first to insist that Auschwitz, and not 1933 or the general character of fascism, constitute the vanishing point of German history. Moreover, he posed the question suggestively as what "might explain the origins

---

[2] Michael Geyer, "Resistance as Ongoing Project: Visions of Order, Obligations to Strangers, and Struggles for Civil Society, 1933–1990," in *Resistance against the Third Reich, 1933–1990*, eds. Michael Geyer and John W. Boyer (Chicago, 1992), 340–341.

[3] The quote is from ibid., 341. For the notion that Jews and their history is "good to think," see Ronald Schechter, *Obstinate Hebrews: Representations of Jews in France, 1715–1815* (Berkeley, 2003), 7, where the reference is to Claude Levi-Strauss's assertion that for understanding societies, totems are "good to think."

[4] Detlev J. K. Peukert, "The Genesis of the 'Final Solution' from the Spirit of Science," in *Reevaluating the Third Reich*, eds. Thomas Childers and Jane Caplan (New York, 1993), 234–252.

of the decision, unparalleled in human history, to use high technology to annihilate certain abstractly defined categories of victims?"[5]

Yet in its emphasis on high technology and abstractly defined categories of victims, Peukert's formulation prejudiced the analysis away from the brutal face-to-face killings that preceded Auschwitz.[6] The "modern," in the sense he intended it, tells us little about the base and brutal slaughters of the *Einsatzgruppen* and the Order Police in countless cities, towns, and villages and at the edge of makeshift pits, ravines, and anti-tank ditches throughout eastern Europe. It also leaves unaddressed the explicitly colonial tactic of concentrating victims in ghettos and allowing them to starve, a policy that hard-line "attrition-ists" advocated against the more economically "rational" occupational authorities, the "productionists," who hoped to use the Jewish ghet-tos to enhance Jewish economic potential in the service of the Reich.[7] Moreover, the initial extermination camps, Chelmno and the camps of Operation Reinhard (Belzec, Sobibor, and Treblinka), killed Jews not with high technology but with carbon monoxide running off internal combustion engines. Put differently, the majority of Jews killed in the Holocaust were not victims of high technology but of archaic forms of murder and ordinary kinds of technology. The Holocaust, Ulrich Herbert has recently reminded us, was "in a pronounced way a process of human destruction of very traditional, indeed archaic forms with a correspondingly high number of direct perpetrators."[8] These archaic

---

[5] Ibid., 236.

[6] This rendering anonymous was hardly unique to Peukert. See the general critique in Alf Lüdtke, "Der Bann der Wörter: 'Todesfabriken.' Vom Reden über den NS Völkermord – das auch ein Verschweigen ist," *WerkstaatGeschichte*, 5 (1996), 13. For a critique of the general approach from the perspective of the new research on perpetrators, Gerhard Paul, "Die Täter der Shoah im Spiegel der Forschung," in *Die Täter der Shoah: Fanatische Nationalsozialisten oder ganz normale Deutsche?*, ed. Gerhard Paul (Göttingen, 2002), 24–27, 41. See, further, Michael Mann, *The Dark Side of Democracy: Explaining Ethnic Cleansing* (Cambridge, 2005), 242. Here the criticism is directed at Zygmut Baumann, *Modernity and the Holocaust* (Ithaca, 1989).

[7] Christopher R. Browning, *The Origins of the Final Solution: The Evolution of Nazi Jewish Policy, September 1939–March 1942* (Lincoln, Neb., 2004), 113.

[8] See Ulrich Herbert, "Vernichtungspolitik: Neue Antworten und Fragen zur Geschichte des 'Holocaust,'" in Herbert, ed., *Nationalsozialistische Vernichtungspolitik 1939–1945* (Frankfurt am Main, 1998), 57. With still more validity, the same may be said of geno-cide more broadly. "For genocide," as Omer Bartov writes, "is, ultimately, also about the encounter between the killer and the killed, usually with a fair number of specta-tors standing by." Bartov, "Seeking the Roots of Modern Genocide: On the Macro- and

forms have a history, in particular with respect to Jews. Finally, most victims were not abstractly defined. The vast majority of those murdered by the Nazis – Jews, Russian POWs, members of Slavic nationalities – constituted peoples against whom prejudice in German society ran long and deep, and this too must be accounted for.[9]

Here German and European relations with Jews are, in fact, good to think. In central Europe, that history was marked by cooperation and coexistence, but also by cataclysmic violence and expulsion. Through-out the early modern period, the right of Christian communities to expel Jews, or to circumscribe their rights, was deeply inscribed in the self-understanding of Christian towns, as revealed in local archi-tecture, religious commemorations, and Jewish ordinances appended to town charters. At the communal level, anti-Jewish sentiment remained rooted in popular consciousness, and this did not begin to change until the force and pressure of Napoleon's armies curtailed the autonomy of towns and cities. Jewish emancipation occurred in this context of defeat. From the start, emancipation encountered popular resistance, in the form of the Hep Hep Riots, and a new nationalism that had no place for Jews *qua* Jews. These two levels of rejection – the locally based and the nationally oriented – coexisted throughout most of the nineteenth century. They occasionally overlapped, but mainly they ran parallel. The first kind of rejection, the community based, drew on a very *longue durée of* anti-Jewish sentiment; its lines of continuity arch all the way back to late medieval expulsions. But the nation-based exclusion was new, as the nation-as-interiorized identity was new. In this sense, early nineteenth-century intellectuals who theorized the nation, and the place of Jews within it, articulated novel possibilities. The most radical among these intellectuals postulated the complete assimilation of the Jews, so that, as Fichte put it, "not a Jewish idea was left in their head." But if

---

Microhistory of Mass Murder," in *The Specter of Genocide: Mass Murder in Historical Perspective*, eds. Robert Gellately and Ben Kiernan (Cambridge, 2003), 96.

[9] For this argument, see now Saul Friedländer, Introduction, *The Years of Extermination. Nazi Germany and the Jews, 1939–1945.* (New York, 2007), xx. With respect to Peukert's modernity thesis, see the early intervention of Marion Kaplan, who argued at a conference in 1998 on "Reevaluating the Third Reich," that "it was good to have German historians fully acknowledging the Holocaust, but it threatened to become a Holocaust without Jews." The quotation is from Charles S. Maier, "Foreword," to Childers and Caplan, *Reevaluating the Third Reich*, xiv, and Maier is here summarizing Kaplan's intervention.

assimilation proved a failure, they considered a solution from the past: expulsion.

Expulsion was one possibility, murder another. Yet while popular violence against Jews increased in the nineteenth century, murder seldom occurred. With some exceptions, this also held true of Europe until the turn into the twentieth century, when the dam of inhibition broke, primarily in Russia, then after World War I in eastern Europe as well. In Germany, that dam would not break until 1938, and even then ambivalence marked the popular response to Crystal Night. Yet the violence, in the form of ritual, had long intimated expulsion and murder, playing it out in highly theatrical rituals of denigration on local stages throughout the German lands. This theater of denigration constituted a long, if thin line of continuity – continuity backward because the play shadowed older forms of social violence and forward because it patterned a relationship between Christians and Jews, implying that expulsion, even murder, always remained possible.

This continuity was not a straight line to mass murder and genocide, for with the exception of the violence of settler societies, these events usually implicate the state.[10] For mass murder to occur, it has sometimes been enough for the state to lose its monopoly of violence, as the killings of Jews in Russia during the Revolutions of 1905, and again in the Ukraine during the Russian Civil War suggest. But in the strict sense of a determined effort to kill all the members of an ethnic group, genocide requires state organization – to identify, locate, and sometimes move the target group, and then to coordinate the killing. In the nineteenth century, by contrast, it was the state, and particularly the German state, that prevented anti-Semitic violence from taking a murderous turn. On this count, the Nazi state represented a decisive break with the German past. Similarly, the continuity of anti-Semitism cannot imply that anti-Semitism was the single causal factor that favored genocidal outcomes, as Daniel Goldhagen argued.[11] Prior to World War I, the anti-Semitic strain in the German right was not demonstrably more powerful than in France or Russia, or as visceral as in the Austrian lands. Instead, the

---

[10] Mark Mazower, "Violence and the State in the Twentieth Century," *The American Historical Review*, 107.4 (2002), 1177.

[11] Daniel J. Goldhagen, *Hitler's Willing Executioners: Ordinary Germans and the Final Solution* (New York, 1997).

radical quality of anti-Semitism in Imperial Germany derived from its position on the political margin. World War I hardly changed this situation.[12] As Sven Oliver Müller has argued, anti-Semitism was neither specific to Germany nor propagated with special sharpness. Even the infamous Jew Count of 1916 betrayed more about old style anti-Semitic prejudices in the Army than widespread antipathy toward Jews (though the Jewish community rightly saw it as portentous).[13] In the course of military defeat, disastrous inflation, and political instability, the Weimar Republic witnessed a deepening of anti-Semitic prejudice and a marked increase in symbolic and actual violence.[14] In this context, the anti-Semitic German Defense and Offense League (*Schutz- und Trutzbund*) ballooned in membership; reaching nearly 200,000 members when it was banned in 1922 – after the murder of Walter Rathenau. Its agitation was not without effect, however, especially on the political right and among military organizations. In 1924, the *Stahlhelm*, originally an organization of former frontline soldiers whose membership was 400,000 strong, introduced an "Aryan paragraph" that debarred Jewish soldiers, regardless of their heroism during the war. A number of other organizations, like the German National Union of Commercial Employees, introduced similar anti-Jewish membership clauses. In this regard, university students proved the most radical. In Prussia, students voted overwhelmingly (seventy-seven percent) to request a clause in university statutes that would declare Germans of Jewish descent "foreigners."[15] The Prussian state denied the request, however. In the Weimar Republic, vitriolic anti-Semitism flourished, but it also encountered resistance, not the least from the state. In the inter-war years, the real killing fields were

---

[12] Sven Oliver Müller, *Die Nation als Waffe und als Vorstellung: Nationalismus in Deutschland und Großbritannien im Ersten Weltkrieg* (Göttingen, 2002), 144.

[13] Ibid., 146. On the response of the Jewish community, Ulrich Sieg, *Jüdische Intellektuelle im Ersten Weltkrieg: Kriegserfahrungen, weltanschauliche Debatten und kulturelle Neuentwürfe* (Berlin, 2001), 87–96.

[14] Dirk Walter, *Antisemitische Kriminalität und Gewalt: Judenfeindschaft in der Weimarer Republik* (Bonn, 1999). Michael Wildt, *Volksgemeinschaft als Selbstermächtigung: Gewalt gegen Juden in der deutschen Provinz 1919 bis 1939* (Hamburg, 2007). On the wrenching effects of the end of the war and the defeat, see Michael Geyer, "Endkampf 1918 and 1945: German Nationalism, Annihilation, and Self-Destruction," in *No Man's Land of Violence: Extreme Wars of the 20th Century* (Göttingen, 2006), 47, "the rhetoric of Endkampf found its most potent enemy in the figure of the Jew." See also Wolfgang Schivelbusch, *The Culture of Defeat: On National Trauma, Mourning, and Recovery*, trans. Jefferson Chase (New York, 2003), 189–288.

[15] Recounted in Herbert, "Vernichtungspolitik," 35, 41.

elsewhere – to the east, where the borders of states were contested, and Jews forced to choose sides with one or the other nationality.

Patterns of either anti-Semitic ideology or of anti-Jewish violence do not, then, answer the question: why Germany?[16] But the converse proposition also does not hold: that an adequate explanation can dispense with an account of the depth of principal enmity on which the National Socialist regime was based and the genocide pursued. Germany became one of the three modern regimes explicitly based on racial exclusion (along with South Africa and the U.S. South during the Jim Crow years) and of these the only one that pursued genocidal policies.[17] It would seem willful to understand race relations in South Africa and the U. S. South without anchoring analysis in the experience of slavery and colonial rule. Likewise, it remains imperative to ground an understanding of how the Third Reich mobilized enmity by considering the longer history of the principal target of the Nazis. This is not just a question of the ideology of the regime but also of the relationship of the regime to the wider population. True, Germans did not give the Nazis the majority of their votes in a free election, though by 1932 the NSDAP had become the largest political party. Moreover, voters supported the Nazis for myriad reasons and virtually no one in November 1932, when the last free election occurred, imagined the terrors of the *Einsatzgruppen* less than a decade later. It is furthermore the case that of all the reasons for supporting Hitler at the polls, anti-Semitism, as such, counted among the least significant. Yet Nazi anti-Semitism hardly deterred anyone, either. This fact is of considerable significance, not because Germans were unique in this regard, but because anti-Semitism had become the common property of ordinary men and women. Not all men and women shared anti-Semitism; not all who did shared it in the same degree: and few shared it to the degree that the National Socialists hoped. Yet as a sentiment, it was sufficiently widespread that it failed to deter in 1933, when the battery of anti-Semitic legislation began, or in

---

[16] Philippe Burrin, *Warum die Deutschen? Antisemitismus, Nationalsozialismus, Genozid*, tr. Michael Bischoff (Hamburg, 2004) 44, remains the most interesting attempt to answer the question with anti-Semitism in view. He sees the specific form of the national question, the religious dimension, and the positive valuation of authority and power as three significant structural factors favoring anti-Semitic outcomes, and of these, the first two, according to Burrin, are specific to Germany.

[17] George M. Frederickson, *Racism: A Short History* (Princeton, 2002), 105.

1935, when the Nazis promulgated the Nuremberg Laws, or in 1938, at the time of Crystal Night. On the contrary, the German population concurred that a "Jewish question" existed and that this question concerned the place of the Jews in a German national community.[18]

It is exceedingly difficult to gauge correctly the response of the German population toward the marginalization, disenfranchisement, and expropriation of Jews and their property. Internal reports on the public reaction to the Nuremberg Laws, for example, suggest support as well as rejection.[19] Contemporary accounts, especially the diaries of Victor Klemperer, similarly oscillate between despair that former friends have cut off ties and optimism because various strangers have signaled solidarity.[20] These accounts give the impression that older people were more likely to show support than younger people. Yet beyond this unsurprising find, we are left with a broad range of attitudes. Historians also differ markedly in their interpretations. David Bankier, for example, argues that "the vast majority of the population approved of the Nuremberg Laws because they identified with the racialist policy," while Otto Dov Kulka insists that the consensus remained incomplete.[21] In this interpretive question, historians cannot escape making subjective judgments. In my own reading of the internal reports, consensus stands out, if sometimes crossed by the dissent of intrepid people – "German-blooded persons who continue to hold friendly relations with Jews and show this in a conspicuous way in public," as one police report from Magdeburg put it in November 1941.[22]

---

[18] Ian Kershaw, *Popular Opinion and Political Dissent in the Third Reich: Bavaria, 1933–45* (Oxford, 1992), 72–3.

[19] Peter Longerich, *"Davon haben wir nichts gewusst!": Die Deutschen und die Judenverfolgung, 1933–1945* (Munich, 2006), 96–100.

[20] On the Klemperer diaries, see Henry Ashby Turner, Jr., "Victor Klemperer's Holocaust," *German Studies Review*, 22.3 (1999), 385–395.

[21] David Bankier, *The Germans and the Final Solution* (Oxford, 1992), 80; Otto Dov Kulka, "Die Nürnberger Rassengesetze und die deutsche Bevölkerung im Lichte geheimer NS Lage- und Stimmungsberichte," *Vierteljahrshefte für Zeitgeschichte*, 4 (1984), 602–3. See also Saul Friedländer, *Nazi Germany and the Jews: The Years of Persecution, 1933–1939* (New York, 1997), 155–164.

[22] Stapoleitstelle Magdeburg, "Verhalten Deutschblütiger gegenüber Juden," (11/11/1941), in *Die Juden in den geheimen NS-Stimmungsberichten 1933–1945*, eds. Otto Dov Kulka and Eberhard Jäckel (Düsseldorf, 2004), 473. This remarkable collection of documents is now the best place to start for scholars attempting to arrive at their own judgment about these vexed questions. For a fair-minded discussion of the differences among scholars, emphasizing that scholars do agree that there was a vast difference between the

If judgments about the general support for Nazi measures remain subjective, it is nevertheless possible to show that many people participated in the persecution of the Jews. In Hamburg, auctions of "Jewish wares" occurred almost every day between 1941 and 1945, as the Nazis auctioned off Jewish clothes and furniture, yard items and books, with more than 100,000 citizens of Hamburg and the surrounding area buying goods and few ignorant of their provenance.[23] In Düsseldorf, an army of civil servants, tax accountants, station managers, and police officers helped when it came time to deport the Jews in 1941.[24] Similar instances of complicity, small and large, occurred throughout Nazi Germany. As Marion Kaplan has forcefully argued, the participation of ordinary Germans in the social isolation and disenfranchisement of the Jews and the expropriation of their property "made Jews suffer social death every day." This "social death" was, moreover, "the prerequisite for deportation and genocide."[25] We often think of attitudes as leading to action. But the reverse can also occur: action, or inaction, can both shape attitudes and have further effects – forcing us to ask whether complicity and passivity brought about a tacit and enabling consensus for expulsion.[26]

The answer is complex, as internal reports of the Security Service (SS) relate general approval, but also significant reaction against the law forcing Jews to wear the yellow star and against the brutality of deportation. Resistance came especially from church groups, and it derived not from general reasons of humanity, but because Jewish converts were involved.[27] As deportations continued throughout the winter of 1941/42, opposition quieted. Yet this was not necessarily the quiet of indifference or the overwhelming concerns of the war. The historian

anti-Semitism of the regime and of the ordinary people, see Browning, *The Origins of the Final Solution*, 388–390, 535–6, fn. 59.

[23] Frank Bajohr, *Aryanisation in Hamburg: The Economic Exclusion of the Jews and the Confiscation of their Property in Nazi Germany* (New York, 2002), 278–9.

[24] Eric A. Johnson, *Nazi Terror: The Gestapo, the Jews, and Ordinary Germans* (New York, 1999), 404–5. Johnson is here citing the research of Michael Zimermann.

[25] Marion Kaplan, *Between Dignity and Despair. Jewish Life in Nazi Germany* (New York, 1998), 5.

[26] See now Michael Wildt, *Volksgemeinschaft als Selbstermächtigung: Gewalt gegen Juden in der deutschen Provinz 1919 bis 1939* (Hamburg, 2007), who argues that participation, at various levels, in anti-Semitic violence and denunciation constituted a self-empowerment from below of the "Volksgemeinschaft."

[27] Peter Longerich, "*Davon haben wir nichts gewusst*," 194–200.

Peter Longerich has suggested another interpretation. As the situation on the eastern front deteriorated, Germans on the home front worried about the consequences of their involvement with the regime's eliminatory measures.[28] If true, did this deepen their anti-Semitism or elicit remorse? One cannot say with certainty. But lessons from history suggest what I believe to be the correct answer. In the thirteenth and fourteenth centuries, host desecration and ritual murder stories often came after, not before, the killing.[29] Is it possible, then, that the apex of German anti-Semitism occurred after knowledge of mass death?

I

German anti-Semitism became a still deeper structuring force when paired with the construction of community. It is the transformation in the conception of community – first defined in local terms, then as nation and nation-state, then as a racialized nation, and finally as a racialized nation-state – that allows us to see the great significance of the long history of anti-Semitism. Scholars overlook this significance when they study anti-Semitism in isolation or consider it as a matter of party politics. But this interrelationship between forms of community and the shape of anti-Jewish thought and practices was utterly central to German history in the long term. The interrelationship was not a German specificity, as similar twining occurred in other nations, especially in eastern Europe, but also in France. The pairing nevertheless counts among the deep continuities of German history.

It counts for reasons that concern the history of German nationalism, in both its ideological and sociological dimension. The construction of the nation, as expression of interiorized identity, occurred at precisely the moment that the place of Jews within an imagined community, local as well as national, was subject to redefinition. The conjuncture was no accident, and a series of German nationalists, from Fichte to Arndt to Father Jahn, theorized the issues together with followers such as Jacob Fries and Friedrich Rühs placing more weight on the Jewish question as

---

[28] Ibid., 194; Friedländer, *The Years of Extermination*, 298–303.

[29] Caroline Walker Bynum, "The Presence of Objects: Medieval Anti-Judaism in Modern Germany," *Common Knowledge*, 10.1 (2004), 3.

such. The idea that only Jews who were no longer Jews could count as German thus flowed into the initial ideological construction of German identity. It also became a founding moment of organized nationalism, with most student fraternities and gymnastics organizations quickly adopting anti-Jewish statutes.

First constructions need not prejudice later outcomes, but subsequent German nationalism exhibited "sensitive dependence on initial conditions," as complexity theorists call it.[30] This happened not in the form of a one-way track, but as a style of nationalism that had a certain pull. This twisted road of nationalism is necessary to emphasize. There were constructions of German national identity that were not exclusionary in a strict sense. During the 1830s, for example, the centrality of anti-French and anti-Jewish sentiment in German nationalism receded. By mid-century, bourgeois nationalists who wanted to encase the German nation in a constitution defined by the rule of law largely subsumed whatever private misgivings they may have had about Jews to the imperatives of constitution-making.[31] This principled constitutionalism even held true for members of the German National Union (*Nationalverein*) of the 1850s and 1860s, despite their assertion of national egoism in the north and east, against Danes and Poles, and despite their willingness to risk large-scale war to achieve national unification.[32] But when unification was achieved (and with it the full emancipation of the Jews), German nationalists turned inward. In the first order, this inward turn meant politics directed against Catholics and ethnic minorities, and it meant a return to the Fichte for whom the state formed national citizens. In the late 1870s, an important shift then occurred, and the generations of historians who insisted on its importance as the "second foundation" of the German Empire were correct to do so. This shift from official to integral nationalism, the nation as twined with the interests

---

[30] Cited by John Lewis Gaddis, *The Landscape of History: How Historians Map the Past* (New York, 2002), 31.

[31] Brian E. Vick, *Defining Germany: The 1848 Frankfurt Parliamentarians and National Identity* (Cambridge, 2002). For the continuing vitality, and wide scope, of the constitutional element of German nationalism after 1848, see Christian Jansen, *Einheit, Macht und Freiheit: Die Paulskirche und die deutsche Politik in der nachrevolutionären Epoche 1849–1867* (Düsseldorf, 2005). Jansen, however, also traces the influence of an increasingly ethnic nationalism.

[32] Andreas Biefang, "'Volksgenossen': Nationale Verfassungsbewegung und 'Judenfrage' in Deutschland 1850–1878," in *Die Konstruktion der Nation gegen die Juden*, eds. Peter Alter et al. (Munich, 1999), 49–64.

of the state to the state as subordinate to a wider and more radical conception of the nation, focused attention on the east and on the place of Jews in Germany. It also opened a space for the very new language of race. Students, especially, took up the new language and embraced exclusionary practices and legislation. When they came to prominence as intellectuals at the turn of the century, they brought together exclusionary anti-Semitism and a social Darwinism that contemplated the eradication of races, peoples, and groups. It is in this period, too, that Fichte enjoyed a genuine renaissance, with the emphasis placed less upon the culture-shaping state than on Fichte's notion of German as an original language and the Germans as a people of destiny.[33] Nationalism, religious exclusion, and racism thus twined, as late nineteenth-century ideas betrayed long-term sensitive dependence on initial conditions and first formulations. After the Morocco Crisis of 1911, radical nationalists like Heinrich Class came forward with sweeping proposals for reform, which included aggressive foreign policy, class-based suffrage, and exclusionary laws directed against Jews that foreshadowed, in a precise sense, the Nuremberg Laws of 1935.[34]

Class's proposals never received official sanction, and if anything the work of parliamentary reform headed in the opposite direction.[35] But here the war proved decisive. It proved decisive not because new thoughts were thought, but because pre-war ideas were now advanced with the possibility of their realization. In his memorandum of September 1914, Class, for example, imagined far-reaching annexations in the west and in the east, the stripping of subject populations of rights, and large-scale population transfers in a vast project of national engineering that would reorder the ethnic complexion of northern Europe. What before the war remained abstract, now took on concrete formulation. Class called it "an ethnic cleaning of the field" (*völkische Flurbereinigung*) necessitating the massive displacement of populations in the newly conquered territories. The "cleaning," which Class imagined

---

[33] Jens Nordalm, "Fichte und der Geist von 1914: Ein Beispiel politischer Wirkung philosophischer Ideen in Deutschland," *Fichte-Studien*, 15 (1999), 211–232.

[34] Roger Chickering, *We Men Who Feel Most German: A Cultural Study of the Pan-German League* (Boston, 1984), 253–298; Geoff Eley, *Reshaping the German Right: Radical Nationalism and Political Change after Bismarck* (New Haven, 1980), 316–334.

[35] The argument in Margaret Lavinia Anderson, *Practicing Democracy: Elections and Political Culture in Imperial Germany* (Princeton, 2000).

would be peaceful, involved exchanging Russians and Poles for ethnic Germans and the expulsion of Jews from the new territories to either Russia (now pushed back to its pre-Petrine borders) or to Palestine (where they would live in a Jewish state under Turkish dominion).[36] But in 1914, civilian leaders could still discount Class as a dangerous ideologue.[37]

The same cannot be said of the Army High Command in the east, the officers of "*Ober Ost*," whose "military utopia" involved reshuffling subject populations. The soldiers, as Vejas Liulevicius has shown, approached the east with the full battery of cultural suppositions, which drew directly from nineteenth-century understandings of the superiority of German over Slavic *Kultur*.[38] The soldiers even imagined that they brought *Kultur* to the lands of the east. But when subject peoples proved recalcitrant, Germans responded with ever-harsher control. In this atmosphere, what had been extraordinary before the war now became normal. Central works of annexationist literature advocated population transfers in order to create ethnically homogenous landscapes.[39] Ethnic experimentation, the thought that anything is possible, began to flourish, with the domination of space (in terms that Ratzel had foreseen in the colonies) central to ideological fantasies. After the war, seemingly lost in the west but won in the east, these fantasies involved the annexation of vast spaces, and the expulsion of peoples. The direct continuity to the Third Reich, in the sense of positing a high degree of identity between the initial and terminal point of the continuum, is evident here as well, with the continuity not to genocide as such but to ethnic cleansing – which, however, often bleeds into mass murder, even genocide.

The centrality of the nationalist imagination to questions of continuity may also be traced in terms of its sociological depth. But here one

---

[36] Heinrich Class, *Zum deutschen Kriegsziel* (Munich, 1917), 44, 47, 49–53.

[37] On this pamphlet, which has as its basis Class's "*Denkschrift*" of September 1914, see Heinz Hagenlücke, *Deutsche Vaterlandspartei: Die nationale Rechte am Ende des Kaiserreichs* (Düsseldorf, 1997), 53–57. See also Fritz Fischer, *Germany's Aims in the First World War* (New York, 1967), 106–108, 166–171, who mentions only the territorial changes that Class proposed and attempts to tie them to the interests of German industrialists. Fischer notwithstanding, whether the *Primat* is ideology or economics remains an open question.

[38] Vejas Gabriel Liulevicius, *War Land on the Eastern Front: Culture, National Identity and German Occupation in World War I* (Cambridge, 2000).

[39] Ibid., 165.

must be careful not to read history backward and impute to nation-alist ideas greater reach than they actually had. In the early modern period, humanists developed a conception of the nation as an emblem of who the Germans were and of where they lived. They did not think of German as an interiorized identity, the prerequisite of modern nation-alism. Nationalism itself did not reach wider circles until Napoleon's armies overran German states, in particular Prussia. In this context, intellectuals like Fichte and Arndt had a profound but limited influ-ence, as they shaped the national imaginations of significant sectors of the Protestant middle class, mainly in Prussia and Saxony. Throughout much of the nineteenth century, not the national utopias of the first hour but a more measured constitutional nationalism held sway – in 1848, but also for the two decades thereafter. In many areas, the idea that being German constituted the full measure of one's identity pene-trated very late, as the best research demonstrates. In the Bohemian city of Budweis, for example, at least sixty percent of the population was bilingual in the 1840s and many were not committed to either Czech or German nationality.[40] In 1848, nation had both cultural and political resonances, with the possibilities of the inclusion of national minorities and Jews more generous than a deduction from Fichte and Arndt would suggest. But throughout the German lands, democratic politics, espe-cially starting in the 1880s, increasingly encouraged ethnic allegiances, making nationality a bridge to politics. What held in a city like Budweis was also true of the ethnic frontiers, which, as Pieter Judson has recently shown, were constructed as frontiers by nationalist activists who set themselves the task of nationalizing peoples whose identities were not national.[41] The state also played a decisive role in the nationalization of citizens – whether through institutions, like the army or the school-room (the site of countless battles with ethnic minorities) or through administrative practices, like naming and counting. Fichte had already discerned legibility of "this is that particular person" as central to the modern state, but Prussian administrators did not count the language of

---

[40] Jeremy King, *Budweisers into Czechs and Germans: A Local History of Bohemian Poli-tics, 1848–1948* (Princeton, 2002). For an early argument for the importance of multiple identities, not as an aberration but as the thing itself, Gary B. Cohen, "Jews in German Society: Prague, 1860–1914," *Central European History*, 10 (1977), 29.

[41] Pieter M. Judson, *Guardians of the Nation: Activists on the Language Frontiers of Impe-rial Austria* (Cambridge, Mass., 2006), 5.

the individual until the 1820s, and even then it was to discern how many subjects could not speak German.[42] By 1861, however, the Prussian Statistical Office undertook a general counting of language and placed it under the rubric of nationality, and in the 1870s Imperial Germany and the Austro-Hungarian Monarchy explicitly used language in order to count ethnicity.[43] As statistics required integers not fractions, this had the effect of rendering increasingly invisible bilingual local worlds.[44]

If the case for nationalism's deep influence cannot be made for the broad, wide, and variegated populations of the German lands, nationalism nevertheless remained important to middle-class sociability and a defining moment of the Protestant public sphere. By the turn of the century, nationalist organizations in Imperial Germany drew millions of male citizens into their orbit, with members signing up to be counted in "national" terms. And if the mentality of members cannot be simply deduced from the public statements of organizational leaders, it nevertheless remains that nationalist organization tilted politics away from the local. In Imperial Germany, this national tilt was especially significant in military sociability, with a considerable amount of effort and energy poured into military parades, monument building and naval and army advocacy. The military also decisively influenced social hierarchies.

This late nineteenth-century militarization and nationalization of public life was less German than historians often assume. Jacob Vogel has illustrated, for example, how in terms of popular militarism Germany and France were "*Nationen im Gleichschritt*," two nations marching apace. Differences notwithstanding, each nation developed a national military cult centered on masculine virtues, readiness to fight, and obedience. Each country also evinced considerable enthusiasm for

---

[42] On Fichte, Jane Caplan, "This or That Particular Person: Protocols of Identification in Nineteenth Century Europe," in *Documenting Individual Identity*, eds. Jane Caplan and John Torpey (Princeton, 2001), 49. Siegfried Weichlein, "'Qu'est-ce qu'une nation?' Stationen der deutschen statistischen Debatte um Nation und Nationalität in der Reichsgründerzeit," in *Demokratie in Deutschland: Chancen und Gefährdung im 19. und 20. Jahrhundert*, eds. Wolther von Kieseritzky and Klaus-Peter Sick (Munich, 1999), 79. Leszek Belzyt, *Sprachliche Minderheiten im preußischen Staat* (Marburg, 1998), 8.

[43] Weichlein, "'Qu'est-ce qu'une nation?'," 79.

[44] Benedict Anderson, *The Spectre of Comparisons: Nationalism, Southeast Asia and the World* (London, 1998), 36–37.

the folkloristic aspects of popular militarism.[45] But in what form this popular militarism culture reached the majority of the population is more difficult to say. When war broke out in August 1914, some interpreted it as a great release, guaranteeing the possibility of a rebirth through war. But we now know that celebratory demonstrations were few, and concentrated in select large cities, with the most visible demonstrations in Berlin. Instead of "a heady excitement," anxiety marked the banal reality of the August days.[46] Similarly, it is no longer self-evident that World War I nationalized, or even brutalized, the masses. Close studies of the experience of the western front point in the opposite direction. Nationalist appeals failed to take root in the mind frame of ordinary soldiers, and such nationalist appeals sometimes proved counterproductive. The Bavarian soldiers studied by Benjamin Ziemann, for example, exhibited little enmity toward Germany's enemies, and relished killing still less. From 1917 on, they suspected that extreme nationalism emanated from those who profited from the war; and in place of victorious peace, they hoped for a swift end to the fighting.[47]

The new research raises profound questions for an understanding of the experience of the war, and the place of continuity in it. It is necessary to pause upon this point since historians have placed significant weight on World War I as the seminal catastrophe inaugurating the European descent into barbarism.[48] Of the profoundly wrenching impact of the war, there can be no doubt. Yet there is now considerable evidence to suggest that not the experience of actual fighting but the nationalist frustrations of those who did not fight proved decisive for the making of groups of men who, by the time of the invasion of Poland in 1939, had already turned into willing executioners of Jews. This is now evident with respect to the Reich Security Main Office (RSHA) – the branch of the SS formed in September 1939 in order to combat the ideological "enemies" of Nazi Germany, including Communists, Gypsies, and Jews.

---

[45] Jacob Vogel, *Nationen im Gleichschritt. Der Kult der 'Nation in Waffen' in Deutschland und Frankreich, 1871–1914* (Göttingen, 1997), 284–291.

[46] The quote is from Gordon Craig, *Germany 1866–1945* (Oxford, 1978), 339. For the corrective, Jeffrey Verhey, *The Spirit of 1914: Militarism, Myth, and Mobilization in Germany* (Cambridge, 2000).

[47] Benjamin Ziemann, *War Experiences in Rural Germany, 1914–1923*, tr. Alex Skinner (New York, 2007).

[48] Early, and with force, Omer Bartov, *Murder in our Midst: The Holocaust, Industrial Killing, and Representation* (New York, 1996), 23.

In his study of the leadership of the RSHA, the historian Michael Wildt shows that more than three quarters of the directing officials, a sample of 221 people, belonged to the generation born in 1900 and after.[49] Steeped in clichés of heroism and hardness, these young and ambitious men found their baptism of fire not during the war but after, with the paramilitary *Freikorps*. They also developed radical nationalist ideas at the universities, where anti-Semitism remained a central element, as it had been since at least the 1880s. But now this anti-Semitism had become an explicitly national-political category, mixed with the notion of Jews as Bolsheviks and as traitors (and although Wildt does not pursue the analogy, its affinity to the post-1905, and still more post-1917, Russian right seems evident).[50] In any case, this generation believed in ruthless dedication to unconditional values, and they became absolute killers, not just in the sense of desk murderers, but also in the sense of leading the *Einsatzkommandos* who descended on the cities and towns of eastern Europe, killing unarmed men, women, and children with staggering brutality.

A second block of evidence comes from the research of Michael Mann, who has undertaken a sociological survey of Nazi war criminals in the context of a still larger study of ethnic cleansing and genocide. Among the 1,581 perpetrators in Mann's study, Germans from ethnically mixed areas and lost territories are overrepresented, and so too are ideological Nazis (those who had long belonged to the NSDAP and had significant careers in Nazi violence). Mann considers murderous perpetrators convicted in postwar trials, plus those who were likely guilty but died in war, committed suicide, escaped conviction, or whose fate was unknown. The sample is not complete and skewed to the higher echelons of the SS and police units, Nazi *Gauleiter*, and senior members of the *Einsatzgruppen*. It is, however, revealing – for its overrepresentation of men (ninety-five percent), and of university-trained people (forty-one percent of the sample, almost ten times overrepresented in terms of the population). His statistics also show a disproportionately high number of ethnic Germans (save for those from the Sudetenland) who lived

---

[49] Michael Wildt, *Generation der Unbedingten, Das Führungskorps des Reichssicherheitshauptamtes* (Hamburg, 2002), 24. On p. 45, Wildt gives the figure of seventy-seven percent.

[50] Michael Kellogg, *The Russian Roots of Nazism: White Émigrés and the Making of National Socialism, 1917–1945* (Cambridge, 2005).

outside the Reich. Alsatians and other western Germans outnumbered the average by a factor of 4.37; ethnic Germans in Poland by a factor of 2.20; and in other eastern areas by a factor of 2.37. Perhaps the most remarkable statistic is of German speakers born abroad, whether from Alsace-Lorraine, Schleswig-Holstein, the Baltic areas, or Poland, and who during the Nazi years lived in the *Reich*. They counted among perpetrators at a ratio of over six times the norm. Mann concludes from this evidence that "virtually all lost territories and threatened borders disproportionately provided perpetrators" and raises the question whether outraged nationalism was not at the root of mass murder.[51] Then there was the problem of war and its aftermath. Mann's numbers are different from Wildt's. In the sample for which Mann has reliable figures for careers in violence, which included 692 men, roughly a third had fought in World War I, but of these nearly thirty percent were in the *Freikorps* afterward (almost ten times the norm), and of those in the *Freikorps*, sixty-eight percent found their way to the Nazi movement before 1933. For later age cohorts, military experience was not nearly as central, but these groups joined the Nazi Party disproportionately either before 1933 or after 1939, suggesting a high degree of ideological commitment. As Mann puts it, "hardcore perpetrators were overwhelmingly drawn from core Nazi constituencies" and "this suggests that most of these perpetrators were probably ideological killers."[52]

The evidence places ideology as such at the center of the picture, as against an understanding of the perpetrators as extensions of autonomous processes of modernity. The vast and variegated new research on perpetrators, while difficult to reduce to an argument, nevertheless underscores that the killers were subjects more acting than acted upon; that these subjects had mental and cognitive predispositions; that they had a will; and that they pushed genocide forward.[53] Nationalist,

---

[51] Michael Mann, *The Dark Side of Democracy*, 227. See Eric Weitz's criticism that Mann is not discussing the dark side of democracy, but of nationalism, in Weitz's review of Mann's book, in *The American Historical Review*, 110.4 (2005), pp. 1138–39. And on the centrality on nation-thinking, which slides into racial ideology, see Eric Weitz, *A Century of Genocide: Utopias of Race and Nation* (Princeton, 2003).

[52] Mann, *The Dark Side of Democracy*, 239.

[53] As Gerhard Paul points out, Christopher R. Browning, *Ordinary Men: Reserve Police Battalion 101 and the Final Solution in Poland* (New York, 1992), whatever one's position on its conclusions, is the work that decisively introduced this paradigm shift in perpetrator research. See Paul, "Die Täter der Shoah im Spiegel der Forschung," 41, 60.

racist, and anti-Semitic ideologies, now fatefully imbricated, played an important role for those who ordered the killings – in Berlin and across Nazi-occupied Europe. Those who killed were not cut all of the same cloth, some murdering from conviction, others because they perceived that the Jews had become the enemy, and still others for base motives of greed.[54] "For the Germans 300 Jews are three hundred enemies of humanity," Kazimierz Sakowicz noted as he observed the killing pits of Ponar, south of Vilnius, "for the Lithuanians, they are three hundred pairs of shoes, trousers, and the like."[55] We know from Christopher Browning's *Ordinary Men* that a special nationalistic or anti-Semitic predisposition was not necessary for killing to occur. We also know from war atrocities, in World War I as in World War II, that German soldiers ruthlessly killed civilians, even when those civilians were not target groups at the center of either nationalist or Nazi ideology.[56] But we have also come to appreciate that the question of threshold (sufficient conditions for genocide to occur) is different than the question of what actually happened in Germany, and here the prominent presence and driving force of a core of ideological killers has come more sharply into view.[57]

[54] Ibid., 61.

[55] Kazimierz Sakowicz, *Ponary Diary, 1941–1943: A Bystander's Account of a Mass Murder*, ed. Yitzhak Arad (New Haven, 2005), 16.

[56] John Horne and Alan Kramer, *German Atrocities, 1914: A History of Denial* (New Haven, 2001), appendix 1, where these are listed. Mark Mazower, "Military Violence and National Socialist Values: The Wehrmacht in Greece 1941–1944," *Past and Present*, 134 (Feb., 1992), 129–158; Sarah Farmer, *Martyred Village: Commemorating the 1944 Massacre at Oradour-sur-Glane* (Berkeley, 1999), 20–28. Michael Geyer, "Civitella Della Chianaon 29 June 1944: The Reconstruction of a German Measure," in *War of Extermination: The German Military in World War II, 1941–1944*, eds. Hannes Heer and Klaus Naumann (New York, 2002), 175–218.

[57] In my opinion, Goldhagen, *Hitler's Willing Executioners*, was right to see the centrality of ideological killers, and the centrality of cruelty to a significant percentage of the perpetrators (with the question vis-à-vis Browning being what percentage?). He was also right to raise the question of why mainly the Jews. Finally, he was right to trace continuities. This is a lot to be right about, especially when perpetrator scholarship remained in its infancy. Yet two problems inhered. The first concerned the way he traced those continuities, assuming the widespread acceptance of eliminationist anti-Semitism before the Nazi *Machtergreifung* and even into the nineteenth century. He also only traced the continuities through German history when, in fact, it is difficult to show the special uniqueness of German anti-Semitism, and murderous anti-Semitism first emerged not in Germany but in eastern Europe. The second concerns his understanding of "ordinary Germans" and his generalization of the killers to the population as a whole. It might be argued that as these points concerned the central thesis, they show the book to be flawed. But I think that Goldhagen must be given credit for placing the question of face-to-face cruelty at

Similarly, a great deal of genocide research has advanced the proposition that genocide can occur when a small but powerful group of individuals carries out the killing, with the support of the population hardly necessary.[58] Genocide happens when the few act on their hate and the many respond with indifference. But is this what happened in Germany? Here the evidence is less clear, both with respect to the range of complicity and the degree of support. It is no longer self-evident, for example, that Daniel Goldhagen overestimated his case when he suggested that the number of Germans who "knowingly contributed in some intimate way to the mass slaughter of the Jews" was "over 100,000 people."[59] When we consider the involvement of the German Army, and take into our purview not only the killing of Jews but also the murder of civilians and the planned starvation of cities and the countryside (in White Russia, for example), the numbers must surely be revised in the opposite direction.[60] The shared knowledge of "belonging to a criminal community (*Verbrechergemeinschaft*) defined in national and racist terms," constituted, as the historian Thomas Kühne has recently argued, a central element of camaraderie on the eastern front and an important factor in the tenacity of the German Army, even as the war was lost.[61] It is also by no means clear that "indifference" best describes the relationship between the population on the home front and genocide in occupied areas. For one, the war brought forth a torrent of anti-Semitic images, with Nazi propaganda offices depicting Jews as the real enemy, and in general terms urging the necessity of their extermination. This torrent became a flood after Stalingrad, so that while it is conceivable that Germans did not know the degree to which the Nazis had organized the

---

the center of things, and for at least asking about the degree to which this cruelty was not merely a result of situational factors, but had a deeper historical mooring. For recent, critical, but also positive evaluations of Goldhagen's contribution, see Wildt, *Generation der Unbedingten*, 221–22; Herbert, *Vernichtungspolitik*, 11.

[58] An excellent summary of this position is Benjamin A. Valentino, *Final Solutions: Mass Killing and Genocide in the 20th Century* (Ithaca, 2005).

[59] Goldhagen, *Hitler's Willing Executioners*, 164, 167. Goldhagen adds: "It would not be surprising if the number turned out to be five hundred thousand and more."

[60] Christian Gerlach, *Kalkulierte Morde: Die deutsche Wirtschafts- und Vernichtungspolitik in Weißrußland 1941 bis 1944* (Hamburg, 1999), 1151. Gerlach estimates that the SS and the police units, including local accomplices, account for only forty-five percent of murdered civilians, whereas more than half can be accounted for by the Wehrmacht.

[61] Thomas Kühne, *Kameradschaft: Die Soldaten des nationalsozialistischen Krieges und das 20. Jahrhundert* (Göttingen, 2006), 205.

killing, it no longer seems plausible to assume ignorance of mass murder.[62] Some historians have even offered estimates of the percentage of
Germans who knew about the killing as just under one-third of the population (and perhaps half of all the adults), with another ten percent or
so having suspicions about it.[63] Even if inflated, such statistics suggest
knowledge of murder more widespread than historians have assumed.
Mainly, the knowledge was about mass shootings, not the extermination camps as such. This knowledge came from many sources, including
soldiers' letters, news and gossip brought back from the front, reports
from employees and workers who had business in the east, and through
contacts in the government and the army. In this fill of information,
the industrial killing in the extermination camps, including Auschwitz,
remained veiled, and it was not easy to perceive a coordinated attempt
to eradicate all the Jews. But this cannot be said of ongoing individual
mass executions. Many Germans knew of them.[64] They knew, in other
words, the method the Nazis used to kill well over a million Jews in eastern Europe. They were hardly indifferent to it; the responses range from
outrage to affirmation to worry, especially toward the end of the war,
when anxiety about accountability increased. That their imagination
did not press to the particulars is not astounding. Nor is it astounding
that few failed to imagine Auschwitz. The idea that not the killers go
to the Jews, but the Jews are delivered up to industrial killing centers –
this, in fact, was without historical precedent.

Yet it remains significant that the killings happened mainly in the east,
where German nationalists envisaged themselves as lords of humanity,
and during wartime, when few willingly criticized their country. The
Nazi occupation of Poland in 1939 began with massacres, as much
initiated by local German minorities (the *Volksdeutsche Selbstschutz*)
as by the Army.[65] Then the Germans concentrated Jews in ghettos. In
this first period of occupation, scant evidence suggested genocide in the
comprehensive sense of killing every last Jew. Instead, as Christopher

---

[62] On propaganda, see Jeffrey Herf, *The Jewish Enemy Nazi Propaganda during World
War II and the Holocaust* (Cambridge, 2006).

[63] Eric A. Johnson and Karl–Heinz Reuband, *What We Knew: Terror, Mass Murder, and
Everyday Life in Nazi Germany: An Oral History* (London, 2005), 369, 393.

[64] Longerich, "*Davon haben wir nichts gewusst*," 222.

[65] Christian Jansen and Arno Weckbecker, *Der "Volksdeutsche Selbstschutz,"in Polen
1939/40* (Munich, 1992).

Browning writes, "Nazi Jewish policy had evolved through a series of final solutions, which first envisioned a *judenfrei* Germany and then a *judenfrei* Europe through expulsion."[66] Historians still debate how policy shifted from expulsion to genocide – with Browning emphasizing that military victory in the Soviet Union gave Hitler the opportunity he sought.[67] In the course of September and October 1941, this meant the abandonment of all hesitation and the embrace of unconditional genocide. This was a new act, perhaps also a new thought, and here there was no continuity. The decision represented a break in German history and in the history of the west. But expulsion did not represent a break. It had been central to the creation of communities throughout central Europe for a very long time. In the history of nationalism, it had already been possible to think in the early nineteenth century, even if dismissed as patently inhumane. By the end of the nineteenth century, however, the discourse of humanity came to coexist with the idea that people could be concentrated into zones, or reservations, moved off the land, or expelled from it. This thought was possible to think in the borderlands of settler societies and in European colonies, where the nexus between white supremacy and the experience of power over others allowed radical experimentation with peoples considered fundamentally different. Such experimentation was more difficult to countenance in the context of Europe, which, whatever else held it together, had become "a grouping of people that as a minimum could be counted on not to enslave each other."[68] World War I eroded even this consensus, as extreme nationalists like Heinrich Class reimagined Europe as an ethnic geography subordinated to the dictates of a *Herrenvolk*, a master nation. Yet even he did not conceive of genocide. His idea was to clear the newly won German space of Jews and push them all into Russia. In his famous letter to Adolf Gemlich, of 16 September 1919, Adolf Hitler did not, in principle, go much further. He insisted that "the anti-Semitism of reason" must place Jews under alien law, but its "final aim must be the irreversible removal of the Jews altogether."[69] By removal (*Entfernung*),

---

[66] Browning, *The Origins of the Final Solution*, 424.
[67] Ibid., 427.
[68] David Eltis, ed., *Coerced and Free Migrations: Global Perspectives* (Stanford, 2002), 13.
[69] Adolf Hitler to Adolf Gemlich, (9/16/1919), in *Hitler, Sämtliche Aufzeichnungen, 1905–1924*, eds. Eberhard Jäckel and Axel Kuhn (Stuttgart, 1980), 89–90. On the importance of expulsion and the creation of reservations, see especially Mark Roseman, *The Villa*,

Hitler meant from Germany and from lands that Germany would come to occupy. It is extremely doubtful that he meant mass murder. That mass murder was the course set was not evident until the war. That systematic murder – of every last Jew on earth – was the policy; this would only emerge in the summer of 1941. Where then does continuity lie? Not in genocide, but in the imagination of expulsion, in the severing of ties to others, and in the violent ideologies, nationalism, anti-Semitism, and racism, that make these things possible to think, support, and enact.

the Lake, the Meeting: Wannsee and the Final Solution (London, 2002), 9. At the core was a commitment to "getting the Jews out of Germany." And on p. 9. "Yet the tide of discriminatory measures that engulfed the Jewish community with such breathtaking speed was sweeping towards the goal of a Jew-free society, not murder."

ACKNOWLEDGMENTS

I first conceived of this book in Regensburg and Halle, but wrote it in Berlin and Nashville. On the way I presented the ideas it contains to audiences in Berkeley, Berlin, Bowling Green (Kentucky), Cambridge (Massachusetts), Göttingen, Knoxville, New Orleans, Oxford, Palo Alto, Potsdam, St. Louis, Urbana-Champaign, and Toronto. Sometimes audiences found what I had to say interesting, other times enraging; in the end, both reactions proved helpful. But it was mainly the subsequent discussions that furthered my thinking, and for these I have many people to thank.

First, I want to thank the wonderful groups of friends and historians in Berlin, including Ulrike Baureithel, Jürgen Busche, Etienne François, Christian Jansen, Hanna Leitgeb, Thomas Mergel, Elke Schmitter, and Siegfried Weichlein, who read parts of the manuscript, or talked at length with me about its arguments. In Nashville, Michael Bess, Bill Caferro, Catherine Crawford, Colin Dayan, Sara Figal, Jim Epstein, Leonard Folgarait, Henning Grunwald, Joel Harrington, Jonathan Lamb, Christian Sinn, David Wasserstein, and Frank Wcislo read chapters, or helped me through areas where my expertise was thin.

The book also has its origins in a series of precise exchanges, for which I am grateful. A letter from Hans-Ulrich Wehler, in response to a review I wrote of his book on nationalism, forced me to return to the eighteenth century and work through positions once again. So too did a late night debate with Jim Retallack and Geoff Eley at Oxford. Jim has also supported this project from its inception, first with a generous invitation to present the first version of "The Vanishing Point in German History" at the University of Toronto, and then by insisting the arguments should be pursued. A spirited exchange after a paper I delivered entitled "When the Sonderweg Left Us" also helped clarify what I was trying to accomplish. For discussions after that talk, which was given in Pittsburgh in 2006, thanks especially to Volker Berghahn, David Blackbourn, Alon Confino, Andy Daum, Ann Goldberg, Sue Marchand, Glenn Penny, and Jim Retallack (again). Finally, an exchange with Niall Ferguson was instrumental in helping me see the outlines of the larger project.

A number of friends and colleagues in the field of German and European history have also aided in the genesis of this book with invitations to present work and generous criticism of it. They include Margaret Lavinia Anderson (and her wonderful students at Berkeley), David Armitage, Ivo Banac, David Bell, Werner Bergmann, Alon Confino, Allison Frank, Paul Freedman, Peter Fritzsche, Rebekka Habermas, Ulrich Herrmann, Stefan-Ludwig Hoffmann (especially for saying when a presentation does not work), Konrad Jarausch, Harry Liebersohn, Vejas Liulevicius, Charles Maier, Uta Poiger, Till van Rahden, Warren Rosenblum, Jim Sheehan, David Tomkins, Cornelius Torp, Corinna Treitel, George Williamson, Tara Zahra, Jonathan Zatlin, and Andrew Zimmerman.

The research for this book was generously funded by a Humboldt Fellowship in 2003, though the project was a different one then. As a Humboldt Fellow, I had the great fortune of working with the late Hermann Rupieper, who exemplified selfless dedication to historical studies and to the students of his home institution, the University of Halle. At Halle, I also had intensive conversations with Manfred Hettling, and these too were formative for my thinking. Then in 2005, I was the lucky recipient of a residential fellowship at the American Academy in Berlin. This was a wonderful experience, with a marvelous group of artists and intellectuals, and it allowed me to think more expansively than I had allowed myself to. Thanks especially to Gary Smith and the superb staff of the Academy – it was in my time there that the book first came together.

When I completed the book, I had the good fortune of supportive editors in Lou Bateman and Eric Crahan, and two critical outside readers, Jonathan Sperber and Chris Clark, who forced me to rewrite. Pieter Judson, whose work has continually challenged my thinking about German nationalism, also read significant blocks of the manuscript. Perhaps I have not met all of their criticisms, but their encouragement and critical remarks have made this a better book. A special acknowledgment is for Isabel Hull – for taking seriously the work of a former student, for a detailed reading of the whole manuscript, for raising questions (some of which I could not answer), and for the kind of last push that significantly improves a work.

My friends Deb Neill and Jan Palmowski have been close interlocutors over the past years, and their thinking and friendship has meant a great deal to me, and to this book. At various points along the way, conversations with my friend and colleague Barbara Hahn have reinforced that writing is all about saying something in your own voice, and not necessarily as convention dictates. All of these friends and colleagues have made this a better book, but one whose mistakes remain my own.

Finally, I thank Meike Werner, who has read this book critically, thought with its questions, and lived with the not-so-occasional absences of its author, and I am grateful to Luca, our son, who distracted me from work as often as it was possible for a four-year-old to do.

The book is dedicated to my Yale teachers: Henry Ashby Turner, who directed my doctoral dissertation more than a decade ago and has been a mentor and friend ever since, and to Peter Gay, for his friendship over the years, and because he has profoundly shaped my thinking about German and European history.

INDEX